Jeff Derksen
After Euphoria

JRP | RINGIER & LES PRESSES DU RÉEL

Jeff Derksen
After Euphoria

Table of Contents

Introduction: All Yesterday's Euphorias

The recent rupture of the present by an economic crisis that cut through the confidence of even the most assured neoliberals—perhaps most dramatically the somber economist Alan Greenspan who was moved to exclaim "I found a flaw in the model of how the world works"—illuminated that these past decades rode the edge of that most mercurial of feelings, euphoria. This euphoria was not simply an effect of a once-booming economy, but had strong cultural and temporal intensities springing from, and altering, the economic ripple. The first intensity was tied to the cultural promises of globalization as a shift that would lift us out of national cultures and into new scales of culture. The second intensity brought a temporal euphoria of the present—a concept and a lived feeling that is both a crystalization of globalization's heroic notion of the present and the triumphal insistence on "the end of history" that was pushed into the popular imagination via the wide-spread influence of Francis Fukuyama's 1989, a concept that "seems to have had to die twice" (after 9/11 and after the economic crisis of 2008).[1] The third most deeply embedded and fiercely inflicted political belief, is the strangely euphoric insistence on the free market and market activity as the engine that will continually churn out surplus value and drive life and capital to new and unlimited possibilities. Even in the aftermath of the economic crisis, this engine, and the global capitalist system, was still largely unquestioned, it simply needed a regulatory tune-up before it got back up to speed. The essays in this collection, written from 2001 to the present, try to think through the intensities and textures of this period to reflect on the possibilities and critical potential of contemporary art, culture, and built space within the long moment of neoliberalism, a moment of building euphoria, a tragic deflation with very uneven results, and now a period of greater unevenness and inequity in which neoliberalism appears to look for new bodies to inhabit.[2]

Despite recognizing the theoretical and experiential difficulties in attaching a cultural dominant to the ascent and grinding decline of neoliberalism, I believe that structures of feeling driven by *euphoria* have characterized this period. Other intensities, more distressingly negative, are also available to give a sense of the range of the lived experiences and "affective attunements"[3] at the tail end of the long neoliberal moment. These terms range from *freedom* to *fear*, from *greed* to *revanchism*, from *triumphalism* to *excess*, but I take *euphoria* as the excitable state that was generated by this distinct and stealthy intensification of an economic philosophy into everyday life. Identifying a period of neoliberalism risks presenting a unified or even monolithic concept of neoliberalism: however, as the essays in this volume reflect, neoliberalism is better conceived of as a dynamic process rather than a rigid and fully enclosed entity covering the earth with its dark shadow. "The *necessary* incompleteness of neoliberalism as a social project," as Jamie Peck, Nik Theodore, and Neil Brenner argue, "ensured that the analytical and political questions around the project's hegemony, or otherwise, were destined to remain unresolved."[4] This incompleteness may also be the enduring strength of neoliberalism. Adding to this,

the awkward term "neoliberalism" does not have a strong
global currency nor a long history (in North America,
the term is rarely used in popular media, yet it is prone to
induce an eye-roll in certain academic and artistic contexts).
As a worldview, it is further abstracted by its merging of
economic theory with a social and cultural program that
meets in both a biopolitical regime and an affective register.

Simultaneously global and place-based, yet fragmented, flexible, and contradictory, neoliberalism is not
a likely engine of euphoria. But the intensity of euphoria is
necessarily cunning and compelling: market euphoria, with
its global promise of prosperity, moved from an economic
imperative to a policy justification to a "social practice" and
lived cultural proposition. To the architects of neoliberalism,
this movement was propelled by the language of social
transformation and liberation: as Elmer Altvater points out,
the Chicago school economist "Milton Friedman called it
a 'neoliberal counterrevolution' against Keynesianism" and
railed against market regulations as "financial repression."[5]
A strong aspect of neoliberalism's affective power is precisely
in this use of the language of *human* liberation and revolution to describe financial reform that redistributed wealth
upward. And this language helped generate a euphoria that
existed as a gaping misalignment between neoliberalism's
promises and its actuality. But the real wildness of these
three euphoric intensities I identify in terms of the social
and the cultural are their human claims, their claims
to universality, and their narrative of liberal inclusion.

Neil Smith has described neoliberalism as "the most
blatantly utopian project of the last 30 years."[6] Yet, as Smith
points out, read from a deeper historical position than neoliberalism itself allows, this project has been widely dystopic.
This dystopic energy has in turn fueled a return to artworks
and projects tied to specific communities and places, and we
have seen new forms of institutional critique and research-
based projects emerge in order to bore through the surface
or *appearance* of the present and *the language* of neoliberalism
to haul up alternative economies, counter-modernities,
minor cosmopolitanisms, and suppressed social and aesthetic
possibilities. As a reaction to these claims of neoliberal uplift
and as a counter move to the overturning of a historical
revolutionary ethos, the essays in this book look at artistic

practices and modes of cultural critique that aim their questions, research, and propositions in direct or tactical manners at neoliberalism's alliance of the economy, affect, and the present.

Negative Euphoria

Despite its triumphalism, the euphoria of neoliberalism is, curiously, negative. This euphoria is not a flash of a shared experience, but the longer and more bullying blockage of other ideas and imaginations of life. From Margaret Thatcher's negation that "there is no alternative" (1979) to Fukuyama's closing of historical change (1989) to George W. Bush's equation of freedom with market freedom (2002), there has been a 30-year run on containing the political imagination. Therefore, I invert the obvious meaning of euphoria and approach it as a negative affect, picking up on Sianne Ngai's use of "negative feelings" that she explores to "read the predicaments posed by a general state of obstructed agency with respect to other human actors or to the social as such—a dilemma [she] take[s] as charged with political meaning regardless of whether the obstruction is actual or fantasized, or whether the agency obstructed is individual or collective."[7] While obstructed agency is different than the form of limited agency (framed as choice, but within a limited set of options, as Slavoj Žižek has insisted)[8] that the discourse of neoliberalism carefully constructs, Ngai's turn on affect allows us a way to read euphoric negations. Here, it is not just that euphoria created an imagination of the real relations we live in (to use this older definition of *ideology*), but that it *became* the affective reaction that produced the imagination of these relations. That is, euphoria is both reflective of the moment and productive of the moment.

The three intensities that I identify are also preemptive, in that they erode cultural and social possibilities other than variations on a liberal democratic consensus based on market values. The euphoria of the cultural level of globalization remained oddly binaristic despite its promises of startling or even new combinations that could block the formation of a unified global culture through new formations of the local, of cosmopolitanism, and of counter-canonical tendencies buried in the flows of the disjunctive global scapes. The euphoria of the present was based on a negation of history and the denial that the future could take a shape other than a global capitalist market tied to liberal democracy. But, the euphoria of the market has proven to be spectacularly negative in a lived, material manner—"a new romance of capitalism with real-world effects," as Nancy Fraser has described it, a romance that thrived on the possibility of euphoria (as all romance must), even as the self-induced crisis of 2008 loomed.[9] The global economic crash-landing from the heights of euphoria has drawn a range of responses as uneven as neoliberalism itself: from tight-lipped acknowledgment to riots in the streets, from contrition to business as usual, and from public austerity to private bailouts.

Art After Euphoria

Today, tales of neoliberalism emphasize that it is emptied of ideas and that its political legitimacy is not just bruised but broken. If, however, "[r]ather than a death knell for neoliberalism, we may be witnessing another historical inflection point in mutating processes of neoliberalization," this should be no surprise, for it thrives on this pattern of "crisis-driven and crisis-exploiting" adaptation.[10] Still sinuously inflected into a wide range of state and policy structures, neoliberalism continues to shape economic policies and urban planning as well as the context for the reception and evaluation of culture and art in particular. The international art market surfed the wave of neoliberal market euphoria, capitalizing both on speculation and contradiction. But as Marx slyly pointed out, even if a table has wooden legs and *a wooden brain*, commodities cannot dance; yet following September 11, art (and other hard commodities such as gold and security apparatuses) as a *commodity* certainly danced frantically up until the financialization crisis. Gold has only just climbed down from its historical heights and art remains a safe bet. This moment of the intensification of the finacialization of art (where it is altered up and own the line due to a new potential as a *safe haven* to park capital in a time of turbulence) has, in combination with the crisis that made the unsteady architecture of the risk economy shockingly visible, been around long enough for the artists, critics, and curators to turn a critical eye to these new forms of capitalization. Such is the intensity of the new speculative economy that what were old truths about the materiality of value have come into sharper relief in this great 35-year shift in the financial imperative of everyday life as it became more and more naturalized. For instance, as the authors of the preface to the "After the Crisis" issue of *Texte zur Kunst* point out,

> The precariousness of the entire art system, which is based on the assessment of value that is not seen in the object itself, and for this reason is built on sand, is now evident to all.[11]

Perhaps what were once beginning points, long since rejected, have now become moments of rupture that allow us to see what is evident. Andrew Witt and Nathan Crompton, in their response to *October* magazine's questionnaire on "recessional aesthetics" put it even more strongly:

> When art is produced and used to legitimize our elites and invest them with the necessary cultural capital for ongoing domination, we should not be surprised, nor necessarily attracted by the temptation to analytically 'deconstruct' the process.[12]

Witt and Crompton cannily refuse the impulse of critique of what by now is obvious as "participation" within neoliberalism—they reject absorption and instead propose practice: "The point is to create exceptional practices that, by their own logic, overturn the decadence we are today being forced to endure."[13] I find the stridency of their language refreshing for it seeks to move past the *effects* of the financialization of art and culture (which is not synonymous with the culture industry) and to look for *causes* and outcomes. If we are going to be instrumentalized, as we surely are, at least let us invert the negation of agency and choose a path *for our agency*.

One of the projects of this collection of essays is to enter *through* the cultural level to point out that, while neoliberalism has failed in its stated economic goals, it has created a cultural revolution by molding the economic as

the mediator between all levels of life perhaps to a deeper
degree than was previously imagined, even if it has done
so with softer culturalized language. Neoliberalism reverses
the utopian horizon of a "cultural revolution" of the 1960s
by reinvigorating the economic base as looming determinate
of the superstructural, yet it does so not by simply reverting
to this classical base/superstructure model, but by adapting
tendencies within cultural critique into an economic logic,
which obscenely enfolds these strata of social life.[14] And,
seemingly on top of that, the economic determinism of
today is more refracted, "reborn and relocated" into global
finance.[15] This revolution complicates the temporality
of the language of any critique of neoliberalism drawing
on an entire set of terms that are now deemed too clumsy
or reductive to assess the present. Not only has the relationship of the cultural and the economic become more
refracted, but the language that we deploy to mark this
relationship and to speculate on its intensities and ruptures
has also been challenged. Even in the manner that economic
values have drifted into the language of cultural values and
served to naturalize these new mediations, this dynamic
doubles back to question the sway of the economic.

As Thomas Locher recently put it, in the context of
artistic research, "The issue is the thorough economization
and governing of culture."[16] The implications are all very
nasty for any imagined semi-autonomous position of culture,
because culture is thrust into an intensified relationship
with the economic that cannot be imagined merely as
over-determined, deadening, or predictable in any soul-
crushing final instance. The final instance never arrives as
it is everywhere. And neoliberalism is adept at absorbing
criticisms of itself and flexing critique into attributes that
more deeply intertwine life, affect, and capital accumulation.
What can be made of the present relationship of culture
and the economic, of course, becomes the crucial question.

Sven Lütticken plays out this shift or reflex in
the relationship between art, the commodity, and the
abstraction of capitalism in a teasing observation that leads
to a productive reversal. Firstly he argues that,

> Works of art are themselves a mute form of political
> economy, offering insights into the changing nature

> of the schizoid entity that is the commodity,
> which today is seemingly dematerializing itself
> into thin air.[17]

And secondly, he proposes, "What matters is the development of commodities that point beyond self-celebratory capitalism."[18] These "inverted readymades" as he calls them "are no longer content to create artistic surplus value, but rather investigate the conditions for a different type of thing, one that is no longer taken as a quasi-natural 'matter of fact, but as a political matter of concern'" with the possibility to "anticipate what a different economy might look like."[19] Read through a neoliberal framework, the work of art is no longer mute in offering its relationships between the cultural and the economic, but it has become a convergence that can open the economic to forms of cultural engagement and critique. This does not develop new or contextual forms of "autonomy, desire, and authorship," as Diedrich Diederichsen argues, but is looped into the production of surplus value (*Mehrwert*) and a law of value that makes art "good for something," even if that something is speculation.[20]

Without looking for an outside to value from which artworks might expend their economies or develop alternative forms of value, Diederichsen delicately proposes that "Artworks and art projects are capable of articulating content and enabling aesthetic experience independently of their commodity form"[21] with the caveat that "the question of value is always (at least partially) thematically embedded as content in a specifically concealed manner, since artworks offer themselves up as fetishes."[22] Curiously, in both Lütticken and Diederichsen's formulations the thing speaks (even if it does not dance), and the commodity or artistic project investigates its own conditions often in order to reconfigure them. Earlier, at the height of the 1970s poetic avant-garde in North America, the writer Ron Silliman proposed that "Poems both are and are not commodities"[23] in order to produce a similar space for the possibility of poetic texts— a space that does not drift to an imagined *outside* of capitalism, nor a space that seeks greater autonomy for a poetic text. Silliman instead aims to open the poem up to a range of productive possibilities within the problematic "that consumption for further production is a moment of production itself—it is action."[24] Silliman's double-time production does not have the commodity speak, but seeks (or the text *seeks*) to alter the relationship between commodity and reader, between consumption and production: the reader is now figured as producer and the text as productive. This linking of the theory of the commodity with a theory of reading gives the poem, *as commodity*, a new "inverted" possibility of the production of social meaning similar to what Lütticken and Diederichsen ask of the art object and artistic practices.

So today a new reversal materializes: to think the cultural outside of the economical is a reduction. This strategy proposes to read through the existing dynamic of the cultural and the economic rather than locating moments and space where this dynamic is diminished. My reversal here is the proposal that renewed and relocated forms of economic mediation are central to the pressure that neoliberalism exerts on the structures of feeling of the present, structures that neoliberalism works hard to make appear natural. As Jodi Dean puts it,

> The fantastic suppositions of neoliberal ideology have become part of the air we breathe, elements of our most fundamental assumptions about how the world works: everyone is an individual with a unique identity; the free market enable us to create and develop those unique identities; everybody wins— there is no alternative.[25]

Having established this foundational economism, the forms of economic repression (to turn Friedman's term to another use) that we see taking shape need not provide answers. Hence massive job cuts or factory closings, or gentrification of working-class neighborhoods, or national austerity plans need no explanation beyond a shrug of the economic shoulder: it simply needs to be done, or (in the manner that neoliberalism so often leaves out human actors), "there is no alternative." Today the twist is that it needs to be done, even if it will not work—as Greece has been told, and as Spain is experiencing—because to not do so is even worse. But turning toward this hard yet naturalized force could lead to a rethinking of the possibilities of culture within and counter to the economic. I am certainly not proposing something new, but simply something necessary—as Stuart Hall pointed out in 1983 (standing Louis Althusser on his head), if we want to establish an open horizon of theorizing to counter the types of closures Dean identifies today, we would be better off to approach "determinism by the economic in the first instance."[26] This could, in turn, open a cultural investigation of the economic as a process that spreads out to saturate social relations in particular material, yet non-guaranteed, and less predictable ways. Within this dynamic cultural-economic context, in which culture is often drawn on to pull capitalism out of a crisis, only to have culture more fully embedded into the crisis, "It is not surprising," as John Roberts observes,

> therefore, that artists, have directed their attentions, then, to both the conditions of their own labor— its similarity with or distance from productive labor— but also, to the ways in which they might find a productive and critical place within this systemic crisis and within the ongoing crisis of the labor-capital relation.[27]

We see this speculative and material investigation in the work of the artists whom I discuss in these essays. Yet the mediations of neoliberalism and its economic logic on everyday life (and on the imagination of the future and the assessment of the past) approach *the economic* in its fullness by turning to its spectrum of effects as well as the intensities of its affects.

My emphasis in these essays is on how artists use the properties of space and the possibilities of time to respatial-ize and renarrate the postpolitical imagination that jumped out from globalization's dream of the dissolution of bound-aries and the neoliberal seizing of temporality through its denial of a future. Many of the artworks and projects that I look at in this collection are grounded in the city and the spatial practices (and territorial problems) of citizens; as such they engage in new situated forms of citizenship, new frontiers of use, and new boundaries of exclusion (including the boundaries of the concept of *citizenship*). But these questions are just as often *retemporalized* or booted back into the swirl of history and the tension of the global present, denying the big freeze that was the present for many. These two forms of investigation and interruption—respatialization and retemporalization—are a repoliticization that opens many of the questions that neoliberalism sought to close.

Globalization After the Long Neoliberal Moment?

In surveying the occurrence of the term *neoliberalism* since the 1970s, Peck, Theodore, and Brenner arrive at the intersection of neoliberalism and globalization:

> neoliberalism might be considered a "post-globalization" keyword, one that has found wide currency since the late 1990s, as a means of *denaturalizing* globalization processes, while calling attention to their associated ideological and political constructions.[28]

While the struggle for supremacy between the concepts *globalization* and *neoliberalism* can be tracked, they are often joined together in a more mutually determining manner in "neoliberal globalization." But the key difference between these two terms is that neoliberalism's cultural project has largely gone unnoticed while culture was a central aspect of globalization. In fact, the cultural aspects of globalization were conceived of as a struggle: this was most clearly and influentially defined by Arjun Appadurai's statement, "The central tension of today's global interactions is the tension between cultural homogenization and cultural heterogeneity."[29] But, in the discourses of globalization, the twinned forces of cultural homogeneity from above and the liberating hybridization of a global-local culture never broke each other down to produce a dynamic global cultural imaginary. The dialectic of global culture reproduced itself at various scales, at times compressing and bending them in ways that seemed to override the nation; yet it was a form of reproduction rather than a new cultural constellation outside of existing models of multiculturalism, recognition, consumption, and specificity. Looked at in retrospect, Appadurai's defining friction of the globalization of only a decade ago has today been thoroughly eroded. In fact this friction was a fuel that drove the expansion of culture into the economic. The great cultural homogeneity based on the universality of US American culture that unified culture and Fordist production, as Perry Anderson argues, "in the sphere of consumption, to offer a single way of life as pattern to the world" ran into the militant exceptionalism of the USA after 9/11.[30] Exporting a model of US American culture globally became a more difficult sell (as several of the works I discuss in these essays pick up and critique). Perhaps the "unified culture" that Anderson identified has been overcome by an abstracted unity of *culture as representation*: this allows national and regional differences and particularities to live in a global model *if* they are imagined to be consumable as representations.[31] In the cultural politics of representation and recognition, a mild version of multiculturalism tied to cultural consumption has crept in as a global model. This is a subtle expansion of Kathryne Mitchell's and Slavoj Žižek's separate observations that multiculturalism is not only compatible with the logics of accumulation in globalization, but also integral as a value-added attribute to cultures, places, and things.[32] In the global cultural landscape, the possibility of new spaces and places of culture have not, unfortunately, produced a counter model that could rewrite the relationship between culture, its reception and circulation, and consumption.

As a result, today there is little discussion of globalization as a cultural process, and globalization itself, in a sense, has broken down into a series of forces and processes rather than being seen as a looming totality evenly covering the globe. This has established a new scalar dance of the national, the regional, and the particular in relation to a more stealthy globalization which could be thought of as *globalization after globalization*. Figured in this way, globalization can be understood not as a stage, but as an on-going tendency within capitalism that is both extensive and intensive, and asserts itself unevenly and is therefore never so total as to be complete in a manner similar to neoliberalism.

In the wake of the economic meltdown and the transformations that the new—yet disturbingly familiar—austerity programs forced on nations and cities, the global dreams of the neoliberals have been rescaled to more localized schemes that are global more in their similarities than in their scope. That is, neoliberal governance, from austerity programs to "the creative city," circulates globally, but is ushered in (or hosted) by nations, regions, and cities: as a result such governance appears more locally shaped and driven. From the call for a one-size fits all economic plan to cut deficits, which was initiated at the explosive G20 meeting in Toronto in July 2010, to the reshaping of cities through the distortion of housing markets or the rebranding of urban territories as *creative* or *sustainable*, a particular form of neoliberal governmentality that migrates globally while being implemented locally is now the hallmark of the intersection of globalization and neoliberalism. Countering this, localized forms of resistance are forced to oppose particular claw-backs of rights or the revanchist redistribution of wealth upward. Yet these localized situations do have the possibility of becoming more and more aligned rather than being unique or particular moments. Curiously, these forms of opposition and the networks of "militant particularisms" have drawn the state back into focus as a target. The very apparatus and scale that globalization was to dispense with culturally, and which neoliberalism was constantly attacking, has seemingly strengthened itself: the state has become more defined, hard-edged, and aggressive in terms of flexing its monopoly on violence (now particularly against protestors as we see from Paris to Athens and from Vancouver to Toronto) and also more ready to assert national borders against migrants, refugees, and to close its economic borders in acts of national self-interest. As a result, the softer aspects of globalization that were attached to the possibilities of cultural dialogue and hybridity now seem to have slid out of view. In some sense, cultural business is back to normal with little instigation of new cultural articulations at the scale of the global. Ultimately the global scale was always treated as too large, outside of sweeping claims of hegemony, as it only sharpened into focus once it was articulated to another scale, such as global-local, or global-urban. Does this now mean that the global, as a scale of cultural and activist imagination, can now be reclaimed from such market sensibilities?

Shock of the Now

The temporal euphoria took shape as a presentism moved
from a right-wing think-tank hypothesis of the end of
history to a temporal frame for governmentality and regulation and then to a cultural frame. Timothy Brennan brings
this neoliberal construction of time in proximity to a trend
in thought that "tends to supplant predecessors by erasing
the history of their own making," which he argues is also

> a characteristic feature of contemporary capitalist
> societies, which are at once *presentist*—that is, viewing
> each moment as the only reality while expunging
> the past in a gesture of calculated anti-historicism—
> and *modernist* in the technical sense of needing
> to judge every current discovery as an utterly new
> departure, an absolute rupture with all that went
> before.[33]

In a sense, this calculated rupture, anti-historicism,
and presentism aimed to set aside or forestall the future
and to selectively mine history to create a path to history's
closure. Of course, this also sets aside the powerful work
within cultural practices, and within the postcolonial imagination, to refigure histories by pulling possibilities out of
the ruins and to lay bare the continuation of the structures
and legacies of colonialism. This in fact is the standard
(and unfinished) work of art engaged with history. The neoliberal imagination of a continuous present therefore is
not a simple reflex against time and history: it sprang from
a euphoria delivered through the idea of developmental
progress at the same time as it aimed to solidify a free-
market ethos bound to liberal democracy as a negation of
other forms of the social.

Finally we have arrived, the neoliberals claimed,
at the perfect moment. But, in reality, this moment was the
brief cresting of extensive and intensive capitalism where
the expansion of the global economy left no imagined
outside (even outer space as a sort of final capitalist frontier
was up for grabs as space exploration was futilely rebooted
under George W. Bush) and the intensification of accumulation strategies bore deeper into everyday life, into the body

(down to the level of DNA), and more robustly and affectively into cultural practices. Neoliberalism managed to create structures of feeling so *deeply economical* that notions of democracy and human freedom were not only tied to market freedom but were the *outcome* of market freedom. This trumping of the economical over the human, which is simultaneous with the equation of the economic and the lived, has been a difficult and strategic cultural project, but one that has not wavered significantly even as the global economy has had to turn its punitive hidden hand to nations, regions, and cities to keep them in line. But this freezing of the present negates the possibility of the future as well as blocking transformation: for are not denials of climate change or the slackening of regulatory structures, such as would have overseen the British Petroleum deepwater drilling disaster in the Gulf of Mexico, a denial of futurity?

The Market Feels Your Pain or, Market Euphoria and Structures of Feeling

In a research-based poem, Aaron Vidaver has brilliantly tracked the manner in which the language of financial speculation and the stock market thickened with emotional or affective resonances.[34] This making affective of the market (and the "marketizing" of affect) is shown in his poem "The Market Prefers" which is a "catalogue of items the market prefers" poached and reappropriated from the media. This poetic catalogue ranges from political assertions such as, "The market prefers a Bush presidency," to seemingly aesthetic judgments like, "But the market prefers a blocky shape," and "Often the market prefers Californian wines." Although in these sentences the market needs no human actors to guide its preferences, the market is not disinterested in its judgments and desires. Vidaver's text does not just poetically materialize a symptom of the monetization of everyday life, but it points to a shift from a quantitative to a lived qualitative difference. As Randy Martin, in *The Financialization of Daily Life* put it in an early text that has its finger on the central cultural aspect of neoliberalism: "The financialization of daily life is a proposal for how to get ahead, but also a medium for the expansive movements of body and soul."[35] More dramatically, Wendy Brown argues that,

> neoliberalism carries a social analysis that, when
> deployed, as a form of governmentality, reaches from
> the soul of the citizen-subject to education policy
> to practices of empire.[36]

This emphasizes how neoliberalism has successfully negotiated the clash between governmentality, a financial regime,
and its grip on the soul, as Brown puts it. Not solely an
economic philosophy, or an ideological position, neoliberalism then takes on the texture of a social practice and
a commonsense that shapes the interface between people,
between places, and between versions of the world.

From a cultural position, it is possible then to ask
if neoliberalism also deploys structures of feelings. But first
Raymond Williams' concept of structures of feeling (and
the pluralization of *structures* is important) has to be slightly
retooled to catch the intensities of the final decades of
neoliberalism. As Williams outlines it, the concept *structures
of feeling* appears to hold both the lived patterns of experience and value in everyday life in conjunction with a general
yet localized tradition *while at the same time proposing* a methodology for analyzing both the lived and the determined.
That is, *structures of feeling* is both a descriptive term that
can be applied to the periods (and the problems of periodization) while also operating as a methodology to identify
a cultural dominant as well as residual and emergent cultural
formations. This tinges the concept of *structures of feeling*
with a curious belatedness: structures of feeling can be
identified in their emergence, but can only be fully grasped
once it has historical momentum and gained dominance.

In this sense, if we approach structures of feeling
as a dialectic of structure and feeling (or "the firm and
definite" and "the most delicate and the least tangible" as
Williams says[37]) in which the lived is altered by the
structured, the euphoria of the market is both produced
and reproduced by the dialectical relationships that
are at the heart of structures of feeling. It is possible to see
the euphoria of the market emerge as such a structured/
lived dialectic because of it.

Steve Matthews describes the relationship of
structures of feeling as a cultural problematic and as a mode
of analysis:

the emergence of a structure of feeling as a concept is an exemplification of the very processes it is designed to reveal, its articulation attended by contemporary uncertainties and difficulties which are in turn its analytical objects.[38]

This is the relationship of art to the economic that I am proposing. Art is simultaneously embedded, shaped by, and tied into a neoliberal regime of accumulation, yet in spite of and because of this condition, it remains both a practice and a possibility. If neoliberalism produces *structures of feeling* that eerily centralize the values and structures of the economic into the heart of our affective/lived lives, artists who turn critically to that supposed anathema of culture (the economic) can also turn to a critique of the production of *structures of feeling* within neoliberalism. Thought of this way, art takes a more dynamic position in the relationship of the social, the cultural, the economic, and the (post)political.

The deficiency in Williams' formation of structures of feeling is that art at times appears as merely a reflection of the already existing structures of feeling. Artistic practices, even positioned as part of culture as a whole way of *financialized* life, are not imagined as *a mode of analysis* of a structure of feeling—such practices can only be part of an emergent, dominant, or residual structure of feeling. As an "aspect" of the cultural, art is not seen as productive of the structures of feeling. Williams writes: "The effective formations of most actual art relate to already manifest social formations, dominant or residual, and it is primarily to emergent formations (although often in the form of modification or disturbance in older forms) that the structure of feeling, as solution, relates."[39] Here there is a residual aspect of one of the "three general categories in the definition of culture" that Williams lays out in *The Long Revolution* at work in this definition of art, or of the function on art: this aspect is the "documentary" aspect of culture, "in which culture is the body of intellectual and imaginative work, in which, in a detailed way, human thought and expression are variously recorded."[40] This aspect of culture is not productive, but is reflective, and the form of criticism that it can generate is "comparative," "historical criticism."[41]

Structures of feeling, then, are built things, emerging out of the struggles over meaning within the cultural and the social, so neoliberalism's shocking mapping of a dry and caustic economic program onto the visceral and lived aspects of daily life is not a secured process, but it is the result of a cultural struggle that both preceded and trailed the economic and social programs of neoliberalism. This social and cultural making of structures of feeling is also the structuring of affect. The relationship of the economic and the affective, and the economic and the cultural has qualitatively shifted over the last 30 years, as many have argued, so that these levels are now embedded and mediated in a manner that is characteristic of the moment. This piercing of the economic into the affective (and vice versa) and the accumulation of a market logic into a cultural commonsense is not a symptom of the collapsing of the categories or areas of life (the new spirit of capitalism absorbing the liberation of blurred boundaries that was the hallmark of postmodernism), nor either a whole new paradigm in which the levels of the social are simply interlaced into a paradigm of liberating flows that pass through the social body, but a more profound entangling of the subject into a world administered through a logic of ownership, of access, of surplus value, and a denigration of nonconformist senses of value.

The Problem of Periodizing, or Neoliberal Times and Beyond

To address the temporal problem that this book steps into by attempting to identify structures of feeling of the long neoliberal moment is to address the question of periodizing, of the possibility of shaping a beginning and an end point for an historical narrative that isolates tendencies of this era in order to examine the relations between its sticky cultural, economic, social, and historical levels. In cultural discourses, periodizing is a suspect methodology in the wake of critiques of historical models, from Walter Benjamin's curiously timeless "Theses on the Philosophy of History" to recent disruptions of developmental models. Earlier, in approaching the 1960s through periodization, Fredric Jameson cautioned that his method of analysis would be both temporal and structural, but with enough breathing

room for wilder mediations to emerge. "Here, in any case,"
Jameson writes,

> the "period" in question is understood not as some
> omnipresent and uniform shared style or way
> of thinking and acting, but rather as the sharing of
> a common objective situation, to which a whole range
> of varied responses and creative innovations is then
> possible, but always within that situation's structural
> limits.[42]

But periodizing, the temptation to grab end points and
events as markers of wholesale shifts, happens all the time:
from Žižek to *The New York Times* to national foreign policies,
September 11, 2001 (or 9/11), was marked as the moment
when things changed. The goal in regards to neoliberalism
is not to narrate the period, or to identify a singular characteristic, but to "produce a concept of *history*"[43] as a gamble
to grasp the period. And, in the present moment, history
as a concept has been a particular target for both artists and
the architects of its demise.

I have chosen to locate the question and time of
neoliberalism within a layering of temporalities that both cut
against each other and extend across several decades to form
this extended moment. Despite its presentism, neoliberalism itself has a long gestation, and is punctuated with
isolated events and ideological cohesion as well as breaks,
contradictions, and contestations (and these are now *generic*
attributes within a cultural language of periods, movements,
and formations). David Harvey chooses Tuesday, September
11, 1973—the day of the Chilean coup overthrowing Salvador
Allende concretizing Pinochet in power—as the beginning
of the neoliberal experiment.[44] Over a different time frame,
Neil Smith tracks neoliberalism back to and beyond neoclassical economics, to

> the revolutionary bourgeois political economy of
> Adam Smith, Kant's cosmopolitanism, the willed
> reason of Rousseau, Hume's practical empiricism,
> and of course John Locke's juridical politics of
> property and rights.[45]

Here Smith also counters the temporality that neoliberalism builds for itself—neoliberalism's self-narration (if we can attribute to it such self-fashioning) has it arrive in the present out of necessity, as a natural development of free market forces and the compelling pull of liberal democracy through the codeword *freedom*. To break this naturalized development of neoliberalism, we can shift from a narrative structure to a poetics: instead of a *bildungsroman* in which neoliberalism comes to age and builds a model home in the global landscape (and welcomes the globally excluded!), a poetics of neoliberalism's structure makes its conjunctures and disjunctures more material and brings them into focus. More recently Neil Smith has proposed that,

> Whereas 10 years ago, the future seemed fixed and change impossible, the global economic meltdown and recession have wrecked this neoliberal certainty, and the social and political future suddenly looks radically open.[46]

Likewise, this period *after* the euphoria generated by the economic, social, and cultural project of neoliberalism also opens up new possibilities.

[1] Slavoj Žižek, "It's the Political Economy, Stupid!" *It's the Political Economy, Stupid! The Global Financial Crisis in Art and Theory*, ed. Gregory Sholette and Oliver Ressler, Pluto Press, London 2013, p. 16.

[2] This *euphoria is* different from both the presentism and the euphoria that Fredric Jameson outlines as a characteristic of postmodernity: "This present of the world or material signifier comes before the subject with heightened intensity, bearing a mysterious charge of affect, here described in the negative terms of anxiety and the loss of reality, but which one could just as well imagine in the positive terms of euphoria, a high, an intoxicatory or hallucinogenic

intensity." Jameson, *Postmodernism, or, The Cultural Logic of Late Capitalism*, Duke University Press, Durham, North Carolina 1991, p. 28. The euphoria that is presently waning is not a "liberation from anxiety" (p. 15), but is negative in its effects.

[3] Brian Massumi, "Fear (The Spectrum Said)," *positions* 13:1 (2005), p. 31–48.

[4] Jamie Peck, Nik Theodore, and Neil Brenner, "Postneoliberalism and its Discontents," *Antipode* 41 (Supplement 1/2010), p. 96.

[5] Elmar Altvater, "What Happens When Public Goods Are Privatized," *Studies in Political Economy* 74 (Autumn 2004), p. 73.

[6] Neil Smith, "The Revolutionary Imperative," *Antipode* 41 (2009), p. 53.

[7] Sianne Ngai, *Ugly Feelings*, Harvard University Press, Cambridge, Massachusetts 2005, p. 3.

[8] Slavoj Žižek. "The Leninist Freedom," http://www.marxists.org/reference/subject/philosophy/works/ot/Žižek.htm (last accessed May 2013).

[9] Nancy Fraser, "Feminism, Capitalism, and the Cunning of History," *New Left Review* 56 (March–April 2009), p. 109.

[10] Jamie Peck, Nik Theodore, and Neil Brenner, "Neoliberal Resurgent: Market Rule After the Great Recession," *The South Atlantic Quarterly* 111:2 (Spring 2012), p. 265.

11] Isabelle Graw, Stefanie Kleefeld, André Rottmann, "Preface," *After the Crisis, Texte zur Kunste* 73 (March 2009), p. 124.

[12] Andrew Witt and Nathan Crompton, "Recessional Aesthetics: An Exchange," *October* 135 (Winter 2011), p. 102.

[13] Ibid.

[14] This, of course, is one of the main points in Luc Boltanski and Eve Chiapello, *The New Spirit of Capitalism*, Verso, London 2005.

[15] Here I am placing two very different texts alongside each other. In *The Aesthetic Dimension: Toward a Critique of Marxist Aesthetics*, Herbert Marcuse casually notes that, "The movement of the 1960s tended toward a sweeping transformation of subjectivity and nature, of sensibility, imagination, and reason. It opened a new vista of things, an ingression of the superstructure into the base" (Beacon Press, Boston 1978, p. 33). J.K. Graham-Gibson in *The End of Capitalism (as we knew it)* outlines a characterization of eight "depictions of capitalism" in which (number seven) capitalism is drawn as "unfettered by local attachments, labor unions, or national-level regulation." "In this formulations economic determinism is reborn and relocated, transferred from its traditional home in the 'economic base' to the international space of the pure economy (the domain of the global finance sector and of the all powerful multinational corporation)." J.K. Graham-Gibson, *The End of Capitalism*, University of Minnesota Press, Minneapolis 1996, p. 9.

[16] Thomas Locher, "Artistic Research: Statement by Thomas Locher," *Texte zur Kunst* 82 (June 2011), p. 128.

[17] Sven Lütticken, "Attending to Abstract Things," *New Left Review* 54 (November–December 2008), p. 102.

[18] Ibid., p. 120.

[19] Ibid.

[20] Diederich Diederichsen, *On (Surplus) Value in Art*, trans. James Gussen, Reflections 01, Witte de With Publishers with Sternberg Press, Rotterdam/Berlin 2008, p. 21–50.

[21] Ibid., p. 44.

[22] bid., p. 44–45.

[23] Ron Silliman, *The New Sentence*, Roof Books, New York 1987, p. 20.

[24] Ibid., p. 30.

[25] Jodi Dean, *Democracy and Other Neoliberal Fanatasies: Communicative Capitalism and Left Politics*, Duke University Press, Durham 2009, p. 73.

[26] Stuart Hall, "The Problem of Ideology: Marxism Without Guarantees," *Stuart Hall: Critical Dialogues in Cultural Studies*, ed. David Morely and Kuan Hsing-Chen, Routledge, London 2006, p. 45.

[27] John Roberts, "The Political Economization of Art," *It's the Political Economy, Stupid!*, p. 65.

[28] Peck, Theodore, and Brenner, "Postneoliberalism and its Discontents," p. 97.

[29] Arjun Appadurai, *Modernity at Large: Cultural Dimensions of Globalization*, University Minnesota University Press, Minneapolis 1996, p. 32.

[30] Perry Anderson. "Force and Consent," *New Left Review* 17 (September–October 2002), p. 24.

[31] And this could, in some ways, be seen as the mode of global representation in *documenta 11*. Marina Gržinić develops a similar but extended argument in "The Genetic Paradigm of Culture," *Situated Contemporary Art Practices: Art, Theory and Activism from (the East of) Europe*, Revolver/Zalozba ZRC, Frankfurt/Ljubljana 2004, p. 124–135.

[32] Kathryne Mitchell, *Crossing the Neoliberal Line: Pacific Rim Migration and the Metropolis*, Temple University Press, Philadelphia 2004; and Žižek in numerous texts, but he initially laid out the critique in "Multiculturalism, or the Cultural Logic of Multinational Capitalism," *New Left Review* 1/225 (September–October 1997), p. 28–50.

[33] Timothy Brennan, *Wars of Position: The Cultural Politics of the Left and Right*, Columbia University Press, New York 2006, p. 128.

[34] Aaron Vidaver, "The Market Prefers," Roger Farr (ed.), *Parser: New Poetry & Poetics* 1 (2007), p. 55–69.

[35] Randy Martin, *The Financialization of Daily Life*, Temple University Press, Philadelphia 2002, p. 3.

[36] Wendy Brown, *Edgework: Critical Essays on Knowledge and Politics*, Princeton University Press, Princeton 2005, p. 39–40.

[37] Raymond Williams, *The Long Revolution*, Harper Torchbooks, New York 1961, p. 64.

[38] Steve Matthews, "Change and Theory in Raymond Williams' Structure of Feeling," *Pretexts: Literary and Cultural Studies*, vol. 10, no. 2 (2001), p. 183.

[39] Raymond Williams, *Marxism and Literature*, Oxford University Press, Oxford 1977, p. 134.

[40] Williams, *The Long Revolution*, p. 57.

[41] Ibid., p. 58.

[42] Fredric Jameson. "Periodizing the 60s," *Social Text*, no. 9/10, *The 60s Without Apology* (Spring/Summer, 1984), p. 178. Here I am echoing Jameson's assessment (from 1981) of Louis Althusser's "structuralism" in order to make a parallel with an analysis of the present. Jameson lays out Althusser's moves in this way: "This is the sense in which this 'structure' is an absent cause, since it is nowhere empirically present as an element, it is not part of the whole or one of the levels, but rather the entire system of *relations* among these levels" (*The Political Unconsciousness: Narrative as a Socially Symbolic Act*, Cornell UP, Ithaca 1981, p. 36). This "entire system of *relations*" has a parallel with Jamie Peck and Adam Tickell's proposition of neoliberalism as "an ideological software for global competitiveness" (Jamie Peck and Adam Tickell, "Neoliberalizing Space," *Antipode* [June 2002], p. 380–404) in that neoliberalism becomes the interface for the relations of the various levels of the structure of global capital.

[43] Ibid., p. 180.

[44] David Harvey, *A Brief History of Neoliberalism*, Oxford University Press, Oxford, 2005, p. 7.

[45] Neil Smith, *The Endgame of Globalization*, Routledge, London 2005, p. 31.

[46] Neil Smith, "The Revolutionary Imperative," *Antipode* 41 (2009), p. 54–55.

How High Is the City, How Deep
Is Our Love?

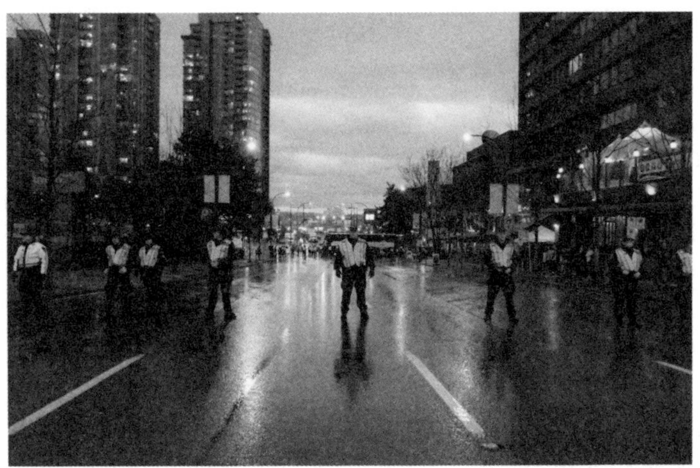

Sabine Bitter, *Vancouver 2010*, 2010
Digital print, 20 × 30 cm

We are often reminded that we love the city, that intimate aspects of ourselves course through the veins of the city we live in, and that a deep affection binds us to the space and places of *our* city.[1] And we *do* love cities; our lives *are* wrapped in and through the spaces and textures and possibilities of our urban experience. By our productive movements through the spaces of the city, and by the making public of streets, parks, galleries, bars, studios, and apartments, through the ways we enliven them, and through the discussion of what is possible in a city, we slowly build up the city's identity and life. Likewise, through the critique of the lack of possibilities, of the enclosures of the possible and the achingly stupid aspects of any city, we also build up a love for the city in another way. But I want to speculate on the place that *critique* has in the texture of the urban and the way that critique engages with the lived experience of the city at

the same time as it hopes to reshape the future city. I also
want to reflect critically on how notions of *affect*—both how
it is thought of in relation to the city and how it is circulated
as a force in urban policy—take this love for the city in
another direction and work toward a short-circuiting
of Michel Foucault's idea of "permanent critique." And in
order to ground this in a policy move that is drifting through
cities looking to rebrand themselves, I take up the tools
of critique to locate Richard Florida's promotion of the
"creative city" as an affect of what Luc Boltanski and Eve
Chiapello identify as the new spirit of capitalism and an
appropriation of progressive critiques of work and human
potential in relation to the utopian leanings of the artistic
avant-garde over the 20th-century.

Completely Urbanized Life and Permanent Critique

The life of any city, and our lives within it, is always
a dramatic testing of the possible against the contained,
a friction of the imagined and what can be made material.
Henri Lefevbre spreads this dialectic across all of society
when he proclaims "Society has been completely urbanized,"[2] but he is equally careful to make *urbanism* a social
practice at all scales. This is not simply a demographic
revolution, however, despite the climbing statistics that
have half of the world's population living in cities while
predicting an even more rapid urbanization, to the extent
that "by 2030, the towns and cities of the developing
world will make up 81 percent of urban humanity."[3] But
urban society is not a demographic argument from Lefebvre;
instead it is a hypothesis that identifies industrialization
as a "process of domination" that has extended the urban
fabric beyond the city, and therefore it is meant to shunt
the term "postindustrial" aside. The urban revolution
refers to, Lefebvre writes,

> the transformations that affect contemporary society,
> ranging from the period when questions of growth
> and industrialization predominate … to the period
> when the search for solutions and modalities unique
> to urban society are foremost.[4]

This also points to the temporal aspect to Lefebvre's urban revolution: it is the condition of the present and an anticipatory hypothesis.[5]

The sinuous energy of Lefebvre's thought on cities is not just his understanding of space as a social practice, nor is it only his emphasis on the life and politics of the street as a defining counter-power to the "from above" urban planning that he saw impose functionality onto the city: Lefebvre also lays out a radical temporality of the city in which cities are always emerging and claiming the present, and can, through critique, grasp a future horizon. Like the Situationists, who drew their inspiration from and against him, Lefebvre argues that critique from the left specifically

> attempts to open a path to the possible, to explore and delineate a landscape that is not merely part of the "real," the accomplished, occupied by existing social, political, and economic forces. It is a *utopian* critique because it steps back from the real without, however, losing sight of it.[6]

Critique then becomes one powerful and lived aspect of the urban phenomenon and the imagining of a city.

Thought of in these terms, critique is not simply a stark or programmatic diagram that would help us understand how power functions in the city—for power is not nearly so diagrammatic despite it being grounded in places and structures. Nor is critique limited to the socially necessary act of pointing out whose voices are heard in city halls or whose ideas are implemented and how other less convenient voices are pushed aside. Rather, critique is a process that is at the very heart of the urbanization of everyday life. In fact, pushed farther, critique can be proposed as a *return to life* through the attempt to "open a path to the possible" by an investigation of what negates the possible.

Critique, therefore, must be thought of broadly, as Foucault does in his reworking of Trotsky's concept and Mao's slogan of "permanent revolution" to "permanent critique of our historical era."[7] As Judith Butler puts it,

> he [Foucault] maintains that the philosophical ethos of modernity involves sustaining a permanent critique

of our historical era (a term that involves a transposition of the Maoist slogan of permanent revolution).[8]

And, by transposing Foucault's transposition, Butler raises
the question: "Could it not be that critique is that revolution
at the level of procedure without which we cannot secure
rights of dissent and processes of legitimation?"[9] With
critique elaborated as a permanent process aimed at securing
dissent and the questioning of the solidification of legitimacy, this concept of critique intersects with Lefebvre's own
permanent critique of modernity in general and modernist
urban planning specifically. With this intersection of rights-
based critique and a critique of modernity and governmentality as it manifests in its urban spatial regime (which itself
can be seen in terms of *spatial justice*), critique shapes the
relationships that we build throughout our lives *within* the
city through its attention to the dialectic of the possible and
the contained and of the real and the imagined. The role of
critique is exactly what can make city life the most energiz-
ing and deeply affective. But critique must be turned toward
affect as well when affect becomes naturalized and moves
into governmentality, or as Foucault put it, "the techniques
of government."[10]

A New Spirit of Urbanism?

Luc Boltanski and Eve Chiapello make a compelling argument
that a new spirit of capitalism was shaped through a dance
of incorporation and evasion of the critiques of capitalism
that came at the moment when imagining the future hit
the streets in Paris in May 1968. Taking that "explosion" as
a shift, Boltanski and Chiapello detail the "sources of
indignation" that heated up two modes of critique—social
critique and artistic critique. I think we can map the claims
of artistic critique—as well as the way that Boltanski and
Chiapello point out that capitalism adapted and absorbed
them—onto the language of urban planning. Crucially,
we also have to grasp this as a move that is strongly affective,
a discourse that asks us to *feel* it and live it even if our
participation in its shaping is minimal and based on a model
of consensus rather than a model of justice and equity."[11]

Artistic critique coalesced out of a critique of *alienation*, an alienation better understood as the hollow distance between everyday life and the promises of postwar capitalism within the dialectic of production and consumption. Central to this critique were the themes of "the poverty of everyday life" and "the dehumanization of the world under the sway of technicization and technocratization," on one side, and, on the other, "the loss of autonomy, the absence of creativity, and different forms of oppression in the modern world."[12] These themes existed earlier as the staple of critique from the historical avant-gardes, and they are the historical themes of the critique of capitalism. They are also themes that are found at different scales and in varied spaces—from the domestic sphere, within institutions, in the work place, and through the city and up to the nation. The development of the themes of artistic critique, Boltanski and Chiapello argue,

> answer to the expectation and anxieties of new generations of students and *cadres*, and spoke to the discrepancy between their aspiration to intellectual freedom and the forms of work organization to which they had to submit in order to be integrated socially.[13]

How do we understand these themes today? While they are both historical and timeless, in a sense, how have these themes of critique been reshaped by the new spirit of capitalism within cities? And, how have these themes been reflected in urban planning of today? What would the "artistic critique" of everyday life in a city be today?

Viewed from the perspective of these questions, the city becomes a dialectic of affect and *enstrangement*[14]: we love the city even though the very things we would love for the city (and, therefore, for ourselves and others) do not yet exist. But as the city is built upon our everyday practices, this enstrangement makes the city strange and distorts our daily lives. At the same time, this relationship creates highly affective forms of collectivity, imagination, and agency, for we also cohere to declare and demand these things for and from the city (to critique rights and legitimacy). These things are often the most basic—such as housing or access to the processes of decision-making. That is, these claims to the city still have their roots in the promises of modernism, which, despite a rejection of their spatial logic, have been replaced by neoliberalism's promise of development and growth (which in reality has accelerated uneven development across spatial scales). To work through this vivid relationship of enstrangement and affect—of deep love for the city yet the unbalanced relationship we have to the grand project for the city—two very powerful *themes* for the city have been mobilized as policy fixes for both "shrinking" or "failed" cities and for cities looking to boost their standing in the neoliberal competition for investment. These themes alter the identity of the city itself and, therefore, ask the people in a city to adapt their own identities, everyday practices, and lives—these themes ask for the love of citizens. These two powerful themes of our times are *sustainability* and *creativity*. When these themes are not grounded in equity and justice, they become programs for the city and extensions of the new spirit of capitalism's answer to the artistic critique of urban life. That is, worse than policy fixes dropped down from above, shined up at "stake-holder" discussions, and then implemented in the grandest modernist fashion (and setting off uneven development within cities between the *creative* sectors and the working-class sectors or the *sustainable* areas and the inefficient and often more-affordable areas), these terms signal a startling reversal of powerful points of critique.

The language of *creativity* and of *sustainability* often represents these concepts as if they are for the city itself, for the good and the life of the city as a totality, rather than the people whose every action makes an urban territory a city. A very lived tension then sparks: we are asked to affectively adapt to a program that has all of the right terms, themes, and perhaps even possibilities, yet it is a program for the city as if its citizens are detached from it. Therefore, we have the enstranged vocabularies of the sustainable city or the creative city, as if these themes, brought down from above, will improve or fix the city itself. But should not a sustainable city sustain life for those who live in it? And should not the creative city make life more creative for all of its citizens?

But these terms and other aspects of urban planning and governance are affectively charged, bringing with them promises of both longevity and a more vital life (again modernism's unfulfilled promises poised on neoliberalism's horizon!). What I am proposing here is that urban governance does not work on the troubled model of ideology and interpellation, as Louis Althusser rigidly laid out in "Ideology and Ideological State Apparatuses."[15] Rather than having citizen-subjects instantaneously interpellate themselves into a structure of power by heeding the call of the Law (figured as the police by Althusser), urban governance makes a visceral attachment to our affective relations with the city. Using Sara Ahmed's model of affect as negotiating both the individual (internal) and collective (relational), it is possible to see that urban governance attaches itself to affectively charged relations that we hold regarding the city, and that this use of affect then mediates what is possible in terms of governance. Often this use of affect is to mediate the most inhuman of governance, to attach it to an affective relation in order to humanize it. For instance, in Vancouver, in the time leading up to the 2010 Olympics, a new law to allow the police to forcibly move homeless people to shelters during severe weather was affectively circulated as an instance of the city caring deeply about the its permanent homeless population. The city, it affectively appeared, cared more deeply about the well-being of the homeless than even the homeless themselves, who were characterized as acting against their own best interests. But this affective tug was blocked by critiques from civil society groups that rightly pointed out that this new street-cleaning law was suspiciously similar to laws invoked by other Olympic cities as the games neared—that, in fact, the law, which was highly contested and therefore not acted on, was designed to hide rather than to help the homeless.

What's Affect Got to Do With It?

In arguing that affect has been neglected in the study of cities, Nigel Thrift posits that "systematic knowledges of the creation and mobilization of affect have become an integral part of the everyday urban landscape," and

> these knowledges are not only deployed knowingly,
> but they are also deployed politically (mainly but not

only by the rich and powerful) to political ends: what
might have been painted as aesthetic is increasingly
instrumental.[16]

Yet from a cultural perspective, there can be no separation
of the aesthetic and the ideological, and, from an urbanist
position, no *use* of affect is non-ideological. There can
be no pure affect; affect is an intensity but not a refuge!
Or to be more precise, no production and deployment
of affect (positive or negative) is non-instrumental, nor can
we understand affect as simply residing within the urban
texture—it is not latent and therefore must be circulated
to have an effect.[17]
　　To be clear, by *affect* I do not simply intend to mark
the emotional attachment we have to the city, nor do
I want to limit the circulation of these strong emotions to
a feeling that emerges out of an individual or that is somehow latent to the city itself. Sara Ahmed, in looking at
affective economies, makes a compelling case to challenge
an idea of affect that isolates emotion to an individual, and,
from an urban perspective, the isolation of an *affective* city
needs to be challenged as well. Instead of a model in which
affect resides inside an individual or object, Ahmed writes
that she is "interested in the way emotions *involve* subjects
and objects, but without residing positively within them."[18]
Ahmed asserts that,

> Rather than seeing emotions as psychological
> dispositions, we need to consider how they work, in
> concrete and particular ways, to mediate the relation-
> ship between the psychic and the social, and between
> the individual and the collective.[19]

This emphasis on the relationship of the individual and
the collective is critical to understanding how cities work,
as well as the manner in which urban governance draws
on our love of the city.
　　Ahmed criticizes a model of the sociality of
emotion that is based on the "presumption of interiority"
and that "assume[s] the objectivity of the very distinction
of inside and outside."[20] In this two-part model, emotions
are understood to either move

"inside out" toward objects and others, or conversely,
"outside in": "emotions are assumed to *come from without and
move inward*."[21] Countering these models, Ahmed argues,

> emotions are not "in" either the individual or the
> social, but produce the surfaces and boundaries that
> allow the individual and the social to be delineated
> as if they are objects.[22]

How can we understand this model in terms of the deployment of affect in neoliberal urban policy? How does a policy
accrue affective value? Governance does not simply circulate
ideas that make their way from affect to ideology (with those
two terms overlapping) to policy, but rather the movement
from concept to policy is bound up with affect. This binding
gives the policy itself an affective quality: "sustainability"
becomes about preserving the city for our children and
grandchildren or about saving the environment and human-
kind. Crucially, this affective binding deflects critique of
sustainability as an accumulation strategy and moves away
from the social justice question of sustainable urbanism.
Read within the terrain of neoliberalism, we can see that
the most *humanly* affective registers (saving the city for
our imagined grandchildren) often hit against the hard edge
of the economic logic of neoliberalism: not only do these
programs that hold so much potential lose their promise,
but, as Margit Mayer points out,

> social, political, and ecological criteria have become
> included [in local economic development policies and
> community-based programs] (while also redefined)
> in the efforts to promote economic competitiveness:
> social infrastructures, political culture, and ecological
> foundations of the city are being transformed into
> economic assets whenever possible.[23]

Let's take the example of *creativity*: this positive
attribute of a city is affectively charged through the constant
discussion and examples of cities as a creative terrain
(What city does not claim to be creative!) and the pleasur-
able possibilities of living in the city as well as tapping into
a central theme in artistic avant-gardes across the 20th

century. Once charged in this way, creativity circulates socially as a positive attribute of a city (Who can be against creativity? Who can say, I want a non-creative city?) that can be embedded in the city rather than a practice already found in everyday life: rather than recognize these practices in the urban terrain, creativity must be brought in, in the form of a highly mobile, and, therefore, potentially temporary class, whose members are understood to reshape the city with their taste, lifestyle, and consumption practices. Creativity, in this form, separates the city from everyday life.

The Right to Creativity

I want to focus on how *creativity* has moved from a term that was central to artistic critique to an urban policy based on a brittle economic understanding of creativity. The notion of the creative city has been formulated and promoted by Richard Florida, and his popular books read as how-to manuals for mayors on the one hand and for home-buyers on the other. Yet what does Florida mean by *creativity*? Merely one paragraph into the paperback edition of his *The Rise of the Creative Class*, he announces that "Human creativity is the ultimate economic resource."[24] This is a shockingly narrow understanding of creativity, and it does not take on much more nuance or texture throughout his work. But most disturbingly, Florida's use of *creativity* is exactly the opposite of what creativity so viscerally meant over the 20th-century within artistic critique. In a reversal, Florida carjacks creativity as an economic resource so it is no longer the antidote to dehumanizing relations and modes of economic production as it historically has been mobilized. Once stripped of its historical context and removed from the actual history of creativity as a central aspect of dreams of life that range from a more meaningful existence and less alienating work to dreams of *autogestion* (self-management) and a new society, creativity turns into the dystopic opposite of this powerful concept. Florida's creativity is not based on equity and justice, for, as he writes, "I had a hunch while writing *The Rise of the Creative Class* that inequity in our society was being exacerbated by the rise of the creative economy," and his research shows that "inequity is highest in the creative epicenters of the US economy."[25] Likewise, his research shows that the creative economy opens a divide between creative labor and non-creative labor (and the class tension in Florida's work is palpable—no working-class labor is understood as anything other than minimally creative), which is replicated economically—the creative class produces low-paying "non-creative" service jobs. Ironically, in cities across Canada, these service jobs are the type of work that many artists, writers, and performers take on to get by.

When read through a history of aesthetics and culture, Florida's commandeering and narrowing of creativity does something very similar to the process that Boltanski and Chiapello attribute to the new spirit of capitalism in terms of critique. In Raymond Williams' forceful, influential argument for an expanded view of culture (and one that has been criticized for becoming too expansive and losing its specific meaning as a consequence), in *The Long Revolution* he tracks the historical separation of art, creativity, and "ordinary social life":

> To see art as a particular process in the general human definition of creative discovery and communication is at once a redefinition of the status of art and the finding of a means to link it to our ordinary social life. The traditional definition of art as "creative" was profoundly important, as an emphasis, but when this was extended to a contrast between art and ordinary experience the consequences were very damaging.[26]

Given this division, Williams proposes that, "The solution is not to pull art down to the level of other social activity as this is habitually conceived."[27] Rather than "lowering" art, Williams pushes for "ordinary activities" to be understood as part of a process of the creative production of everyday life—the result is that "we create our human world as we thought of art being created."[28] This leveling of art and life is not the same move as that of the Russian Futurists, with their call of "art into life," for, in Williams' view, this process does not involve a radical transformation of art or life, but rather a *recognition* of the thread of creativity that stitches them together into the texture of culture as a whole way of life. Despite his breezy configuration of life, Florida resorts to a traditional isolation of *creativity* as the attribute and

practice of a particular class. In essence, in contrast
to Williams (and in contrast to any progressive or engaged
art practice), Florida pulls *creativity* out of life as a whole
and deposits it in the lifestyle of the creativity class.
Florida's dystopic appropriation of the Futurist slogan
is "Art into lifestyle."

Florida's conceptualization and location of the value
of creativity is exemplary of the new spirit of capitalism
and neoliberalism in relation to both critique and to the
utopian leaning of art. As Jacques Rancière puts it,

> If the concept of the avant-garde has any meaning
> in the aesthetic regime of the arts, it is on this
> side of things [the aesthetic anticipation of the
> future], not on the side of advanced detachments
> of artistic innovation but on the side of the invention
> of sensible forms of material structures of life to
> come.[29]

Or, in other words, the avant-garde has meaning beyond
itself when it aims to look for novel and appropriate
ways to embed art and the politics of the aesthetic into
life (therefore transforming life) rather than seeking
degrees of autonomy for the aesthetic.

Manfredo Tafuri framed the avant-garde in a similar
manner earlier, but he sharpened the point of the avant-
garde's attention to relations of production and work;
he writes " … there has existed no avant-garde movement
whose own 'political' objective was not, implicitly or
explicitly, the liberation from work," including the
Russian Productivists and Constructivists who proposed
a "new work" that was collective and planned.[30]
Tellingly, for Florida, it is this liberation from work
he understands as noncreative that defines the creative
class and produces value for the creative city. But,
again, this is possible because Florida cannot imagine
Williams' recognition of the creative aspect of *all work*
or the transformation of the relations of work in society
as a whole. Florida does include the caveat that

> Creativity in the world is not limited to members
> of the Creative Class. Factory workers and even

the lowest-end service workers always have been
creative in certain ways.[31]

There is no masking that Florida frames this limited
creativity as *less valuable* than the creativity of his class (for
he includes himself in the creative class). Ultimately Florida
argues that this simple creativity needs to be integrated into
the creative economy rather than "bringing back the factory
jobs of the past."[32] In this, we hear the echoes of neoliberalism's response to unemployment in the productive sector.
Of course, those "factory jobs of the past" (with their
relatively decent wages) have gone elsewhere, as someone
has to *make things*, but with punishing wages and conditions.
      As Jamie Peck points out in his biting critique of
Florida, creative city plans and the creative economy do not
solve issues of inequity and the right to the city; rather,
"[c]reative strategies have been crafted to coexist with these
problems, not to solve them."[33] Peck describes the use of
creativity in urban planning as an easy fix:

> The creative cities thesis represents a "soft" policy
> fix for this neoliberal urban conjuncture, making the
> case for modest and discretionary public spending
> on creative assets, while raising a favored bundle of
> middle-class lifestyles … to the status of urban-
> development objective.[34]

Florida's thesis is a nexus of the incorporation and evasion
of the critiques of capitalism pushed in the most dramatic
manner (life and death!) by the artistic critique: what was
once a devastating critique and a hair-raising rallying call for
action in one's everyday life becomes a migrating policy
designed to exit alongside the contradictions and inequities
it produces.

Conclusion: Artistic Critique in the City

In terms of how I have written about affect here, creative
strategies try to take the very aspects that we love about the
city—street life, alternative modes of production, mobility,
and movement by choice—and incorporate them into an
economic force at the same time as it blunts artistic critique

aimed at capitalism and everyday life. But this idea of creativity also contains or curtails other forms of *creativity* such as collective forms of production, or nonhierarchical ways of organizing cultural production and creative practices, or ways of thinking about culture outside of an economic imperative, ways of grasping culture that see it as an alternative and less predictable method of thinking. Ironically, for Vancouver—a city that is proud of, and banking on, its creativity and its lifestyle—the form of creativity imagined and rendered by Florida would run some of the more resilient forms of cultural life out of town. In Vancouver, the artist-run network was based exactly on a strategic separation of the artistic (or creative) from the imperatives of the economic. This separation was to open a space of critique as well and was based on artistic forms of soft autonomy and self-management.

We often read that we are living through a great moment in the transformation of the world economy. We are living through neoliberalism as a failure on the grandest scale, but because of this "great transformation," we are also living through the rewriting of culture. And, this, too, is a question of scale—where once culture was imagined in Canada at the national scale, and then at the regional scale, it is now imagined at the urban scale. The modernist cultural plan of the nation has given way to the public-private cultural model of the city. Today, an exportable form of urban governance and planning with which Vancouver has branded itself is seen as the city's achievement, as its marker within the global-urban nexus. Yet, urbanism in Vancouver is not as positively public as the language of urban planning hints at—many of the necessary public acts in the city are to make a claim for what is lacking, or to try to block bad governance, or to ask for unfulfilled promises to be met. Within the consensus model of urban planning that is now dominant, the range of its imagination does not include more radical planning that would allow decisions to drift downward to those who will be the most affected. Neoliberal governance drifts upward—it avoids the streets, as Lefebvre would say—to nonelected private groups or boards and public figures in the field of urban development or finance: this drift upward is what has distorted urbanism in Vancouver, as it has in so many cities. As John Punter dryly lays out

in *The Vancouver Achievement*, with the shift away from
large-scale public redevelopment to large-scale development,
"urban planning as public policy" was also transformed
to "safeguarding," "review practices," and "design principles"
rather than participatory planning with a sustained public
input. The public aspect of planning becomes based on mini-
mums rather than "vision," yet all the time speaks of vision
and risk (so much so that these two terms are honorifics for
developers). Punter unquestioningly sees this shift as being
a move from unpopular modernist planning to postmodern
urban design distinguished by private development that is
"more likely to respect the scale, grain, and character of the
locality and to reinforce its positive rather than its negative
qualities."[35] Yet this division of public modernism and
private postmodernism is not so clear in practice—private
development and redevelopment has been at a massive scale,
a scale much more common to modernist planning, and
as it is private, there are few chances for meaningful public
input or any impulse toward publicness in the architecture
or plan beyond what can be bought by the city in terms of
public art (as an added value) or another form of trade-off. In
Vancouver, it often appears that we have a form of public-
private modernist planning that erects postmodern architecture. In this formula we even lose the aesthetics of modernism to ornamentation, unusable setbacks as private-public
space, and a myth of the human scale.

This parallel between modernist urban planning's
drift to postmodern private-public urban design has also
altered the model and use of public art in our cities.
Perhaps, then, we also need to recalibrate the understanding
of public art—which so often is the product of public–
private partnerships—to think through the possibilities
of it as an *urban art* and, therefore, part of the texture of the
city. Urban art could then engage in a dialectic of closure
and possibility that is characteristic of the life of cities.
Pop art, public art, and the politics of the creative city
share more than is comfortable to acknowledge if they work
toward rebranding a city, or being a policy fix as Peck
argues, rather than taking on a more active and challenging
role in imagining the city.

The right to the city continues as an intense global-
urban theme as we enter this new decade. Artistic critique

and its history of emphasizing the creative possibilities
of everyone's life has a lot to say about the transformation
of cities today. The deployment of affect in urban governance is itself embedded within the new spirit of capitalism's
appropriation of artistic and social critique's force.
But artistic critique is both discursive and material as well
as affective and public. Perhaps through it we can then
ask the city to love us, and to love equity and justice.

[1] I began writing this reflection on Vancouver in Caracas, Venezuela, a city seemingly impossible to love yet utterly compelling. Seen as one of the most dangerous cities in Latin America, it is thick with a past of colonial city planning, of modernist plans broken by both the corruption of dictators and the popular will of the people. It is a city held in the hands of spectacular nature, yet a nature that seems to deliver little to the majority of people. But today the official Socialist City Plan of Caracas has enabled citizens to develop a robust form of self-management, or *autogestion*. Urban Subjects, a cultural and urban research collective formed by Sabine Bitter, Helmut Weber, and myself, visited barrio communities that had taken self-governance to a degree that would be impossible in North America: community councils in Caracas organize solutions to housing, health, food/nutrition, transportation, culture, sports, and many other aspects of their communities through a non-consensus form of participatory democracy that is aided by all levels of the city and state, as well as the military. For an indication of this mode of planning, see Farruco Sesto's "Conceptual Notes on a Design for Cities of Socialism" (2007), at http://mrzine.monthlyreview. org/2007/sesto241007p.html (last accessed May 2013).

[2] Henri Lefebvre, *The Urban Revolution*, trans. Robert Bononno, University of Minnesota Press, Minneapolis 2003, p. 1.

[3] Cf. the UNFPA report "State of the World Population 2007: Unleashing the Potential of Urban Growth," at http://www.unfpa.org/swp/2007/english/introduction.html (last accessed May 2013).

[4] Lefebvre, *The Urban Revolution*, p. 5.

[5] Ibid., p. 4.

[6] Ibid., p. 6–7.

[7] Cf. an online version of Trotsky's 1930 "The Permanent Revolution" at http://www.marxists.org/archive/ trotsky/1931/tpr/index.htm (last accessed May 2013). Also, Judith Butler situates Foucault in relation to Mao in her extensive reading of Foucault in "Critique, Dissent, Disciplinarity," *Critical Inquiry* 35, no. 4 (Summer 2009), p. 773–795. Gerald Raunig provides a rereading of both Butler and Foucault in "What Is Critique: Suspension and Recomposition in Textual and Social Machines," trans. Aileen Derieg, at http://eipcp.net/transversal/0808/raunig/ en (last accessed May 2013).

[8] Judith Butler, "Critique, Dissent, Disciplinarity," *Critical Inquiry* 35, no. 4 (Summer 2009), p. 773–795.

[9] Ibid., p. 795.

[10] Michel Foucault, "Governmentality," Graham Burchell, Colin Gordon, Peter Miller (eds.), *The Foucault Effect: Studies in Governmentality*, University of Chicago Press, Chicago 1991, p. 101.

[11] In a video of a panel on "Radical Urbanism: The Right to the City," held at the City University of New York Graduate Centre on December 12, 2008 (and available at http://www. youtube.com/watch?v=DkKXt6lTTD4, last accessed May 2013), Peter Marcuse argues that a consensus model of urban planning is based on a "win-win" situation, that the plan will help everyone. But the real issue, Marcuse points out, is a change in power relations and in that there must be a "win-lose" change. In order to redistribute power, some must lose power in order for others to gain it.

[12] Luc Boltanski and Eve Chiapello, *The New Spirit of Capitalism*, trans. Gregory Elliot, Verso, New York 2005, p. 170.

[13] Ibid.

[14] I am using the word *enstrangement* here rather than the more common *estrangement* due to the specific avant-gardist history of the word. My usage stems from the translation of the Russian Formalist Viktor Shklovsky's use of the Russian neologism *ostraniene* in his classic *Theory of Prose*. An earlier translation was *estrangement* (see *Russian Formalism: Four Essays*, Lemon and Reis (eds.), University of Nebraska Press, Lincoln, Nebraska 1965), but a new translation form Benjamin Sher argues in detail for the specificity of *enstrangement* (see "Translator's Introduction: Shklovsky and the Revolution," Benjamin Sher in Viktor Shklovsky, *Theory of Prose*, Dalkey Archive Press, London 1991, p. xix).

[15] Louis Althusser, "Ideology and Ideological State Apparatuses," *Lenin and Philosophy and Other Essays*, trans. Ben Brewster, Monthly Review Press, New York and London 1971, p. 121–176.

[16] Nigel Thrift, "Intensities of Feeling: Towards a Spatial Politics of Affect," *Geografiska Annaler* 86 B (2004), p. 58.

[17] Nor can we privilege the city as the scale that is more intensely affective than any other scale—certainly during the Olympic games in Vancouver we saw a shift in the scale of affect from the city (always positioned centrally as a place of pride) to the nation (channeled through the nationalism of sport and particularly hockey as "Canada's game"). But this affective scale shift simply produced a nonreflexive form of nationalism that was resistant to any challenge or questioning.

[18] Sara Ahmed, "Affective Economies," *Social Text* 22, no. 2 (2004), p. 118.

[19] Ibid.

[20] Sara Ahmed, *The Cultural Politics of Emotions*, Edinburgh University Press, Edinburgh 2004, p. 8–9.

[21] Ibid., p. 9.

[22] Ibid., p. 10.

[23] Mayer, "Contesting the Neoliberalization of Urban Governance," Helga Leitner, Jamie Peck, Eric Sheppard (eds.), *Contesting Neoliberalism: Urban Frontiers*, The Guilford Press, New York 2007, p. 91.

[24] Richard Florida, *The Rise of the Creative Class*, Basic Books, New York 2004, p. xiii.

[25] Ibid., p. xv.

[26] Raymond Williams, *The Long Revolution*, Harper Torch Books, New York 1961, p. 37.

[27] Ibid.

[28] Ibid.

[29] Jacques Rancière, *The Politics of Aesthetics*, trans. Gabriel Rockhill, Continuum, London 2004, p. 29.

[30] Manfredo Tafuri, *Architecture and Utopia: Design and Capitalist Development*, trans. Barbara Luigia La Penta, MIT Press, Cambridge, Massachusetts 1976, p. 57.

[31] Florida, *The Rise of the Creative Class*, p. 10.

[32] Ibid.

[33] Jamie Peck, "The Creativity Fix," *Fronesis* 24 (2007), p. 174–192. Amended version reprinted as "The Creativity Fix," *Eurozine* (2007), www.eurozine.com.

[34] Ibid.

[35] John Punter, *The Vancouver Achievement: Urban Planning and Design*, University of British Columbia Press, Vancouver 2005, p. xxi.

Art and Cities During Mega-Events: On the Intersection of Culture, Everyday Life, and the Olympics in Vancouver and Beyond

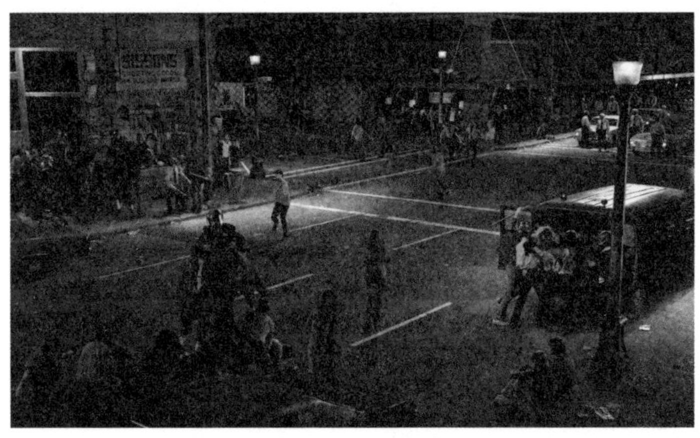

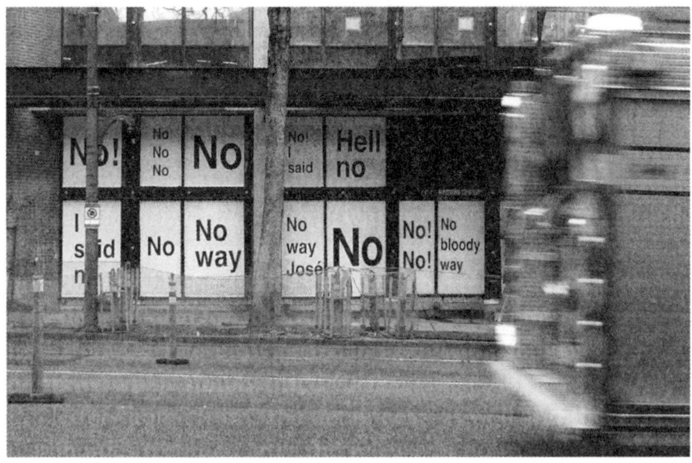

Stan Douglas, *Abbott & Cordova, 7 August 1971*, 2008
C-print, 117.8 × 290.8 cm

Ken Lum, *"I said No!,"* 2010
Site-specific installation, vinyl signage

I.

On the plywood cladding that encloses one of the many stalled construction sites in the city center of Vancouver, British Columbia (BC), a spectral figure speaks from a block of posters. This ghost from the recent past, identified as Premier Bill Bennett, addresses urbanites and tourists as citizens who have a pride of place and a civic duty. While this address would be familiar only to those who recall the devastating days of BC's Thatcherite 1980s period, the poster bears the familiar blue logo of Expo 86, the World Fair held on what became the largest waterfront development in North America, which miraculously produced no public profit for the city, but was passed off to developer Li Ka-shing to embed Vancouver into global capital by using land and space (real estate) as a raw exportable resource.

This Expo poster, one in a series of reproductions from the archive of Expo 86 and part of artist Jeremy Shaw's project Something's Happening Here, reiterates a government statement that coaxes citizens into the excitement of a world's fair; but the address comes from a beleaguered position of a city that imagines itself on the edges of global capital, and a city that desperately wants to bring that capital in through this "unmatched opportunity, a once in a lifetime chance, to showcase our province to the world." Ironically, this excited view of capitalist opportunity—that has its eyes set firmly on the present as the exceptional moment that cannot be missed, as a moment that all stops must be pulled out for—is exactly, and uncannily, the moment that the city, and its now more wary citizens, find themselves in as the 2010 Winter Olympics descend, literally, on Vancouver as the next big opportunity, as the big opportunity that is the exception.

Shaw's public project is reinforced by the uncanny intersections of these two mega-event fueled moments in the globalization and neoliberalization of Vancouver. But, these mega-events open the situated example of Vancouver beyond the global-local boosterism and city-to-city competition that neoliberalism breeds. More tellingly, these events spark Vancouver as a volatile node in the global-urban nexus in three ways. Firstly, history and the present collide in an overdetermined manner: the still unsettled colonial past of Vancouver haunts the very notion of land and, crucially, of ownership (that bedrock of neoliberalism) through the land claims of the First Nations people. This legacy of dispossession also haunts the security of the Olympics, for the First Nations have a radical history of road-blockages and stand-offs, and they bare a powerful slogan "No Olympics on Stolen Native Land." Secondly, the trajectory of neoliberalism raises crucial questions: What new shape of neoliberalism will be wielded by the local governments and the global players (from the International Olympic Committee to the financiers) now that neoliberalism itself is perceived to be powerful yet at the end of its long regime—"dead, but dominant," as geographer Neil Smith describes it, or as "zombie governance" as Jamie Peck recently called it.[1] Thirdly, there is the growing cultural question: What will be the role of culture, in this exceptional moment, in the transformation of the texture and possibilities of urban life, and in the possibilities of producing a counter-discourse to the mega-event? Add areas of deep poverty and chronic homelessness, highly organized and wonderfully critical civil society groups and activists, and a concentrated group of global elite players who have an intense engagement with real estate, urban development and art, and Vancouver emerges as a ground zero for the conflicts that neoliberaliza-tion thrives on and the crisis within it. The city is catalyzing into a platform for new claims to that Lefebvrian rallying cry, "the right to the city."

The content of this series of four columns cannot be predicted beforehand, for this unsteady mix of actors and interests, of floating neoliberalism and grounded opposition, of activists and rights advocacy groups and the $900 million Integrated Security Unit, creates an event within the mega-event that can not be foreseen.[2] These columns will be part reportage on how things unfold, but they will also try to theorize the tactics of neoliberalism as its zombie body again plants it feet in this "sustainable" and "creative" city. I will also locate the ways in which activists, artists, and civil society groups counter the coercion and force that have already produced "free-speech zones" (dubbed "protest pens"), a ban on signage that does not celebrate the Olympics, the enclosure of public spaces used by the poor and homeless, and a proposed bill that could put the homeless in shelters against their will and their rights.

Public space in Vancouver, long since fragmented and policed and altered by the transformation of space into a speculative commodity, is now distorted by the Olympics and the push of the mega-event as a gentrifying force in the poorest working-class neighborhood and as an acceleration of real estate as the economic engine throughout the city. While public space can be seen as a dead issue in this late neoliberal moment with the public sphere evaporated into "P3s" (public-private partnerships), it is this space— or this production of space—where possibilities brew. Yet the fate of the possibility and shape of particular spaces is not the key outcome; rather it is the kinds of publics (counter, neoliberal, activist, etc.) that will emerge through this struggle over space.

The political and cultural history of Vancouver is
punctuated by what Michael Warner calls "counter-publics"
and what Sven Lütticken has better described as the "secret
publicities" of avant-gardist formations.[3] These two acts—
one that estranges existing public space and the other more
utopian in its radical futurity—are necessary at the present
unsteady moment. But another form of a public is now
effectively operating within the exceptional time of the
mega-event. Spatializing Sianne Ngai's notion of "negative
affect" that springs from a context of "obstructed agency,"
I think we can identify negative publics whose tactics are
reactions to the clamp-down of critique and dissent and the
restrictions on making space public.[4] Negative publics can
be thought of as an act rather than a community or tendency
that fits into the existing fragmented and competitive public
sphere. Negative publicness does what counter-publics
do—present oppositional discourses and refuse to be
absorbed into a dominant commonsense—but it also shows
the limitations of existing public space and forms of publicness. As an act, negative publicness effectively tests these
spatial, social, and political relations—and they have the
possibility to produce space for unlikely allies and alliances.
Along with the many reactions to surveillance and enclosures
in Vancouver, there have been acts of negative publicness on
the cultural front. Countering the official Cultural Olympiad,
Fuck the Cultural Olympiad: Art & Anarchy, defined itself
as "not an art show, but the opening of a cultural front"
in direct opposition to the limits of institutionalized art. But
this event also unleashed a dialectic with the possibilities
of cultural critique that is social rather than institutional,
a critique that has been, for the most part, soft in Vancouver.
Over the course of this four-part series, I'll report on the
types of publics—and the cultural, social, and political
acts—that emerge out of these contested, branded, penned-
in, lived, and potential spaces.

2.

The Olympics in Vancouver began by marking itself as the
"sustainable games," but more pressing social issues around
housing, gentrification, and displacement quickly moved
to the forefront through the push of civil society groups and

activists. Tied into an existing populist resentment to the Olympics as a corporation and a supra-governmental organization, the push-back against the security force operating in the city and the new networks of surveillance is shaping the resistance to the Games. Security feels like the dominant Olympic concern, and the urban terrain of Vancouver is fragmented, enclosed, and altered daily as blue fencing shrinks the areas lived in by the city's impoverished population. At the same time, fresh surveillance cameras are blossoming throughout the city and streets are sealed as the International Olympic Committee builds a locked-down temporary city within this city. Combined with the 16,000 strong security force to come, the Olympics are taking on the feel of concentrated security occupation on "stolen native land" and on urban space pulled out of daily life.

In this rapid and alienating production of space, struggles over the public sphere and public speech brew as the types of negative public acts that I described in my last column—acts that test the boundaries of publicness— mark and contest the limitations on publicness in this time of mega-event exceptionalism. Speech acts are spatial acts in this moment, and even the rumor of an activist action causes the Olympic organizers to shift venues for events and announcements, to the point that the Olympics have little public contact. On the softer cultural front, the Cultural Olympiad produces space in ways different than the blue fencing barriers, the white tarps of temporary buildings for media, and the closed-off "red zones." Through an expansive public art program, the Cultural Olympiad is "mapping and marking" the city in a rush to add more public art to "brand Vancouver." Compared to other cities, this is a belated program, but the cultural aspect of the Olympics is not a temporary add-on designed to draw more tourists to the mega-event; instead it signals a highly localized programmatic shift driven by the migrating global policy of "the creative city."

The idea of the "creative city," shaped and promoted by Richard Florida, ties flawlessly into neoliberal urban governance as it caters to one class at the expense of others by proposing a cultural fix to social and economic problems.[5] This program—and Florida's heavy use of indexes of crea- tivity—foregrounds culture in the neoliberal competition between cities and the race to brand cities around a dominating identity of creativity—identities often at odds with the city's history. With sustainability and eco-density as the new signifiers of a green consumptive lifestyle, Florida's brand of economic creativity laces human nature into Vancouver's famous and lavishly represented naturalized landscape. In this scenario, artists are not the bulldozer blade of gentrification—in fact artists are not needed—but creativity as an economic engine becomes the rationale for gentrification. This marks a new role for culture in the new global stage of gentrification: culture is no longer only the accelerant—the starting fluid—of gentrification, leaving only a trace once its job is done; rather culture is a spin-off of creativity refigured as an accumulation strategy.

Within this altered cultural landscape of the city, several new works of public art gain sharpened meaning from the Olympics context and disturb the intention of art in the public sphere within the creative city. The public sphere has been fundamentally rearranged here, existing more as a private-public amalgam, but it has been tightly squeezed by the restriction on public speech and anti-Olympics signage that comes from the IOC and the city. The IOC Charter bans any "demonstration or political, religious or racial propaganda in any Olympic sites, venues or other areas" and through clumsy city bylaws this seemed to extend to any statement negative to the Olympics, even if it was a sign in the window of this "city of glass." A legal challenge to this closure of free speech was successful, but the threat is still potent. In a public artwork in the window of the new Audain Gallery in the Woodward's building in the heart of the Downtown Eastside—a site that is symbolic of the scale the transformation of the city—Ken Lum has mounted a sly and effective textual work. *I Said No* is a powerful speech act of a negative public with 12 different exclamations of disagreement ranging from a simple "NO!" to "No way José" and "No bloody way" addressing the street. Contradicting the affirmative nature of most public art, *I Said No* amplifies the right to say no, the very right which the IOC and the city have tried to erode. Cannily, this work relies on different public frames of meaning to give it a concrete address—it is a public work stripped of its referent, but it draws on the public to produce a particular meaning. At this site, and at this time, the possibilities of meaning are powerful and multiple, but I'm reading it as a smart tactic that works in three ways. Firstly it uses public space to say "No!" to the erosion of the ability to say "No!" but, read within the dominant frame of public discourse, it is also a specific rejection of the Olympics (the very thing that cannot be said no to!). And thirdly, it reflects the rejection of the many demands of housing, poverty reduction, and equity that civil society groups and activists have directed at the city and the IOC. *I Said No*, with its multiple yet grounded address, is filled with public meaning.

In the courtyard directly behind this temporary work is Stan Douglas' massive photomural, *Abbott & Cordova, 7 August 1971*. On a looming scale, Douglas' work is a super-realist reproduction of a riot that erupted on the adjacent street corner. Known as the Gastown Riot, this clash was really a police riot, complete with the batons, helmets, and horses, as the police set upon hippies who had gathered for a "Smoke-In" to claim the area as the center of the city's lingering and less political 1960s counterculture. Drawn from Vancouver's rich radical past of riots, the mural represents the current fear and expectation of police action against anti-Olympics protesters. So, while the mural does the public-art work of cinematically commemorating a historical moment, it also frames the present distortion of public space and the right to the city. But the mural is also tied into the intensified relationship of public art and private real estate as it has been used as a marketing feature for the speculative resale of private condos in the building.

Both of these works point to a creativity other than the narrowly defined form the neoliberal policy of the creative city sells—and both of these works make a claim to city space. Perhaps the greatest and most creative claim to space, and the right to the city, however, will come out of the restrictions on protest and speech as activists, in response to the clamp-down, devise smart and effective responses. The Olympic Resistance Network designed a series of posters that pick up on the contradictions between the Olympics Charter and the action of the IOC and its sponsors—each poster cites a contradiction and asks publically of the IOC, "Do You Hate the Olympics?" In a semantic twist, these posters are not only pro-Olympic

Charter, at least in the way it trumpets universal human rights, but also sharp critiques of the actually existing Olympics. In their fanatical control of visual and textual language, the IOC has alienated the Olympics from the city; on the other hand, activist groups have been able to tie causes and communities together that will lead to a 5-day convergence timed to the Olympic opening. The expectation for those days is a very different type of creative city.

3.

Earlier, I reflected the thick anticipation that the Games would occupy the city as an overwhelming zombie force, clamping down and clogging up the streets with the $900 million Integrated Security Unit, the powerful yet disengaged apparatus of the Olympic Organizing Committee (VANOC), and international tourists. Countering this, a convergence and coalition of artists, activists, civil society groups, and advocates for social justice appeared as a crest of opposition aiming to wrestle the city back, with all of its contradictions and possibilities, from the flat and affectless vision of the city as Brand Vancouver, a nature-drenched lure for those global citizens bold enough to lay down some capital in a sustainable city vibrating with the post-Fordist pleasures of investment and tourism. But, just as Henri Lefebvre opens his speculation on the events and situations of 1968, "Events belie forecasts: to the extent that the events are historical, they upset calculations."[6] To rework Lefebvre for the situation of the Olympics and the explosive, affective, and annulled events throughout the city, what was forecast did not always materialize and the calculations of the opposing sides were less incendiary than the frenetic lead-up promised.[7]

The Games hit the ground as a massive situation exactly in opposition to Debord and the Situationist International's sense: the situation of the Games was not mean to disrupt the familiar, but to accelerate and exacerbate both the inequities and aspects of everyday life in the neoliberal city—from the enclosure of space and the controlled access to space, to "police presence" and the monopoly of violence, surveillance, and most euphorically, consumption and cultural nationalism.

In the first week the spectacle looked to be heading for an official disaster—the sparse snow for the alpine events (nature failing the natural city!), the low number of tourists, the callous reaction to the death of luger Nodar Kumaritashvi, the lack of street events without five-hour line-ups, and the criticism of it all by (surprisingly!) the sports media, sped up the limp boosterism based on a belief in speech acts ("It will be the greatest Games ever!") and made space for deeply moving mobilizations and effective actions. I am tempted to build a marvelous catalogue of events prizing possibility from sleepy hegemony—but I will hold back and only highlight three events before turning to the cultural scene. The 19th Women's Memorial March for missing and murdered women wound through the contested areas of the city, growing to 5,000 people taking over the streets to arrive at the steps of the police headquarters to call out the police on their shocking inaction. Although purposely separated from anti-Olympics marches, the event illuminated the unevenness of justice and access in the city and clashed against every official representation of Vancouver beamed globally.

The Vancouver Media Co-op also kicked into high gear as a space of representation of all anti-Olympic actions, from the planned to the spontaneous to the mercurial— such as the temporary blockage of a bridge by the Salish Katzie First Nation. Generating the alternative news, VMC ignited the urgency of events and seized the representation of the present, particularly during a rally for housing a coalition set up the Olympic Tent Village on a lot used as a parking space for VANOC vehicles. The Tent Village ran as a highly visible symbol and as a self-managed site for several weeks—under police surveillance—and was a lever to negotiate housing for 40 homeless folks who took shelter there. Unlike marches, the tactic was not disruption but autogestion or self-management, which as Lefebvre (my go-to theorist for this situation) observes "is born and reborn at the heart of a contradictory society."[8]

The city, therefore, was not pressed down under the sheer weight of surveillance, security, and mega-event euphoria, but the unevenness, the contradictions, and the possibilities of the city were exaggerated. Within this clamor, varied cultural scenes emerged under the city's strategic use of the Olympics to showcase (a preferred verb of neoliberals) Vancouver as a localized creative city welcoming cosmopolitan capital. A range of tactics—from provocations and convergences to avoidances and capitulations—shaped up within this cultural showcase. The capitulations were gestures of official culture that saw the Olympics as a populist opportunity—the most crunching example was slam poet Shane Koyczan who performed during the truly unimaginative opening ceremony, hauling out every retrograde trope of Canadian cultural identity. In counterpoint to the forced inclusion of the situation, Artspeak Gallery mounted an effective refusal to participate, with Lucy Pullin's *I Would Prefer Not To*. The gallery windows were blanked out by reflective blinds that bounced light back at viewers, but denied visual entry into the gallery space. For Pullen, this refusal illuminated "the blind spot in every spectacle," but the window also gained meaning within the urban landscape. Artspeak is on a gentrifying street where restaurant owners effectively blur the relationship of inside and outside by using glass facades: the neighborhood people who use the street as part of their living space are now pressured to "move on" as they are seen to interfere with the "customers" inside. This "big window gentrification" is a recent tactic in the urban frontier of Vancouver.

The Candahar Bar, a reconstructed Irish bar by Theo Sims, hosted talks and performances that actively broke the contract of the Cultural Olympiad. Most slyly was the exhilarating Cranfield and Slade performance of riot songs drawn from the UK, American, and Vancouver punk history. The band seized the situation on the streets, detourned it, and ignited an affective event that powerfully set the speech act of "Fuck You" (from Vancouver's legendary Stiffs' song, yes, "Fuck You") against the jargon of neoliberal populism. Cranfield and Slade harnessed the tension of the potential riot (which never materialized other than a small clash between the police and the black bloc in the first week) in a convergence with the now-invisible history of urban punk politics. It was a strong shout-along reminder—with "superior passional quality" as Debord would say—that another city is possible.

The most transformative cultural events came through Video In Video Out (VIVO), an artist-run center,

which refused Cultural Olympiad funding to stage a series
of seminars, workshops, pirate radio broadcasts, and nightly
events under the banner of "Safe Assembly." VIVO became
the transversal site of artists, poets, intellectuals, and
activists where the urgency for exactly such an alignment
coincided with the necessity of assembly and transgression.
During the "Nightly News" events, where VMC screened
daily events, this urgency often boiled over into an inter-
generational antagonism as the tactics of civil society
groups, cultural groups, and the black bloc-tactic folks
clashed on the effectiveness of marches and policy pressure
versus the eruptive smashy-smash of symbolic store windows.
The lines of solidarity short-circuited and broke the idea
of the activist convergence as a consensual network; what
emerged was more transversal in the manner that Gerald
Raunig defines it, as " ... lines that do not necessarily even
cross, lines of flight, ruptures, which continuously elude
the systems of points and their coordinates." Despite real
moments where the convergence of art and action were
imagined as possible, these lines revealed other faults—
and ultimately raised the question of whether all tactics
needed to be resolved with a coalition.

4.

The language of mega-events is always the language of legacy
and transformation. But, in Vancouver, the imagination of
the legacy and the shift in the city displays both the limits of
the neoliberalization of cities and its socio-spatial characteristics. In this sense, the specific imprint that the Olympics
pressed on the city, despite the particular and dynamic
political and cultural responses to the force of this mega-
event, have also folded Vancouver deeper into a global model
of urban governance. The stadiums and the transportation
infrastructure, and the Olympic Village complex, are the
visible aspects of this legacy, but the phantom force—shifts
in governance and subtle rearrangements of the circulation
of power—are the more calcified legacy. Even as neoliberalism fades and exists now as a machine that recirculates
rusted and failed policies through different scales and places,
it still is able to play off the global and the particular in
a way that reshapes cities spatially, politically, and culturally.

Trying to track the way that the mega-event dropped down from above—like a long-lost modernist plan—and the mobilizations and counter-proposals that sprung up from community organizations, I began this series by speculating on the contestations of public space and on the forms of publicness that could emerge out of the intensification of policing and security measures that are now the kevlar-dressed symbols of mega-events. In the Olympic moment, new forms of publicness based on rights to housing were ultimately overridden by an older form of cultural nationalism that took to the streets. This identity-based celebration blanketed the optimistic urban mobilizations that civil society groups had set in motion long before the Games. Issues of sociospatial inequities in the city receded from the view of an imagined global public (and much of the politics contra the Olympics was based on bringing images to this public via the global media, using a visual programming of political space). The most visual, and visually compelling, protest—the Red Tent Campaign—that highlights the homeless crisis is an act of publicness that has endured because it also extended itself nationally.

Other acts of publicness did not go unnoticed by the heavily financed surveillance. The massive Olympic security budget was recently trumped by the 1.2 billion dollars spent on G20 security in Toronto: these two mega-events (for the G20 is a mega-event now as well) flowed into one extended security event. Community organizers who were highly public in anti-Olympic politics were targeted and snatched up by police in Toronto and slapped with conspiracy charges. The mass arrests in Toronto (up to 1,000 people) were the largest in Canadian history, larger even than the late-night sweeps of the War Measures Act in 1970 during the actions of the Front de libération du Québec. With this turn of deep antagonism to the publicness, of both black block tactics and milder democratic demands (and in Toronto the police put on more of a show of force to the "good" protestors), the terms of counter-publics, wild publics, and diverse publics, and other nuances lose the force of their argument. Sitting with wrists zip-tied, they tend to look the same. Acts of negative publicness, acts that demonstrate the limits of publicness, risk the danger of being an endgame of struggles for publicness itself in this atmosphere. In the neoliberalized city, the idea of the public is off the streets. Publicness has been atomized and attached to ownership, and participation in "the public" is now based on property ownership. As a result, the public was told to stay home during the G20—to be out was to invite arrest—and in Vancouver the public was invited to party on the city's streets while to live on the street was to invite arrest.

Beyond claims to publicness that are met with huge security forces, what other spatial and cultural politics can emerge? Could a shift in the frame of such a politics be a legacy of this joined mega-event—the Olympics and the G20? Parallel to the anti-Olympic movement in Vancouver (a movement against the type of governance that brought the Olympics) a "right to the city" movement spearheaded by issues of housing, access, and democratic processes cohered. This program emphasized access to space, such as the right for the homeless to be in the street or to camp in parks, but it was also about the right to shape the politics of the city. The right to the city is, then, as Mustafa Dikeç argues, " … not the right to urban space, but to a political space as well," so that the right to the city is " … a way of actively and collectively relating to the political life of the city."[9] A dramatic legacy of mega-events has been exactly the distortion of urban political life: the usual channels and guidelines of governmental process become even more subservient to private agencies and institutions, and democratic accountability becomes more and more difficult to locate. Mega-events therefore alter the processes that produce the city both spatially and politically. A call to the right to the city under these circumstances is made both more compelling and more troubled. But Dikeç extends this sense of the right to the city to a spatial justice that focuses

> not on space per se, but on the processes that produce space, and at the same time, the implications of these produced spaces on the dynamic processes of social, economic, and political relations.[10]

The Olympic Village in Vancouver, hunched on the postindustrial waterfront, is an aluminum-clad symbol of neoliberal governmentality and of a specific production of spatial injustice. From its ever-shrinking promise of social housing, to its post-crisis financial structure that had the City bail out hedge-fund backed developers, to its web of private-public arrangements based on private profit and public risk, this new building also marks the long reterritorialization of the waterfront as an elite space, burying its working-class history deeper into the mud to have the waterfront transformation emerge as a real-estate gamble that hopes to shape the city's future yet again. Class anxiety around the complex, particularly about who deserves to live in the subsidized housing, also marks the shift in the constitution of the public. And the nervousness around the "non-owners" who could live in the building (subsidized or renting at market rates) catches the antagonism that the socio-spatial program of neoliberalism has built. So, when people who did not want to buy a condo, but rather protest this string of broken social promises, tried to enter the open house, set up to display the spaces on sale, the police erupted, roughed up some people, and then "locked down the area," which ended the event they there were commissioned to guard—sales of condominiums. This minor event illustrates the spatial and class tension that the Olympics have accelerated in the city, and it marks the shift in the recognition of the public and acts of publicness. As neoliberalism's political legitimacy fades and as it tries to reshape itself during a crisis of its own making, a call for spatial justice is a strategic opposition that can also help characterize neoliberalism, and show that it is never fully formed but is, instead, in process.[11]

Given the spatiality of neoliberalism and the transformation of the status of the public, what can public art orient itself toward? The Germany-based artists Köbberling and Kaltwasser were commissioned to do a public artwork on a fallow yet semiotically rich section of land near the Olympic Village. Opting for entropy rather than legacy, Köbberling and Kaltwasser have constructed a sculpture made out of temporary building materials left over from the Village itself: the wheat-board architectural sculpture will decay with time, and weather and transform into a plant nursery that will be "claimed and nurtured" by residents of the newly redeveloped waterfront area. The intention is that, once grown, the plants can be transplanted within the development by the residents. The tensions here between the community impulse, instigated by the artists, with its metaphors of reuse, decay, and renewal, and the production of a public of owners (always depicted as a community) pushed by the profit imperative that the building is defined by, will no doubt be played out over time. As is common with mega-events, social contradictions and spatial production move from the streets to the waterfront.

[1] Jamie Peck, "Postneoliberalism and its malcontents," lecture at "The Future of Neoliberalism" seminar, Simon Fraser University, October 5, 2009.

[2] This text was originally published as four columns to cover the cultural scene in Vancouver during the 2010 Winter Olympics for *Camera Austria* in issues 108/109/110/111 in 2009 and 2010).

[3] Michael Warner, *Publics and Counterpublics*, Zone Books, New York 2002; Sven Lütticken, *Secret Publicity: Essays on Contemporary Art*, NAi Publishers, Rotterdam 2005.

[4] Sianne Ngai, *Ugly Feelings*, Harvard University Press, Cambridge, Massachusetts 2005.

[5] Jamie Peck, "The Creativity Fix," http://www.eurozine.com/articles/2007-06-28-peck-en.html (last accessed June 2013).

[6] Henri Lefebvre, *The Explosion: Marxism and the French Upheaval*, trans. Alfred Ehrenfeld, *Monthly Review Press*, New York 1969, p. 7.

[7] Henri Lefebvre, *State, Space, World: Selected Essays*, trans. Gerald Moore, Neil Brenner, Stuart Elden, ed. Neil Brenner and Stuart Elden, University of Minnesota Press, Minneapolis 2009, p. 149.

[8] Gerald Raunig, *Art and revolution: Transversal Activism in the Long 20th-Century*, trans. Aileen Derieg, *Semiotext(e)*, Los Angeles 2007, p205.

[9] Mustafa Dikeç, "Justice and the spatial imagination," *Environment and Planning A*, vol. 33 (2001), p. 1790.

[10] Ibid., p. 1793

[11] Jamie Peck, Nik Theodore and Neil Brenner, "Postneoliberalism and its Discontents," *Antipode* 41 (2009) p. 94–116.

Citizens of the [World] [Nation] [City] Unite and Take Over!

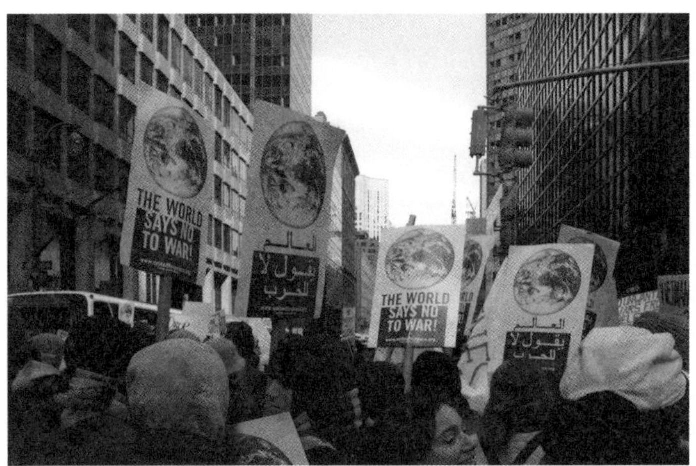

Andrea Geyer, *Parallax*, 2003
8-channel slide installation, 50 minutes

We use the term "globalization" to cover such a broad range of processes— including the complex of transnational organizations that service global capital—that there is sometimes the tendency to ignore new possibilities that have been generated during this era of globalization.
—Angela Y. Davis[1]

Even though cities and nations have received detailed attention in the conceptualization of globalization, these two scales have moved in and out of focus under that lens. Curiously, at times the view of globalization has left little standing other than the all-inclusive global and the alluring local. But somewhere between these two scales, or spinning out of them, is the globalized city—an urban territory given global status in its capacity because it is read as a hub of central control and management needed to link the network of spatially dispersed economic activity. Here, a global city is synonymous with a concentrated financial center, where certain types of financial work get done, yet where other forms of capital accumulation go unrecognized. "The things a global city makes," as Saskia Sassen writes, "are services and financial goods."[2] Gone, in this over-valorizing of finance, is more material production. Gone too, or only ignored as the above epigraph from Angela Y. Davis suggests, are other forms of production—cities as spaces of sociability and social reproduction that include the cultural and resistances to the logics of globalization.

These claims to the city are not new whether they emanate from a concept of urban territory as the network of social practices on "the street," or as a social condenser where contradictions, diversity, and cultures heat multiplicity into insurgency. This tendency to imagine insurgency or a new politics being generated as the diversity amplified by globalization is concentrated in the urban territory, relies on that mix to articulate itself into a social force able to negotiate "the regulation of a carefully modulated freedom."[3] This regulation, as Thomas Osborne and Nikolas Rose propose, grew out of the city as a laboratory of liberal government as well as the site of discipline and subordination—the beach may well be under the paving stones. Yet, this regulation of freedom exists alongside the narrowing of the *types of freedom* available and the international spread of a revanchist city.[4]

At another scale, the notion of the weak nation state grew in globalization theory to propose its demise and the lubricated fallacy of a borderless world. The bound nation was locked into a hopeless conceptual competition with mobile flows—and this within a theoretical framework that, at the cultural level, favored the dynamism of dispersal and multiplicity no matter how metaphorical or unsupportable after a glance at a global realpolitik. John Urry nails down the logic of the submerged nation-state:

> Global flows across societal borders make it less easy for states to mobilize clearly separate and coherent nations in pursuit of societal goals.[5]

The devastating irony here is that nation-states *were able* to mobilize (hierarchically of course) their relations coherently into a neoliberal dynamic of global capitalism.

The weak nation-state view has been countered
by a point of view that rightly points to the state's own role
in competitively implementing the treaties, laws, and
agreements that have built the current financial globalization. State activity even includes its participation in dena-
tionalizing particular state functions. But the oscillations
of the strong state/weak state views pass over the point
that both forms of state exist simultaneously and that
globalization is not a smooth event covering the earth's
surface, but is hierarchical and riddled with rivalries. What
is tragically neglected is that the relative power of the state
is a potential apparatus to regulate or resist globalization,
to provide another national program at the urgings of
citizens, or simply to be a scale at which citizenship claims
and resistance are imagined—*despite* the coercive aspects of
state apparatuses and local elites, and heat from the International Monetary Fund, the World Bank, and transnational
agreements.

Making Spaces Stranger

These two scales—the city (both the regional and the global
city) and the nation—have emerged from the rapid and
sustained strong-arm reshuffling initiated by the American
imperial project after September 11, 2001, as scales dramatically transformed. Following her narrative tabloid, *Interim*
(2002), Andrea Geyer's *Parallax* (2003) focuses on the scalar
dynamics of the city, the nation, and citizenship to register
and estrange the transformations that the new moment of
American empire has wrought. These transformations have
been brought about by coercion and force, but the US, the
world's policeman or "freedom of the market" cop increasingly prefers force as the immediate solution to security and
the quest for capital accumulation. When force overtakes
coercion at the national scale, and within the urban territory, it becomes most visible.

While the scales on which socio-spatial relations are
fought out are always interlaced and dialectical—and the
scales of the nation and the city are central—there has been
a different tension in spatial relations since September 11,
2001.[6] Specifically, the terrorist attacks on New York City
shifted rapidly from a global/local act (even geopolitical and

architectural) to a universal and then a national problematic. The result has been to nationalize the effects of the attacks, to harden an "American" national identity, and to split the world around this concretized national space. This is reflected in Bush's decree that nations are either "for us or against us," in aggressive and unilateral US foreign policy, and in domestic repression. Nations are transformed into allies or threats, light or shadows. The political management of this comes clear as new nations are included in the biblical "axis of evil," and as old allies become new antagonists (illustrated in the suspicious eyes cast toward France, Germany, and Canada by the US). Borders, in this new geopolitical spatial arrangement, are no longer just symbolic of trade barriers, but are seen increasingly as lines demarcating security zones.

This is the tension between the space of global capital flows, the space of the nation, and the restrictive space of "anti-terrorism." In a reassertion of the role of states, terrorism—while described as a global network— is primarily imagined as developing in "failed" or "delinked" states, then breaching their borders to spread throughout the world. Nations as containers and generators of terrorism (Iraq, Syria, Iran, North Korea, etc.) are targeted, or national borders and immigration/refugee policies are pressured to harden (as in the case of Canada and the European Union) to US determined standards. This is a shift from a US-led world order based on national development, to one based on national containment, punishment, and primitive accumulation.[7]

But as the effects after September 11, 2001, have hardened around a national subject, there are immense repercussions to the discourses of identity and of liberal multiculturalism—the very platforms of insurgent citizens and a product of the global city. There are repercussions for other forms of citizenship as well, but much of the "antiterrorist" policing within the US is in the global city. No longer is terrorism imagined as the disgruntled loner out in the woods or former government employee (postal worker, soldier), but it is shaped as a transnational network of cells of "Middle-Eastern men" hidden primarily in the uncontainability of the global city where they can receive support from the local community or simply blend into the ethnic and racial mix of the city. The racist basis of anti-terrorism and national security was evident in the mass F.B.I. and police sweeps of people identified as members of the generalized category of "Middle-Eastern men."

Anthony Vidler has asked if Americans' experience and building of urban public space will be altered as a result of 9/11: "Will a desire for 'defensible space' radically transform the city as Americans know it?"[8] Certainly the semi-private spaces that make up the "public spaces" of the US, and New York City in particular, have been somewhat altered, although not to the extent that was predicted—in part because of the capital outlay an urban transformation would necessitate. In concert with this traffic barrier and duct-tape security, what has certainly been dramatically altered is the way in which groups targeted by the FBI ("illegal aliens," "foreign nationals," "Middle-Eastern men," "Pakistani-Americans," etc.) experience urban space in America. The experience of American spaces by "racially-profiled" groups is now one of increased surveillance, repression, and loss of rights.

Geyer's *Interim* catches both the mechanisms of surveillance and repression and the cheap and provisional manner in which "security" has been off-loaded to New York City in the midst of a city and state fiscal crisis. In one photograph, the art-deco entrance to the Waldorf Astoria hotel is guarded against protesters of the World Economic Forum by a small events sign that neatly spells out "No Entry," and cement traffic barriers on the street. Another photograph shows a solo orange traffic pylon sitting in a doorway of the Port Authority Bus Terminal fulfilling an unknown function. This improvised strangeness of an American urban landscape on perpetual "elevated alert" is made harsher in other photographs with security lighting glaring onto street scenes and formations of police on foot and on horses. Geyer's photographs, taken from middle distance, embed the police into the urban landscape, making them a structural urban aspect rather than an event of street photography. In *Parallax* the strangeness and the repressive apparatus are together, with a photograph of a cop with his riot-helmet visor up, while standing solemnly beside him are two horses also with riot visors, ready to defend the nation against its own citizens.

The "I [heart shape] New York" t-shirts were popular enough in the years following 9/11 that they were sold for three for $10 by street vendors—they were the wearable version of the sentiment that was circulated in the media, "We are all New Yorkers now." But the changes in the urban territory and in geopolitics run counter to these popular claims. In an intense dialectic of inclusion/exclusion, citizenship in New York City and the US is not as open as the boosters proposed. But reversed exclusion has also become true culturally: this time it is US culture that is being rejected. It is not easy for American culture to pose itself as the universal global model or single way of life after it hardened itself post-9/11. The "formulaic abstraction" (as Perry Anderson calls it)[9] of US culture into a global universal has fueled the cultural wing of US hegemony in the past. But with American exceptionalism turning to unilateralism, its global coercion turning to military force, and cultural universalism hardening into a national particularism, a cultural crack is opening in the American hegemonic project. US culture, and its concentrators of culture, its cities, are looking strange rather than preferred. *Interim* and *Parallax* present this strangeness in its everyday urban guise.

The Scales of Citizenship

> Yet, the nation-state is the name of that crude episteme that will not go away. The culture-subject-agent trinity remains as necessary as it is impossible.
> —Gayatri Chakravorty Spivak[10]

Parallax sets in motion the dynamics between the nation state, the urban territory, and geopolitics through the concentrated figure of the citizen. The textual material of *Parallax*, drawn from the global media, runs through the risky transnational movement of people, racism, and the coercion of identity, the invocation and manipulation of democracy at national and global levels, class, gender, and the militarization of the US economy and culture, policing and prisons as a form of social management and oppression, but also forms of resistance at the individual and urban level (from protest marches to librarians shredding documents). Much of it reports on the contradictions and strangeness in US culture.

By interlacing a range of news reports that spiral upward from the urban to the global, with a narrative that takes place in the city with a "female protagonist," two aspects of urbanism are interwoven in *Parallax*: the production of the urban territory by forces of capitalism; and the on-the-ground or everyday practices of life, social reproduction, and the governance of the city.

The questions that emerge from the visual and textual information of these works are: At what scale can claims to citizenship be made? What scales are the most effective to make those claims? It is also important to ask: What are the dynamics or relations that give rise to making these claims?

Paralleling the competing views of globalization, there are competing models of the citizen. First, there is the view that the nation-state, while historically central in the production of citizenship, has been challenged as the only mechanism or site where citizenship can be imagined, formed, contested, and benefited from. The dominance of the nation-state as the scale of citizenship is reterritorialized by claims of citizenship at an urban and global scale. In a less spatialized manner, a national citizen is also set in tension with emergent "post-national" citizenships: cultural; minority; ecological; cosmopolitan; consumer; mobility; and the all-encompassing, citizen of flow.[11] Curiously, this list separates aspects that would be included, along with many other markers, within the notion of citizenship at any scale. Globalization, in this argument, has led to a breakdown of the universal liberal citizen embedded in the nation-state, and replaced it with a particularized catalogue of attributes: globalization's hegemony leads to particularization.

The particulars are not necessarily localized or even spatialized, but are tied to categories of social life. Global citizenship presents a catalogue of types of citizenship, but an undifferentiated geography: it assumes the global as the dominant scale of the citizen. Rather than asking what type of differentiated citizen might be effective, we can rescale the question and look for a model of citizenship that is not based on a static notion of space, but one which is more dialectical, in which citizens would act on a number of scales. This model of citizenship would engage with the spatial relations of globalization by looking to participate at the scales on which globalization is formed and at which it operates. The nation-state is obviously one such scale.

Secondly, the city has historically been a site of citizenship and a space of government. Due to its density, its thickening of social and cultural relations, and its multiplicity, the city is seen as producing the "new spaces of citizenship"[12] that also complicate the nation-state's relation to citizenship. But it also imagines resistance coming from the claims of new citizens based on their particularized demands. What is often not obvious in this view are social transformations initiated by citizens asking for the rights and services they have been told they have, but can not access. These claims could powerfully mesh with so-called new claims and with claims at other scales. As we increasingly see, social action can be spurred by forces external, yet tied, to the individual—forces such as the repression of rights, invasive surveillance, heavy-handed and racist police activities or, at another scale, claims for imperial wars.

Much of the visual and textual information in *Parallax* (and to a different degree, *Interim*) illuminates how the promises of citizenship, burdened as they are with the liberal compact but still offered as a horizon, are part of that "carefully moderated freedom" that relies on the dialectic of inclusion/exclusion, and that is moderated through coercion (media construction of fear), corruption (Florida vote rejections, Enron, Haliburton, etc.) and force (FBI, Giuliani's "broken windows" policy of urban policing adopted internationally). As the forms of force taken after 9/11 that took way access to the rights of citizenship for Arab-Americans show, the dialectic of exclusion/inclusion can reverse itself, revealing that the politics of recognition are ultimately defined by the blind ideology of those who do the "recognizing."

Coercion does not necessarily generate counter claims to citizenship and rights—but force, in its crudeness, can. This has taken on an active politics in the movement for cities to resist the US federal government's USA Patriot Act (Uniting and Strengthening America by Providing Appropriate Tools Required to Intercept and Obstruct

Terrorism Act) and its extension, following the logic
of Hollywood movie sequels, USA Patriot II. Troubled that
the Act is in conflict with civil rights, and in some cases
directly in conflict with cities' civil rights codes, over 140
cities and municipalities (and so far three states) have passed
legislation opposing or criticizing the Act. Even before
the Act was passed, the police in Portland, Oregon, refused
to comply with the FBI investigations of Middle-Eastern
students as it contravened state laws. Rather than the urban
taking the place as the site of citizenship as the state fades
in its capacity to provide citizen rights, in this instance
cities have risen up against the state's overriding of rights.

Simultaneous to this state-urban tension, a global-
urban alliance against hegemonic state power has formed.
When millions of people gathered in cities on February 15,
2003, to protest the immanent war on Iraq, the incredible
coherence of the event was brushed aside by the US government. As Geyer reminds us in *Parallax*, Bush was recorded
as commenting

> that he disagreed with the millions of anti-war
> protesters who turned out in 300 cities worldwide on
> Sunday, and that he would press the United Nations
> Security Council to pass a new resolution intended
> to authorize war with Iraq.

In the glib and taunting way that characterizes US hegemony, Bush tellingly despatialized the protests and negated
citizenship at any scale, calling what others saw as a mobilization of a global citizen a "focus group": " … allowing the
protesters to influence him, he said, 'is like saying I'm going
to decide policy based upon a focus group.'"[13]

From the memorable blue and black flyers to the
media coverage, cities were foregrounded as the site of this
act of global citizenship and global public opinion. The
scales of citizenship are most effectively imagined and
materialized, in actions such as this, as the sites and spaces
where the political relations between social actors, govern-
ability, and claims to global society are contested, modulated, and transformed.

A global neoliberal model of the citizen is being
exported and embedded into jurisdictional structures

through coercion and force by the US. This citizen is based on, as Bush put it in his editorial "Securing Freedom's Triumph" on the anniversary of 9/11, "the hope of democracy, development, free markets, and free trade."[14] The paramount form of freedom in this model is an economic freedom with rights tied to free trade—a citizen has the right to live in a nation with free trade or corporations have the right to trade freely. This neoliberal citizen is not organized around overlaps of commonality and purpose that bind the liberal compact of citizenship, nor articulated through overlaps in scale, but is a passive construction that would ultimately rely on the logics of the market. Perry Anderson argues that such a citizen is a political catalyst for the hegemony of capital that

> does not require mass mobilization of any kind. Rather, it thrives on the opposite—political apathy and withdrawal from any cathexis of public life.[15]

Geyer's recent works engage with this withdrawal, denaturalizing it by pointing to its strangeness as it is materialized in cities and instrumentalized in the media. Out of the cultural cracks, Geyer's projects counter the formulaic abstraction of hegemony (and of neoliberal promises) and show the spaces balanced between coercion and force. Meshed into this balance are the contested scales of a new globality ("another world").

[1] Angela Y. Davis, "Inside/Outside: Women at the Borders of Globalization," *au.la: Arquitectura y Urbanism en Las Americas* (Spring 1999), p. 108–120.

[2] Saskia Sassen, *The Global City: New York, London, Tokyo*, Princeton University Press, Princeton 1991, p. 5.

[3] Thomas Osborne and Nikolas Rose, "Governing Cities: Notes on the Spatialization of Virtue," *Environment and Planning D: Society and Space*, vol. 17 (1999), p. 737–760.

[4] For the limitation on the types of freedom cf. Slavoj Žižek, "What Can Lenin Tell Us About Freedom Today?" *Rethinking Marxism* 13/2 (2001), p. 1–9, and (for a very different view) George W. Bush, "Securing Freedom's Triumph," *The New York Times*, Op Ed, September 11, 2002. For the revanchist city program, cf. Neil Smith, *The New Urban Frontier: Gentrification and the Revanchist City*, Routledge, New York 1996.

[5] John Urry, "Globalization and Citizenship," *Journal of World-Systems Research*, vol. 2 (1999), p. 321–324.

[6] For an overview of the scale debates in critical geography cf. Erik Swyngedouw, "Neither Global Nor Local: 'Glocalization' and the Politics of Scale," K.R. Cox (ed.), *Spaces of Globalization*, Guilford, New York 1997, p. 137–166.

[7] Cf. Steven Sherman, "The Attacks of September 11 in Three Temporalities," *Journal of World-Systems Research* XI/1 (Winter 2003), p. 141–169, regarding the relationship of hegemony and development. It's available online at http://www.jwsr. org/wp-content/uploads/2013/05/jwsr-v9n1-sherman.pdf (last accessed June 2013).

[8] Anthony Vidler, "Aftermath; A City Transformed: Designing 'Defensible Space,'" *The New York Times*, Week in Review, September 23, 2001, Section 4, p. 6.

[9] Perry Anderson, "Force and Coercion," *New Left Review* 17 (2002), p. 5–30.

[10] Gayatri Chakravorty Spivak, "Megacity," *Grey Room* 01 (Fall 2000), p. 8–25.

[11] John Urry, "Globalzation and Citizenship," p. 321–324.

[12] James Holston, "Spaces of Insurgent Citizenship," Arjun Appaduria, John Holtson (eds.), *Cities and Citizenship*, Duke University Press, Durham, 1999, p. 155–173.

[13] George W. Bush quoted in Richard W. Stevenson, "Threats and Responses: The White House; Antiwar Protests Fail to Sway Bush on Plans for Iraq," *The New York Times*, February 19, 2003.

[14] George W. Bush, "Securing Freedom's Triumph."

[15] Anderson, "Force and Coercion."

Urban Facts & Global Forces: Toward an Urban Poetics of the Global

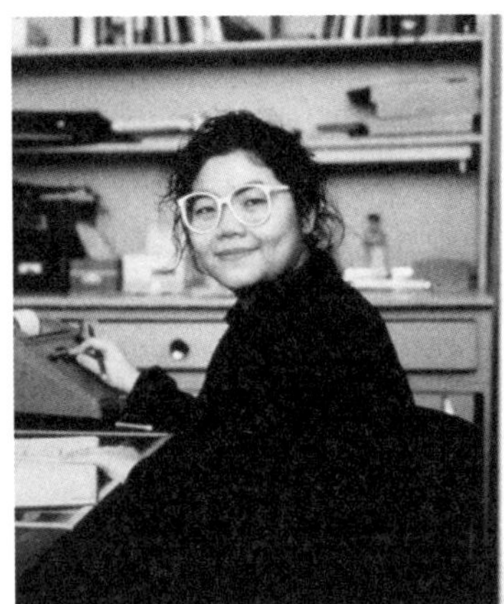

Ken Lum, *Melly Shum Hates Her Job*, 1989
Chromogenic print, vinyl lettering, 124 × 230.3 cm

People came quickly to expect me on the same spot. I became a sign.
—Ken Lum, "Living Statue Tries Experiment," *The Surrey Leader*, July 5, 1978.

The Urban Gone Global

Alongside a main feeder route leading to Vancouver from Surrey— a former farming community that the urban development of Vancouver transformed into a sub- urb, which then morphed into an Edge City with its greenbelt areas, industrial spaces, office and hous- ing complexes joined by a gridded highway and road system studded with nodal monster malls—Ken Lum stood for four days during the morning rush hour, a static figure in jeans and a grey hoodie, glimpsed briefly, as working-class and white collar commuters rounded a curve and sped under the overpass. Same time, same place. On the fifth day (corresponding to the working week), Lum positioned a white outline of this figure. The ironically named *Entertainment for Surrey* (1978)—ironic because even among suburbanites, Surrey was held up as all that was boring and raggedly violent about the unevenly developed edges of the metropolis area—cues up a forceful problematic that goes beyond the subject's positioning within space.

Rather than retreating to the national trope of the figure in the naturalized landscape, this early work of Lum's places the subject (and then a sign) within *the built environment*. "*Entertainment for Surrey*" breaks from "a lyrical, romantic, expressionist, subjective, but above all asocial and bourgeois landscape art that has been the dominant tradition" in British Columbia, as Robert Linsley argued. This turn to the subject within the urban structure of the Vancouver metropolis follows in the wake of previous breaks: a localized narrative that begins with Robert Smithson's 1969–1970 visit to Vancouver which lead in turn to an investigation of the suburban edges, suburban seriality, and urban possibilities. But, by corresponding to "the spatio-temporality of economic globalization [which] can already be seen to contain dynamics of both mobility and fixity,"[1] this compact early work of Lum's establishes a relationship between the urban and the global with its own dynamic of fixity (the static figure), mobility (the commuters as a form of mobile capital) and space built for the ends of capital.

In Canadian cultural history there has been an axis foregrounding space and place—and the figure or subject's position within that—rather than on examining the built environment and on how daily life is developed at an urban level. This does not mean that there has not been a project—forceful at times, halting at others—within the national culture to identify an urban culture, but that the discourse of urbanism is not as developed as narratives of space, place, and identity. These concepts of national space and place are not, within the cultural field, a reflexive knowledge: spatial scales are rarely examined as ideological and constitutive, but reflective of existing spatial and social relations. Behind and beyond that, spatial relations are not understood as constructed by the capitalist logic of accumulation; rather, the focus has been on naturalized space as a determinant of national psyche and, by extension, of the national culture. Space was concretized as a cultural and psychic determinant,

but the determinants on the production of spatiality itself
were rarely investigated. This emphasis on space follows
the strategic and colonizing rejection of time and history,
and it also buried the urban under the weight of this timeless space.[2]

Even in the specific art history of Vancouver—where
Lum lives and works—this discourse of urbanism has been
halting. Despite a narrative that names a culturally dominant mode of production and then posits an anti-tradition
and the promise of urban cultural production, an urbanist
poetics remains emergent. The belated break from the
dominant lyrical representation of the landscape in the 1970s
(pinpointed by Jeff Wall as Ian Wallace's *La mélancolie de la rue*
[1973], and expanded upon by Rodney Graham's *Illuminated
Ravine* [1979] and Lum's furniture sculptures) builds upon
the aspects of a "defeatured landscape" that Scott Watson
sees growing out of local and transnational confluences in
the early 1970s.[3] But in this narrative, the counter-tradition
remains negatively defined, blocked by necessity of avant-
garde ruptures and discourses of site and place rather than
expanding on the potential of an urbanist project. Even in
the moment of Watson's "defeatured landscape,"[4] the urban
is given a static role as semiotic and as "typology and
abstraction" rather than process. Robert Linsley asserts the
again-belated project of urbanist art practices as an anti-
thesis. The tyranny of Vancouver as "place" and as "the
local"—or positing it as a nonplace—continues to over-
shadow an urbanist discourse based on the city as an urban
phenomenon tied into globalization. Vancouver seems to be
seen as the sum of its space and sites and their representations rather than the sum of its everyday *uses* of built environment in relation to its historical economic and social
determinants.

If a model of uneven cultural development is invoked,
a model which does not narrate an uncontested, unified
modernism (grandly transnational or parochially regional)
giving way to a more diverse and fragmented postmodernism
(imagined as more racially diverse yet less class-defined;
more service oriented, less based on production) following
an aesthetic break, then the struggle for spatial understanding at a national and an urban level can be linked
to other diverse yet powerful global factors. Tellingly,

the stuttering emergence of a new spatial understanding
in cultural production in Vancouver coincides with shifts in
global capital that are tied to changes in the production
of spatiality. As Neil Smith points out, "The transformation
since the 1970s has involved not simply a spatial reorganization of the global political economy but a restructuring of
the very scales at which different kinds of political, economic,
and cultural activities are organized."[5] This is not a micro
to macro relationship—of economic globalization to local
cultural production—but a register of a different spatial
understanding. As Smith goes on to argue,

> although the different geographical scales constructed
> as a framework of accumulation were conceived of as
> mutable and not permanent, the rapid transformation
> of the nation-state as economic actor, however
> selective, marks a crucial evolution of global capital-
> ism that in turn highlights the global-urban nexus.[6]

From this new global-urban relationship, a new urbanism
seeps up as cities again become "production platforms," but
within a global economy rather than a national economy. The
scale of cities undergoes a shift here as well, as production
nodes—factories, workshops, home works, and other forms
of labor that have formed in these "flexible" times—are
dispersed throughout the metropolitan area. Despite this
dispersal, this "global city," "emergent city," "cosmopolis," or
"metapolis" is a condenser of global forces and an amplifier
of global effects.

    This global-urban nexus does not propose a stateless
"global/local" world where corporations conduct electronic
business instantaneously with no regard for supposedly
out-dated and permeable borders—a world imagined as
placeless when dynamic flows replace static space. However,
it does reposition the dominant nationalist discourses
of space that have buried the urban in Canadian cultural
discourses. Moving from the scale of the subject and
the domestic, through corporate and business "cultures"
in relation to the subject, and up to issues of migrancy
and diaspora, Lum's work is itself a form of geographical
knowledge that traces a subject's intersection with the
global and the urban. From the static domestic furniture

sculptures which leech out the use value from sofas and chairs in order to turn them into *art* objects (with their value generated through uniqueness, scarcity, and cultural capital) and to reinvigorate them as social signs that carry symbolic capital that is followed up with the refunctioning of mirrors as art in his *Photo-Mirror Series* (1997), to the logo portraits that capture their subjects in time (a function of portraiture) so they can be placed in a spatial relation to logos or text in order to draw out the social-cultural relations of people to "corporate culture" (the friendly term for capitalism), to the image-text works which freeze representation and language into an "urban fact" by drawing on avant-gardist strategies and urban signage, there is an insistence on disjunction and conjunction, of recognition and misrecognition that jambs together the subjective and the structural, the aesthetic and the social, and the urban and the global. But having been removed from the distinctly national and the particularities of the regional, this work is not without sites. What emerges in *place* of the national and the regional scale in Lum's work is a compressed and interlaced scale of the urban and the global.

Eclectic Atlases for the Urban

However, a representational problem emerges between urbanism and cultural production. As Rosalyn Deutsche argued,

> [Urban discourse], though critical, generally adopt[s] a classic realist approach, treating the image of the city as a mere reflection or distortion of the "real" city or as an object that either reveals or disguises under-lying spatial realities.[7]

However, within the recent emphasis in urbanism, which privileges process and imagines the city as an accumulation of collective uses of the built environment within the spatial relations determined by capital, there is a move toward documentation and critical art projects which emphasize use, both within architecture and in urban phenomenon.

Stefano Boeri calls these new representational strategies of the city's evolution and mutation "eclectic atlases." Not only visual, Boeri includes research reports, textual descriptions, critical essays, archived material, and so on in this category, anything that adds to the paradigms of viewing urban phenomenon. An important aspect of Boeri's paradigm shift is the notion of the "urban fact" from architect Aldo Rossi's *The Architecture of the City*. For Rossi, "fatti urbani" is the intersection of typology and history that asserts: "[c]ertain functions, time, place, and culture modify our cities as they modify the forms of architecture ... "[8] Boeri inflects this idea with a greater dynamism, less the deep embeddedness of time in space, but more forcefully urban facts as "spatio-temporal events that leave a wake in time and cast a shadow on society."[9] Urban facts are temporal and spatial condensers of lived relations and are accumulations of lived urban experience. The effects of globalism and everyday experiences agglutinate into urban facts which (although spatially rooted) are filled with the dense tensions, time-worn activities, major crack-downs, mercurial eruptions, as well as all the pressurized or mundane determinants and perplexing indeterminancies of globalization. Lum's works add to the eclectic atlas of urbanism by staging urban facts that reflect and constitute global facts with the understanding that the urban dynamic is a part of the global dynamic—but is more tightly packed with and reflective of the temporalities and uneven spatial development of globalization.

Eclectic atlases work on the "bottom up" theory of urbanism where the city and its regions are defined by the sum of the acts of the people who inhabit the space, that it is a dynamic process of the use of space that is not reducible to a single collective mode of conceiving space. This pluralism of uses, however, does not have to reject global-ization's deterministic shaping of the urban—both spatially and experientially—nor does it turn the urban into a jumble of isolated events. What is compelling in Lum's work is the arrest of social processes, where space and the subject are held in a temporal moment that highlights rather than reduces both the dynamic and the deterministic factors. Like urban facts, Lum's pictures are both synchronic and diachronic, time-based yet having a fixity, showing not so much contradictions and antagonisms but the process of the urban as people, ideas, and capital move and agglutinate into the contemporary urban territory. The staged moments of the pictures can be both internally and outwardly mundane (as in *Hum hum hummm* [1994]), internally traumatic (as in *Don't Be Silly, You're Not Ugly* [1993]), or even comically enthusiastic (as in *Melly Shum Hates Her Job* [1989]) yet they operate from the tension between scales: between capitalism and the subject, between the urban and the global. As Scott Watson observed of an art historical impulse in Lum's work, "They are really big miniatures."[10] Projected onto the social field, this takes on a denser, more material meaning.

That Lum's cropped photographs in the image-text works provide only shards of generic architecture and the urban territory reinforces the eclectic atlas view that the urban is a collection of facts and phenomenon driven by processes and forces and not a totality that can be grasped or mapped at once. The brick and granite wall with its horizontal construction cut across by the diagonal wooden staircase that a child with a backpack relaxes across aimlessly in *Hum hum hummm*; the lack of depth and a granite wall topped with concrete details behind *Rebecca Rosenberg* (1990) as she sings on the street with a rolled up magazine as a mock microphone; the public phone beside a store with a yellow awning and sandwich boards on the sidewalk in *You Don't Love Me* (1994); again a phone booth and close sidewalk scene with the fat typography of the "2001 Futon" sign as the angry rocker shouts (or does he just think it?) *Fuck You! You Asshole!* (1993). These closed-in pictures of urban facts are rarely broken by an elevated or "zenithal" view. *Nancy Nishi, Joe Ping Chau, Real Estate* (1990) depicts two Asian real-estate agents posing on a balcony of residential high-rises and a glimpse of a body of water in the background. Again there are not enough details given to exactly identify the city (except for locals), but this is not about recognition of a particular city but a linking of the zenithal view with the commanding view of capital. Released from urban facts, this scalar shift to the zenithal view does not view the urban as an agglutination of events and uses within social, economic, and spatial determinants, but instead the city is surveyed as a commodity—urban materiality is turned into immaterial commodity speculation. This contrast is jokingly (though effectively!) grounded with the typeface of "Real Estate" replicating 3-D stone or concrete letters. The generic yet specifically recognizable locations and details of these pictures emphasizes an urban context, the people, and the situations and processes at work, rather than spectacular architecture, astonishing density, or beautiful typologies.

There Is No Place Like Home (2000) is a scalar shift not just in the view, but also in the art object itself. In this piece, the optimistic transnationalism of *Youth Portraits* (1985) is replaced by a critique of an easy cosmopolitanism more concerned with frequent-flyer points than the possibilities of a transnationalism of linked cities, and the liberal multi-cultural dream of dialogue is replaced by the struggles over space that define the urban as well as the national scale.[11] Produced with Vienna's innovative Museum in Progress, this massive billboard work (making Lum's other image-text works into miniatures) again holds in balance the tensions of fixity and mobility that characterize the current moment of globalization. Covering the entire wall of the Kunsthalle Wien, which *was* situated on a major traffic circle in the city's center, the six text-image panels of *There Is No Place Like Home* literally formed the static image in the urban landscape. But the images and text foreground the effects of mobility as it is registered through differently defined social positions. The potential didacticism of the image-text format is made socially unstable by the oscillation between representation and ambivalence set into the relationship of text to image. Are we reading images and text that represent a particular social-subject position (the joyous white tourist, the introspective Muslim woman; the angry Asian immigrant; the lined face of someone living in poverty; the unhappy frowning Black girl; the shouting white worker threatened by job-loss because of immigration) or are we reading our own social assumptions about these social categories back into the image? While Lum's construction of urban facts within globalization does condense and lock a situation in time, there is never a reduction of social-subject position to identity that is outside of the very social forces that identity is formed in and against. The multicultural expectation of a diversity of identity—of a national or urban mosaic— is forced aside by a cataloguing of the diverse social forces that position the subject within globalization. Again reassert-ing the domestic (as the furniture sculptures do) and the subject in relation to identity (as the photo-mirrors do)

There Is No Place Like Home shows "home" to be a contested and unstable site due to the domestic's location in the urban/global nexus.

Outro

Lum displays urban facts as global facts, as formations and intersections that are forced by globalization—but not without a "life" of their own—and therefore also as internal psychological events. The shift in eclectic atlases and in Lum's project is not toward a truer vision, nor toward a more complex or plural understanding (the liberal cultural project), but in a cataloguing of forces, effects, and practices which, when arrested, can be arranged into a form that gives a materiality and a denseness to these forces. Again this is about fixity and mobility: the mobility of money, the limited mobility of people and ideas, and the fixity of capital, as well as the photograph as fixity of this process. But in an urban poetics of the global, this fixity is a tension and not a stasis.

[1]   David Harvey, *Spaces of Hope*, University of California Press, Berkeley 2000, p. 262–263.

[2]   Officially, I would argue, Canadian culture has been constructed along concepts of space and place and once that was no longer effective in identifying the national subject, state multiculturalism and the politics of diversity were mobilized to fulfill the national sign. Multiculturalism, however, is not a discourse of urbanism in that it mobilizes around identity in relation to difference, in which particularized identities are collapsed into a national universal; ironically within the "unity in diversity" rhetoric, these differences are made ultimately cultural rather than formed by the pressures of history and capitalism. Hence particularized differences are collapsed into a national universal: what we all share is difference, etc. Not only bypassing history, this shift from space/place to identity bypasses the built environment. The Canadian cultural project has been a spatial project, but its scales have not included the urban.

Other factors—both regional and national—have blocked the development of an urbanist discourse for cultural production. On descending scale, here is a possible overview of these factors. An imagining of modernism as a unified project rather than an unevenly developed (both spatially and temporally) project which establishes the Romanticism/Modernism/Postmodernism narrative that obscures emergent urbanism (and critical modernisms) in the postwar period; the lack of a robust understanding of the constitutive effect of modes of production on urbanism and not merely on the natural landscape; official state multiculturalism's emphasis on identity at a national level rather than the transformative effect of immigration on cities ; the foregrounding of the bureaucratic structure of Canadian art and its relationship to corporate and state structure (See Ken Lum's "Canadian Cultural Policy: A Problem of Metaphysics," *Canadian Art* [Fall 1999], p. 78–83); the emphasis on regional sensibilities, and their relationship to transnationalism and not urbanism; the conflation of architecture with the urban; the elision of the domestic from the urban, which excludes critical feminist practices; the adoption of the flanuer as emblematic urbanist which obscures an array of social relations, identities, and uses of city space (particularly those of production).

[3]   Jeff Wall, *Ken Lum*, Winnipeg Art Gallery, Winnipeg, 1990. See Robert Linsley, "Landscape and Literature in the Art of British Columbia," Paul Delaney (ed.), *Vancouver: Representing the Postmodern City*, Arsenal/Pulp Press, Vancouver 1994, p. 193–216.

[4]   Scott Watson, "Discovering the Defeatured Landscape," Stan Douglas (ed.), *Vancouver Anthology: The Institutional Politics of Art*, Talonbooks/Or Gallery, Vancouver 1991, p. 247–266.

[5]   Neil Smith, "New Globalism, New Urbanism: Uneven Development in the 21st Century," *Working Papers in Local Governance and Democracy*, 99/2, p. 4–14.

[6]   Ibid., p. 6.

[7]   Rosalyn Deutsche, *Evictions: Art and Spatial Politics*, MIT Press, Cambridge, Massachusetts 1996, p. 213.

[8]   Aldo Rossi, *The Architecture of the City*, trans. Diane Ghirardo, Joan Ockman, MIT Press, Cambridge, Massachusetts 1982, p. 163.

[9]   Stefano Boeri, "Eclectic Atlases: Four Ways of Seeing the City," *Daidalos* 69-70 (1998/99), p. 102–113.

[10] Scott Watson, "Hey, That's Not Funny," *Art & Text* 50 (1995), p. 49.

[11] "A meaningful cosmopolitanism does not entail some passive contemplation of global citizenship … The cosmopolitan point is, then, not to flee geography but to integrate and socialize it. The geographical point is not to reject cosmopolitanism but to ground it in a dynamics of historical-geographical transformations." David Harvey, "Cosmopolitanism and the Banality of Geographical Evils," *Public Culture* vol. 12, no. 2, issue 31 (2000), p. 529–564.

Making and Breaking Neoliberal Spaces
Jeff Derksen and Neil Smith

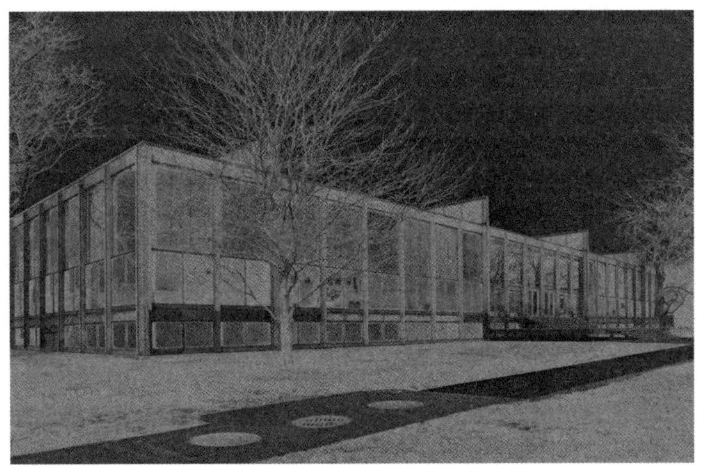

Sabine Bitter/Helmut Weber, *Bronzeville*, 2005
Part of a series of 11 solarized photographs, each 50 × 75 cm

The cultural debates about modernism in the late 1980s were complex, but in many quarters came to revolve around the temporality or periodization of modernity itself. "When was modernism?" quickly dominated the question, "What was modernism?" This debate emerged in response to postmodernism, a seemingly new "cultural dominant," as Frederic Jameson dramatically designated it, signaling an apparent tectonic shift in our cultural sensibilities. At issue was whether modernism was radically shattered, surviving only in the shards of the "aesthetic populism" and competing cultural claims of postmodernity, or whether postmodernity represented a mere interruption (even irruption?) in the incomplete Enlightenment project of modernity. On one side, some privileged the temporal march of aesthetics, identifying the emergence of a new cultural logic woven into a new stage of capitalist development;

on another side, historical narrative was vigorously eschewed altogether. Like automatic weapons fire, newly fashionable spatial rather than temporal allusions peppered texts on all sides, and yet today in the troubled temporality of postmodernity, that has slipped from noisy dominance into ubiquitous absorption, and despite the early emphasis on architecture in the modernism debates, a curious thing has happened. The spatial lexicon remains, but in most places it is radically unhitched from any critical analysis of globalization—from the cultural, political, or economic spatiality of contemporary social change. Globalization promises a "level playing field," of course, or as *New York Times* columnist Thomas Friedman proposes, "a flat earth."[1] The debate over temporalities, displaced into a language of space, is today mulched back into a more conservative stage theory: space is again annihilated by time. It is not postmodernity that transformed modernity or refigured the modernization paradigm; rather the failed ideological project of modernity and modernization has been reinvented in the ventricles of globalization.

The continuity of the processes and patterns of uneven spatial development, from the era of postwar modernization theory to that of globalization, carry forward a certain "satanic geography" wherein the benefits promised from twinning social development to economic growth rarely if ever arrive. Systematically mistranslated on its way from beautiful theory to earthly practice, social development passes from a guaranteed result of economic neoliberalism to an optional byproduct whose non-fulfillment can always be blamed on the translator.[2]

The great dystopic divide of exacerbating inequalities and social misery, and the expanding distance between rich and poor people and places, is built into the utopic DNA of neoliberalism from the beginning; the playing field is neither geographically flat nor socially even between economic profit and the betterment of everyday life. Rather, it is a mountain range in the process of dramatic uplift. From modernization theory to neoliberal globalization is not a seamless transition, however, and a new satanic mistranslation is put in place: economic development is no longer a goal of state policy, but a matter of "free trade"; free trade in turn becomes the corner stone of human rights

and democracy, and social development is repositioned as
the natural result.

This return to a certain 18th-century liberal promise
eschews other forms of social and economic organization—
local community development, regional cooperatives,
national currency control, international unions, world social
justice politics—as unnatural. Ideologies of free trade,
competition, flexible labor, "active individualism," and
self-responsibility have become the social imaginary of
neoliberalism.[3] If modernization theory failed in its mission
(economic and social) and was reinvented as globalization,
neoliberal globalization has dropped the proactive language
of modernization for naturalized stridency of privatization
and the market. Yet the master narratives of modernity,
imagined as shattered and unmanageable across the postmodern terrain, have nonetheless returned as the neoliberal
master narratives of privatization, marketization, and individualization. Modernism's utopia of "impersonal equality"[4]
and its colonial legacy is strikingly similar to the utopic
neoliberal "free market" and its competitive landscape of
turbo-inequality. "Actually," says Masao Miyoshi, the "global
economy is merely a maximum use of world resources via
maximum exclusion," and places and regions that do not
promise super-profits are ignored.[5] They can always be pulled
in again when active underdevelopment has reduced wages
and rents, and shifts in resource economies or government
largesse open new opportunities for super-exploitation.

Through enforced deregulation, structural adjust-
ment, trade, and other laws, and outright dismantlement,
this continuation of modernization (without even the paper
promises of the impersonal equality of modernity) in
the garb of globalization (and not merely the workings of
transnational corporations) has opened previously contained
national spaces to global economic sway. From the inside,
by corollary, national agendas of social development are
increasingly relinquished and privatized.[6] As Elmar Altvater
points out, the privatization of "health or educational
services, old-age pensions, water and waste disposal systems,
and social security or public security" has dominated debates
between nations, within nations, and in cities.[7] And as Pierre
Bourdieu put it, the program of privatization is a program
against forms of collectivity.[8]

The raucous geographies of actually existing neoliberalism are highly uneven and dissonant, yet the gap between the promises of modernization and the creative destruction of the neoliberal moment is a space of junked utopias, overlapping temporalities, and revived or relentless forms of socialization, as well as the implementation and absorption of neoliberal restructuring, and counter-models of organizing. *Live Like This!* traces Sabine Bitter and Helmut Weber's long-term engagement with the processes restructuring the city into this uneven landscape of neoliberal spaces, national spaces, and self-organized communities. Launched from multiple geographic scales, these processes are not new, but have followed a jagged path toward market discipline and the shift to the city as a monochromatic site of consumptive practices and real-estate opportunities flanked by austerity programs and social exclusion for under-consumers. This shift, incomplete and in process as it is, has been built on a long process of erosions, exclusions, dispossessions, and reconfigurations of the urban landscape that has gone hand in hand with the global neoliberalizing of production sites, the emergence of the new non-places (such as Free Trade Zones and Guantánamo-type gulags), and a general ideology of the privatization of public goods set in opposition to forms of collectivity. While not uniform in its impact on cities, the urbanization of neoliberalism has made cities the "geographic targets and institutional laboratories" of neoliberalization.[9] This creative destruction of cities, and the creative resistances it produces, are represented both coolly and analytically in Bitter and Weber's works, mediated through the rationalizing optics and perspectives of architecture and photography and artistic practices more broadly. But it is more accurate and acute to say that the projects in *Live Like This!* represent the sites where the global project of neoliberalism hits localized and nationalized contexts, and is either absorbed into the culturally and place-specific contexts of Europe, North America, and South America, or is met with forms of living, organizing, and dwelling that reject or confound the market-driven policies and atomizing effects of the neoliberalization of urban space.

A touchstone in Bitter and Weber's investigation has been the transformation of modernist spaces and the widening disjuncture between the beleaguered promises of modernity and the lived effects of neoliberalism. But this transformation is not the replacement of one failed social utopia with a more exclusive economic utopia, rather it traces the transformation of the nature of social promises over the last half century. In addition, the much-criticized history of modernism and the unearthing of alternative modernities, particularly of modernist architecture and urban planning, provides a condensed studio for revisiting the modernity debates and understanding the kinds of losses and victories that have seeped into the groundwater of globalization. Masao Miyoshi hit on this when he reminded an audience of architects that, "Modernism— with all of its ills—was at least mindful of those left outside architecture. Urban workers had their housing projects, though ugly, unlivable, and finally useless. Today's industrial cities eliminate those rational monstrosities and, with them, homes for vast numbers of people."[10] Although Miyoshi's account suggests a rather uniform modernism, one with insufficient national or local variation in style and intent, and with perhaps a premature closure of the "finally use-less," Bitter and Weber have focused on the spaces of modernity which have been gradually transformed from "rational" urbanizations meant to house or warehouse the working-class and the poor into spaces where more collec-tive, even transformative, forms of living have forced their way to the surface. Resilience, reworking, and yes, resistance in the face of everyday neoliberal life, have, of necessity, inscribed themselves in the landscape."[11] These often self-organized communities are, in a sense, the unintended and disassembled legacies of modernization, spaces where the decades-long organizing and everyday life has produced a culture and literacy which has so far been able to deflect the neoliberalization of space that has inflicted dispossession and privatization to different degrees.

A number of crucial intersections of the discourses of modernity and neoliberalism are amplified in Bitter and Weber's investigations of modernist spaces and urban regimes in Brazil, Venezuela, Vienna, and former Eastern Bloc countries, and in the implementation or resistance to the neoliberalization of space in the Netherlands, Caracas, and São Paulo. In Gdansk, Poland, their city-wide billboard project, *Meeting at the LOT* draws its title from everyday

speech of people who live in Gdansk—the steel and glass
pavilion that was the former headquarters of the national
airline LOT is a popular place to rendezvous before moving
on to other parts of the city or hopping on the nearby
transit. But this building, embedded as an urban fact into
the city, is now the intersection of local modernism and
global neoliberalism. Built in 1961 as an international
furniture showroom, this modernist building housed the
regional headquarters for LOT in 1970. This national space
was downsized after 1989, and LOT now shares the building
with the mixed and more transient businesses of a mobile
telephone shop, a fast food outlet, an auto club, and a photo
store. This one building, a relatively undistinguished, but
nonetheless elegant example of the international style, has
been altered from an ample and representational space
to house the ambitions of a national industry—and national
airlines were highly symbolic of a nation's place in modernity—and become a site for less stable service industries.
Such service industries spring up in cities as competition
has driven industry elsewhere, or respatialized production,
or has filled in spaces opened after the downsizing or
collapse of more regulated national ventures.[12]

While neoliberalism may appear as a fragmented
phenomenon taking hold in particular localities, Jamie
Gough argues that neoliberalism inhabits "not only institutions and places but also the spaces in between" and hence
it sets the rules of how places interact.[13] The neoliberalization of urban spaces is not simply a matter of deregulation
then; it is also brought about by local regulations when
public policy picks up the DNA of neoliberalism. Bitter and
Weber's project on Almere, a polder city in the Netherlands,
engages with the relationship of the total plans of a model
city that then shares striking similarities with unplanned
and deregulated cities.

After exhaustive research, Almere's plan was born of
a state development authority under the Ministry of Transport and Public Works as a consumption-side plan giving the
residents the "lifestyle" they want.[14] Yet this individualization
in the state-planned town of Almere is similar to forms of
individualization found in North American suburbs where
planning is dominated by developers. For Bitter and Weber,
research that began on the serial suburbs of Calgary,

Alberta—called the "Texas" of Canada because of its oil and right-wing politics—led to almere.txt (2000). Without geographical boundaries to block its sprawl Calgary is, in terms of area, one of the largest cities in North America. The uncontrolled suburbs at its edges trickle out and are punctuated by gated communities hunched into the foothills west of the city's business center. Its polynulcear layout is made from far-flung malls connected by high-speed "trails." Even today Calgary does not require a public meeting for the development of a new suburb, yet spatially it resembles (on a different scale) the highly planned Almere. This similarity demonstrates the conjunction of state, urban planning, and "consumer preferences" within the neoliberalization of urban territories.

While these forces converge in Almere, Bitter and Weber also give powerful examples of places where the process of neoliberalization is rejected as an ideology and as a social practice. *Caracas, Hecho en Venezuela* (2005) began as a research project on the relationship of the modernist rationale of the Carlos Villanueva housing blocks, commissioned by the former dictactor Pérez Jiménez, that cut a rational line through the steep and irregular hillsides ringing Caracas, and the self-built and seemingly temporary barrio *ranchitos* which cohere into an irregular and organic mass on the hillside. Or at least this is how the language and logic of modernist architectural discourse would dramatize this condition. However, the spatiality of 23 de Enero is not the outcome of a failed modernity and the resourcefulness of the underclasses, it is a continuation of modernization into neoliberal globalization marked by spatial struggles and an increased rural-urban diaspora. What is remarkable at the moment in Venezuela is the confluence of the state and the people and organizations of the barrios (and the underdeveloped countryside) against a deepening of the inequities of neoliberalism and the assault on collective, community, and public formations and goods. Confounding the naturalized language of neoliberalization, and the flattening of the geography of globalization, *Caracas, Hecho en Venezuela* reveals public history of modernist architecture in relation to the neoliberalization of urban and national spaces.

In a series of black and white images entitled *Super Citizens* (2003), scenes from various pro-government, union, and independent media rallies set within the spectacular modernist urban landscape of Caracas are mediated through software to abstract the architecture while foregrounding the citizens. These photo-sketches, responding to a moment of social optimism and a degree of functioning unity at a national scale due to the promise of the redistribution of wealth, access to land, and the constitutional possibility of an active and participatory democracy (which included a public process for the rewriting of the Constitution, to the point where the Constitution itself became a popular book, an actual "pocket book" carried by people and read on busses, etc.). As Gerald Raunig notes, "The Constitution introduced 'participatory democracy,' and the 'protagonist role' of the people, including a complex version of human rights and the rights of women and Indigena, and generally followed an anti-neoliberal course."[15] Yet, in the near monopoly of the media of Venezuela and the exceptional criticism of the national project and cartoonish characterization of Chávez in the North American media, the media images circulating transnationally were of opposition marches: images of the poor and highly mobilized majority are rarely seen—except in the documentary *The Revolution Will Not Be Televised*, which filmed the mass rallies outside the presidential palace that, in some part, overturned the 2002 coup attempt against Chávez. Bitter/Weber's images are, in part, images of a curious formation—an anti-neoliberal "pro-government" (or, at least pro-participatory democracy) demonstration that understands the stakes to be the shape of democracy nationally, as well as the *articulation* of an anti-neoliberal project regionally and globally. Raunig defines a "non-conforming mass" as a mass that is "neither formless nor uniform … a mass organized in difference: a permeable, fluctuating, dispersed mass."[16] For Raunig, non-conformity is created by an inward and outward dialectic. Outwardly this takes the shape of "non-conformity in non-agreement with the form of how it [the mass] is governed," while "[i]nwardly non-conformity in this negation of any positive sense of community means the permanent differentiation of the singular."[17] This outward-inward dialectic is in effect in these images, but the outward non-conformity based on "non-agreement" of how the people are governed is flipped: there was (at that point) an agreement (to a strong if contingent

degree) in the "pro-Chávez" majority on how they were
governed, and the protests were organized to demonstrate
the actual mass of support (as a protection of *el processo*
against another coup attempt) as well as a "nonconformity"
to the form by which they *would be governed* if there was a
coup. That is, the dialectic is not just inward and outward
within the non-conformist mass, but there is a temporal
dialectic that is nonconformist with neoliberal harmonization of governance.

The cityscape in which these demonstrations are set
is sketched out as a drawing (highlighting the straight lines
of international modernism), while the human actors, the
"super citizens," are visible as photographs: the figure and
ground here is citizen and architecture, and well as transnational (architecture) and national (citizen). Reminiscent
of the socially optimistic (if not utopian-leaning) projects of
architectural groups from the late 1960s such as Superstudio
and Archigram, these drawings record people in the street
while proposing the city as a platform for social transformation. This "universal" aspect is laced into the particular
national project of participatory democracy in Venezuela,
while opening an optimistic space against universal neoliberalism. Rather than an either/or spatiality, the problem of
"too large and too small" is addressed spatially by joining
the global, national, and urban scales: the globalized city is
the platform for national rights as well as the global claims.
The modernist city program, rendered more rational by the
aesthetics and perspectives of an architectural drawing, does
not clash with the social program of the demonstrators: the
modernist architecture is not a deadening determinate on
the shape of everyday life; and the kernel of utopianism that
came along with the bad politics of modernist urban
planning (particularly in Venezuela as dictators rationalized
the city to saran-wrap the poverty "spilling from its hills")
is recoverable in some form.

Bronzeville marks a switch from the tension of
modernity and neoliberalization to a reinvestigation of the
tensions of race and space, and of the tropes and promises of
modernism that drive "urban regeneration" and gentrification. Bitter and Weber begin from the historically dense site
of Mies Van der Rohe's first large scale project in North
America, the Illinois Institute of Technology (IIT) on

the South Side of Chicago. Reading what is acknowledged as
a masterpiece of modern architecture in its full historical
and social context, Bitter and Weber turn to the work of
the writer Gwendolyn Brooks—the first Black woman to win
a Pulitzer prize and a central figure in a group of younger
cultural workers in the "Black Megalopolis" who "were
sowing the seeds of Chicago's 'cultural front,' one that would
give birth to a distinctive black radicalism that relied on
an improvisatory spirit of local collaboration, 'democratic'
radicalism, class struggle, and race-based 'progressivism'"
from the 1930s to the 1970s.[18] Brook's long poem "In the
Mecca" is an engaged sociological text of the residents
of The Mecca, a turn of the century building that began as
luxury apartment housing for Chicago's elite in 1891 and
finally was demolished by IIT to develop the Mies campus
in 1952. At that time, The Mecca was described in a *Harpers*
magazine article as "one of the most remarkable negro
slum exhibits in the world"[19] and it met the wrecking ball
despite the organized protests of its 700 occupants. Brooks
racializes the modernist tropes of light/lightness and rational
design versus darkness/blackness and disorder to build
a poem structured on epic ascents and descents that intro-
duce the actors of the poem floor by floor, as the narrator
walks up The Mecca. The people of the poem, and of the
building, are connected to one another by their engagement
in the life of the building as well as the forms of racism
and economic repression that they meet. The dramatic cast
of the poem stacks a dynamic argument of the various
debates within the Black community at that time—from
Black Nationalism and uplift, to economic analyses of racism
in relation to class. But the opening lines of the poem set
the denseness and pointed ambiguities of the language, while
establishing yet demolishing architecture as a claim to truth:

> Sit where the light corrupts your face.
> Mies Van der Rohe retires from grace.
> And fair fables fall.

Using the opening epic address to the audience (and echoing
Homer's *The Odyssey* and Ezra Pound's *The Cantos*), Gwendolyn
Brooks establishes the modernist qualities of light and its
"master builder" as also ideological with three charged

words—corrupts, grace, and fall. Describing light as corrupt and having the unquestioned Mies "retire from grace" (inevitably the later verb "fall" is also in effect here), Brooks throws the modernist rationales for knocking down The Mecca into sharp question. The opening lines of this urban poetics are a tight knot of race, modernism, language, and ideology.

Inspired by Brooks' work, Bitter and Weber's *Bronzeville* project (2004/2005) revisits the space of The Mecca and reiterates Brooks' relation of modernism, light, and race. But Bronzeville also links the process, started with Van der Rohe's IIT campus, with another phase of so-called "urban regeneration" in the south side of Chicago. The transition from modernism's rationalized plan to the endemic gentrification of the South Side is part of the creative destruction that neoliberalization brings. It also marks the centrality of gentrification as global-urban strategy in neoliberal globalization.

Globalization, for all of its opening of the world and its deepening of national and local connections, or its erosion of nation-scale politics, focuses its transformational powers on cities, and therefore coheres dramatically in the textures and rhythms of daily life and the production of urban space. Urban landscapes, in Bitter and Weber's work, are born out of the fact that cities are at the center of global change, as the intensification of globalization over the last 30 years has also been an acceleration of urbanization. *Recent Geographies* (2007) captures the emergent urban landscapes as they are remade by social, economic, and urban transformation. The shift subtly caught in Bitter and Weber's work is that "global cities" are obviously not just the major financial and media command posts, but that peripheral cities (peripheral in the global imagination, but still in the orbit of global capital) such as Belgrade and Vancouver, and the edges of cities themselves (such as the banlieues of Paris and the state-modernist New Belgrade, across the Sava River from the old city) have become globalized in conflicting and spectacular ways. These minor globalized cities and zones, if we can call them that, are altered and molded by the hands of globalization and neoliberal governance, yet (and not paradoxically) they are cities that are deeply textured in their particular, beautiful, and transitional ways. The urban texture

of such cities takes on the layers pressed into them from
globalization—and the drastic reworking of the city in
the global system—yet the layers of past planning, and the
vectors of past ways of living (or culture) still resonate in
the city space.

Recent Geographies begins with images of architecture
and urban space from the postmodern aspects of Paris,
downtown Los Angeles, the state architecture of Romania,
and Canada's representative postmodern city, Vancouver.
Mixing and juxtaposing these images, Bitter and Weber
focus on postmodern architecture found in urban
territories and economies that are seemingly incompatible:
city space planned and produced by socialist Yugoslavia,
the social housing on the fringe of Paris which erupted in
riot and flames by the socially dispossessed, the highly
mediatized urban core of Los Angeles, the grand boulevard
of Bucharest, and the Pacific Rim cosmopolitan city of
Vancouver.

Curiously, in these recent geographies of globalization
and neoliberal spaces, postmodernism emerges as a mobile
style that has crossed very different and even contradictory
economies and spaces—a style that is called upon to
represent very different social and spatial logics and social
visions. In one collage in *Recent Geographies*, a grand
boulevard in Bucharest bends seamlessly into the social
housing project, Abraxas, by Ricardo Bofill in the banlieues
of Paris (a building central in Terry Gilliam's dystopic film
Brazil which warned of a totally administered modernity).
In another collage, the Genex Tower, an intensely postmodern gate to postsocialist Belgrade and a former state
import-export company, merges into Moshe Safdie's new
public-private library of Vancouver, a building that is itself
a postmodern collage of a Roman coliseum, a shopping
complex, and library. Rather than holding architectural style
as a marker of an economic and cultural logic, through
their collage method and through their research (the careful
choosing of buildings and sites), Bitter and Weber show
how the cultural logic of architecture is itself produced anew,
carrying its sedimented social and spatial meanings into he
long moment of neoliberalism.

Curiously, postmodernism seems to have returned—
despite its damning architectural critiques and its theoretical

relegation—as a logic of neoliberal globalization. Why is this style so often turned to, as cities are being remade and creatively destroyed, as one way of urban life is overlaid with a new one (a new one that often descends from above with little discussion or consultation from citizens)? In cities such as Vancouver, there is a postmodern sameness to the new cityscape, a cityscape driven by the logic of real estate that finds its representation in a variant of postmodern architecture. But this postmodernism, while linked in some global manner, as *Recent Geographies* shows, is not identical to the postmodernism in New Belgrade, in Bucharest, or on the volatile peripheries of Paris. However, by using collage as research, Bitter and Weber show the precise tension between difference and sameness produced by neoliberalism in globalized cities.

The geography of actually existing (or lived) neoliberalism is nuanced into visibility in Bitter/Weber's works, recalling the disjuncture of the promises of modernity and the project of neoliberal globalization while simultaneously presenting the spatial and social logics that powerfully link them. In these overlaps and gaps, new spatialities, new relations, and new struggles brew.

Jeff Derksen thanks Mark Novak for, among many things, discussions of Gwendolyn Brooks' work.

[1] Thomas Friedman, *The World Is Flat*, Farrar, Straus and Giroux, New York 2005.

[2] Neil Smith, "The Satanic Geographies of Globalization: Uneven Development in the 1990s," *Public* Culture, vol. 10, no. 1, issue 24 (Fall 1997), p. 169–189.

[3] Jamie Peck and Adam Tickell, "Neoliberalizing Space," *Antipode* (June 2002), p. 380–404.

[4] Ian Angus, "Modernity and Its Discontents," *Topia* 13 (2004), p. 145–151.

[5] Masao Miyoshi, "Outside of Architecture," Cynthia C. Davidson (ed.), *Anywise*, MIT Press, Cambridge, Massachusetts 1996, p. 38–47.

[6] Peck and Tickell, "Neoliberalizing Space," p. 380–404.

[7] Elmar Altvater, "What Happens When Public Goods Are Privatized," *Studies in Political Economy* 74 (Autumn 2004), p. 45–77.

[8] Pierre Bourdieu, *Acts of Resistance: Against The New Myths of Our Times*, trans. Richard Nice, Polity Press, Cambridge, 1998.

[9] Neil Brenner and Nik Theodore, "Cities and the Geographies of 'Actually Existing Neoliberalism,'" *Antipode* (June 2002), p. 349–379.

[10] Miyoshi, "Outside of Architecture," p. 38–47.

[11] Cindi Katz, *Growing Up Global*, University of Minnesota Press, Minneapolis 2004.

[12] Jamie Gough, "Neoliberalism and Socialization in the Contemporary City: Oppositions, Complements and Instabilities," *Antipode* (June 2002), p. 403–426.

[13] Ibid., p. 387.

[14] Petra Brouwer, "Boom Town Almere: Form Follows Lifestyle," *Archis* 11 (1999), p. 10–19.

[15] Gerald Raunig, *Art and Revolution: Transversal Activism in the Long Twentieth Century*, trans. Aileen Derieg, *Semiotext(e)*, Los Angeles 2007, p. 65.

[16] Ibid., p. 58.

[17] Ibid.

[18] Bill V. Mullen, *Popular Fronts: Chicago and African-American Cultural Politics, 1935–46*, University of Illinois Press, Urbana and Champagne 1999, p. 10.

[19] John Lowney, "'A Material Collapse that is Construction': History and Counter-Memory in Gwendolyn Brooks' 'In The Mecca,'" *Melus* 23/3 (Fall 1998), p. 3.

The Flâneur Could Not Take the Monorail: Representing Vancouver in Three Temporalities

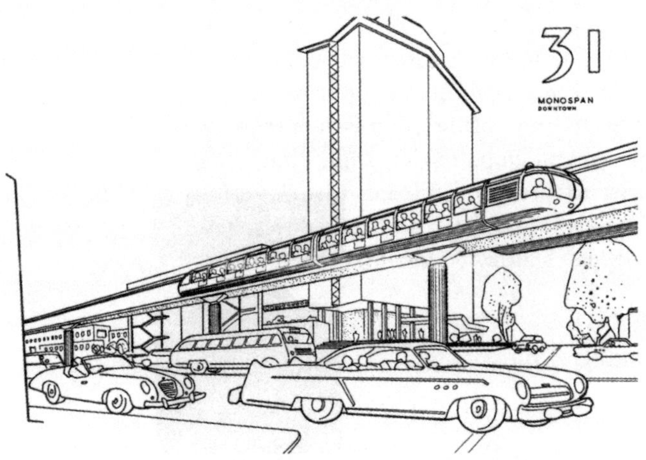

Dennis McNulty, *one second of a possible future/monospan twin-ride*, 2008
Inkjet print on paper, sound, and electronics, dimensions variable

*In the midway of this life we're
partner with,
I awoke to find me in a dark wood,
Where not only was the only way fixed,
It is hard to speak of what it was,
All the exits went waylaid, thick end
of ever Covered trace
Of an even stray path, then up in the
rain, Lo! Skytrain.*
—Gerald Creede, "Detach"

The inherited narrative that poses
the modernist imagination of a city
as a rational machine for living,
propelled by the dream of development, ran smack into the sensual
life of the streets and the unpredictability of everyday life. To
negotiate this contradiction of the
modernist logic straight-line, and
the unpredictability and possibilities of the street, literature and
then the visual arts picked up the
emblem of the flâneur as the
detached yet secretly engaged navi-
gator of the city. Today that modernist dream of the city, and the
19th-century device of the flâneur,

is further twisted by two recent and very prosaic qualities
that are characteristic of the neoliberal city. These twin
urban tensions of a containment-security-surveillance
complex and a consumption-speculation-expansion complex.
This first complex—a containment-security-surveillance
complex—worries over the excess of publicness (such as
rallies, marches, and other forms of civic protest), the
production of unruly spaces, and the excesses of life. This
complex has expanded, as a counter measure, an industry of
surveillance systems and rehearsed police tactics to deal with
new social actors and public speech. The second complex—
a consumption-speculation-expansion complex—tries to
guide the creativity of everyday life into intensified affective
relations tied to consumption: publicness is then acted out
through consumption and its spaces. In this complex, the
heat of everyday life in commerce is drawn off into a turbo-
charged capitalism, tied into the whirling speculation of real
estate, as well as the shaping of the city as a space of consumption. Of course cities always have been deeply shaped
by economic factors, but the intensification today is that
cities themselves are used as *an accumulation strategy* rather
than the site of economic activity. Hence, cities continually
look for ways to expand, either through actual building or
through the making of a bubble market and the elevation of
real estate to a key organizing principle of everyday life. This
has also altered notions of *home* and *dwelling*, shifting them
from more affective relationships to economic imperatives.

    In this scenario, the empty apartments in the city
I live in are never idle: even as they sit uninhabited they can
make or lose money for the owners who have bet, short- or
long-term, on the housing market. In this sense, they are
neither homes nor dwellings, but investment platforms. The
dialectical struggle that emerges here is over the production
of space by social actors and the conquest of space as a
commodity. For Henri Lefebvre, this has altered both space
and the inhabitant: "He [the inhabitant] is reduced not only
to merely functioning as an inhabitant (habit as function)
but to being a buyer of space, one who realizes surplus
value."[1] Habit, that squelcher of life and art from the Russian
Formalists and their notion of *banalization*, is now figured
as the force to resist in the urban, as the Situationist
International continually pointed out. This also brings

artistic practices directly into the urban dialectic, for art and literature have taken habit and banality as processes to be investigated, reworked, and overturned.

From Place to Process and the Problem of Representation

This shift in urbanization, largely predicted by Lefebvre in the 1970s and wonderfully documented and analyzed since, creates a conundrum in the way that cities are represented culturally. For urbanism, this question of representation amplifies *an illusion* in Lefebvre's terms:

> Like classical philosophy, urbanism claims to be
> a system. It pretends to embrace, enclose, and possess
> a new totality. It wants to be the modern philosophy
> of the city, justified by (liberal) humanism while
> justifying a (technocratic) utopia.[2]

This produces a "blind field" in which urbanists, although they "live it [the city], they are in it, but they don't see it, and certainly cannot grasp it as such."[3] More than a criticism of planning and the rationalization of the city, Lefebvre points to the impossibility of grasping the city as a totality. This is not due to the city being an ephemeral wonder, but, Lefebvre argues because, "in bureaucratic capitalism, productive activity completely escapes the control of planners and developers," and "space, as product, results from relation-ships of production that are taken under control by an active group."[4] In this relationship of control and representation, another dialectic emerges, the aspects of life that escape control and those which become banalized.

Prior to Lefebvre, Kevin Lynch proposed a rational-ized approach to this problem of representation in his classic study of the image and *imageability* of the city. For Lynch,

> Like a piece of architecture, the city is a construction
> in space, but it is one of vast scale, a thing perceived
> only in the course of long spans of time. City design
> is therefore a temporal art, but it can rarely use
> the controlled and limited sequence of other tempo-
> ral arts like music. On different occasions and

for different people, the sequences are reversed, interrupted, abandoned, cut across.[5]

What Lynch catches here is the how the temporal aspect of cities—whether they emerge from urban design or whether they evolve from a Lefebvrian dialectic—is uneven and cut across by layers of development, the interventions of social actors, and the stuttering of urban processes. In keeping city design separate from architecture, Lynch hopes to keep this process open, not terminating in "a final result, [but] only a continuous secession of phases."[6] Unfolding the city over time, and moving closer to Lefebvre's term of *urbanization*, Lynch opens a tension within the representation of the city *as process*. But, through *imageability* Lynch gives us is

a concept … [that] does not necessarily connote something fixed, limited, precise, unified, or regularly ordered, although it may have these qualities.[7]

Through the case studies of the experience and image of cities (in particular Boston, Jersey City, and Los Angeles) Lynch turns to the techniques of "field reconnaissance and citizen interview," as well as "photographic recognition tests, actual trips in the field, and by numerous requests for directions made of passers-by in the streets."[8] From this fieldwork, and from his proposal of the city as a multi-temporal process, Lynch's imageability catalogues a more subjective experience of the elements of urban space— from edges, paths, districts, nodes, and landmarks, a shifting image builds up.

Shifting from Lynch's 1960s cities—before the explosion of urban upheaval and before the intensification of urbanization brought on by the acceleration of globalization—to today, the image of globalized cities becomes even more vexing, and the temporality of urban space even more layered. More layered because the creative destruction of the urban territory is felt in a deeply material manner, and more vexed because globalized cities also fall into what Slavoj Žižek locates as a "'danger' of capitalism." Writing on urban violence in Paris and New Orleans (in France's fiery fall and in the days of devastation after the flood of New Orleans in 2005), Žižek argues that, capitalism, through globalization, is "depriving the large majority of people of any meaningful 'cognitive mapping.'"[9] Crucially for Žižek, the inability to map one's position within global capital is not ontological, but produced by capital's production of space and spatial relations. This establishes a scalar dialogue with Lefebvre's accusation that urbanists cannot grasp the city, despite being in the middle of urban processes, because urban life itself, despite the determinations of capital, is always in excess of a complete image and of complete understanding. For Žižek, it is global capital that has overturned a grasping of totality and fractured the possibility of Fredric Jameson's unfinished concept of cognitive mapping; but for Lefebvre—true to his wild dialectics—the complexity of everyday life resists such a mapping.

The Question and Spaces of Representation

An aesthetic or artistic question arises from the difficulty of grasping, mapping, or even codifying urbanism today: has this work of cataloguing and representing urbanization and the city moved from urban planners to artists? Has the *imageability* of the city passed over to artists whose aesthetic practices can grasp the contradictions and overlapping temporalities of urbanization? But the dark side of these questions suggests that urban planners are merely technocrats for urban development programs, that they have no plan for the city other than to strengthen it as an accumulation strategy, that their social imagination is to manage the inequities of the neoliberal city rather than to imagine an equitable city. But on a productive aesthetic side, these questions suggest a shift in the *knowledge* of the city and a complication of the ideological act of representation.

Peter Lang, arguing that "new urban conglomerates" today "defy […] any of the standard formulas underlining the late modern rules of urban determinancy," arrives at such a role for artists: "The new breed of multidisciplinary artist is a far more prescient gauge of the dramatic transformations affecting society than his or her more rigidly focused professional counterpart, and clearly serves to instigate a debate on the subject of the contemporary city and its impact on new forms of cultural behavior."[10] It is important here to not propose artists as a trans-historical instrument for gauging urban life—such as the device the flâneur turned into—but to catch the alteration, over the last half-century, of the shape of urbanism itself and how it has become both increasingly unruly and difficult to represent, map cognitively, or be fully known. At the same time, cities do expand and mutate under new sets of determinants, and new technological mediations; but the dialectic of determination, and of the twin tensions I outlined at the beginning of this essay, have shifted the representation of urban processes from the planner to the artist.

This in turn opens the modes of representation of a city to a wide field of artistic and aesthetic approaches. The explosion of urban art seeking to represent an urban imagination and processes of the city—from site-specific work, new genre public art, to research-based work and the mass of photographic strategies—is a dynamic symptom of this. In his works *one second of a possible future/monospan twin ride* and *the view from now/downtown parkade* (both 2008), Dublin-based artist Dennis McNulty delves into the aesthetic representation of Vancouver through the use of three different aesthetic interventions. Crucially, these works approach the problem of the representation of space through three temporalities: a possible future drawn from the archive of city planning; an unstable linguistic landscape of the present; and the complex overlapping time of the shifting of urban economies from industrial to real-estate via idleness (or from production to speculation).

But I have been too passive in my verbs here, for no representational act merely *approaches* a city—rather such an act is more actively *generative* of the city. Artistic practices then are spatial practices in the way that Andy Merrifield invigorates Lefebvre's term:

> Spatial practices invariably relate to *perception*, to people's perceived take on the world, on *their* world—particularly their everyday world. Spatial practices make sense (and nonsense) of everyday reality, and include routes and networks, patterns and movements that link together spaces of work, play, and leisure.[11]

Merrifield's emphasis on perception and movement is canny in relation to McNulty's work on Vancouver, for the three temporalities that these works produce through the representation of space are largely based on various perceptions of movement. But, grasping the city through uneven and overlapping temporalities, *one second of a possible future/monospan twin ride* and *the view from now/downtown parkade* also play off of a relationship of *movement* and *development*.

One second of a possible future/monospan twin ride revolves around a 1957 plan for a monorail in Vancouver's downtown by the architect and designer Wells Coates. Despite his participation in CIAM and an important role in British modernism, his enduring designs (for instance the "D-handles," which you probably used opening a door today) and the Isokon Flats in Camden (inhabited, at one point, by Walter Gropius), Coates certainly remains under-recognized internationally and almost unknown in Vancouver.[12] In 1957 Vancouver was a still a rough, material town, a city standing on an economy based in fish, lumber, mining, ship-building, and manufacturing. Coates' design of a raised monorail on an inverted T of cast concrete, which made the trains appear to float, would have been extremely space-aged at that time. Which is perhaps why it was never built. Even today a monorail is emblematic of a nostalgic and unrealized technological future: that is, the monorail is a temporally tricky image of a future that is still in the past. But Coates' proposal was actually a practical solution for its present. In the late 1950s Vancouver was actually dismantling its urban transport: its two inter-urban train lines and the streetcar system were shut down in September 1958.[13] Coates' monorail would have filled the time span between when there was no rapid transit in Vancouver other than busses, and the brief moment when there was a monorail. Ironically, the only monorail that Vancouver has had—which ran as a temporary amusement in movement from May to October 1986, and was built by the Swiss company with the appropriate name of Von Roll—was on the grounds on Expo 86, the global mega-event that was to bring Vancouver into the future by opening it to the new impulses of globalization. That is, it was to bring Vancouver out the world of resources and *stuff* to a world of the buying and selling of space.

Ironically, for a city that had denied such an innovative and beautiful transportation system as Coates', the theme of Expo 86 was transportation. This set off a rush to provide the city with an actual rapid-transit system. As a result, the Skytrain hastily built—at first a one-line transit system raised on concrete tracks that gave it its name (a name suitably mocked in Gerald Creede's poem "Detach," which echoes Dante to invoke the humor of naming a raised transit system Skytrain: "…*then up in the rain, / Lo! Skytrain*").[14] Curiously, even though Skytrain was an emblem of the arrival of a new form of global modernity for the city, the Skytrain's lines partially overlap with the interurban train line that ran from 1902 to the late 1950s.[15] With this type of spatial layering of the city, which Lynch was concerned with as well, the question of the difficulty of the representation of urban processes is again raised. To this McNulty has added an extra conundrum: How to represent an aspect of the city that was imagined, planned and proposed, but never realized? This is also a temporal question: for Coates' monorail represents the modernism and a possible future that Vancouver never had. This modernism, drawn from the lost archive of city planning, arrived belatedly, exactly at the height of corporate postmodernism (so shiningly represented by Vancouver's waterfront architecture) with Skytrain, only due to the global push of Expo 86.

To represent the city and the movement of Coates' monorail through city space, McNulty takes an image drawn by Coates, and used in his research report on the monorail plan, and pushes this architectural drawing through the frame. This sequence of 24 drawings, which forms part of a piece entitled *one second of a possible future/monospan twin ride*, mimics the motion of the monorail, but the image itself simply passes through the frame. The cityscape in Coates' drawing is dominated by one building looming in monumental perspective: a sleek tower that was once the B.C. Hydro headquarters designed by Thompson, Berwick, Pratt in 1955, and a "testimony to the high ideals of modernism."[16] Today, the signature office tower of the electrical company that was state-run but is now partially privatized, was retro-fitted as apartments and renamed The Electra. Its apartments circulate through Vancouver's real-estate market, changing hands as space and the idea of living is magically turned into capital. In this frame, McNulty's representation of the modernism that was never to arrive—the monorail and its sense of mobility and futurity—passes by the modernism that moved from the state to the market. The movement in this drawing then is not just the clean representation of the monorail cutting sharply through the cityscape, but it also gives us the elements of a movement from a Keynesian welfare state to a neoliberal state, and from a publicly owned industry that produces something socially necessary (electricity) to a privatized economy that produces immaterial surplus value. In terms of artistic representation, McNulty's use of Coates' architectural renderings *mimics* movement, yet provocatively *represents* another more obscured form of development and transformation.[17]

The second temporality of *one second of a possible future/monospan twin ride* is constructed from a sound work rather than images. Yet this sound work also strains at spatial representation. Devised as a soundtrack to the images of Coates' monorail, this work is narrated by Karen Kelm, who was the official voice for Skytrain's original line, the Expo line, but whose calm announcements were replaced as the system expanded with other lines. Kelm worked for B.C. Transit at the time and was conscripted for the job because she had some theater experience. Yet Kelm's voice may have been one of the most familiar of all public voices in the city—her affectless voice announced each stop ("The next station is [pause as the computer selects the appropriate station] Stadium") up and down the line from Waterfront to New Westminster. McNulty's approach to debanalize both Kelm's voice and the Skytrain ride itself was to have her narrate a dense soundtrack edited from McNulty's field recordings of his travels along the Skytrain lines and his walks through the stations and their vicinities. Kelm, listening to McNulty's recordings of the sounds of the stations, the whirls and clicks of the Bombardier-built trains, and the voices of the passengers, attempts to create a linguistic-visual image of the ride: her attempt is necessarily speculative as she guesses what the sounds could be, as a result (and in combination with the soundtrack's layered editing) each articulation is abrupt or unsure. What does it mean, in terms of representation, to have the steady, assured, yet disembodied voice of a transit system brought back into the spaces and sounds of that system and to try to recreate it? In terms of the tension between urban designers' representations of the city and artist's representations of the urban, this soundtrack is directly shaped by the voices, movements, and bodies of the citizen/inhabitants using Skytrain. Kelm, the voice that represented predictability, here is thrown into another register by the uncertainty of the urban movement and life. Unlike the surety of the old station announcements, here Kelm makes perceptual leaps (through McNulty's editing):

> Boarding the train … clicking sounds all around doors close … an engine accelerating train moves away outside … something's coming … slowing down at an outdoor station … foreign language—an accent! … teenagers joking around …

This soundtrack also throws off the flâneur as an artistic device for it is not a 19th-century idling walk, nor a Situationist derive designed to overcome the city's overly administered spaces through an excess of purposelessness, but a temporally askew narration between the future that Coates imagined and the present (his future) that the city has.

The third temporality that McNulty constructs is also done through research, site selection, and sound in the work *the view from now/downtown parkade*. But this temporality is nearly glacial in terms of urban process and globalization: it is the slow swing from an industrial waterfront to a speculative waterfront, from a working dock to a post-port real-estate zone of cheap post modernism and "preserved" heritage buildings … and with a market, always with a public market and ample parking. The waterfront on the Fraser River in New Westminster, a former city now integrated into the suburban texture of Vancouver where *the view from now/downtown parkade* was situated, represents this transition, this creative destruction punctuated by moments of optimistic development and demolition and then periods of rusty stalling. The layers of developmental miscalculations and miscues by city planners and small-time developers are literally stacked side by side and on top of each other on this waterfront: the unused industrial spaces hover between the working-dock past and the limited imagination of waterfronts today which rely on public walkways and condominiums. In New Westminster this decay also includes a paddle wheeler that was once a casino when gambling was the only imagined economic engine; a postmodern public market with pink and teal details, including the perplexing po-mo use of industrial scale pipes merely for ornamentation; and a two-story public parkade that separates the downtown from the waterfront and shrouds the waterfront street in darkness. The parkade is largely unused, and persistently rumored to be slated for tear-down or redevelopment (as a farmers market, naturally). On this unloved structure that could stand as one of that city's industrial-modernist monuments, McNulty set up a mobile sound unit from the back of car and staged a proprioceptive electronic soundwork that echoed through the minimal and narrow parkade overlooking the wide Fraser River. The relationship between the digital scratches, tweeps, droning, and bleeps (reminiscent of the Mego Record artists such as Jim O'Rourke and Fennesz) and what Stuart Hall described as the slow rusty sound of deindustrialization, is a relationship that again steps into the conundrum of representation of urban processes. Can sound, unfolding as it does in time, represent an urban process? Or, with less directness, is Dennis McNulty's site-specific sound piece an *objective correlative* of this movement from working-docks to post-Fordist development failure? The answer lies closer to the impossibility of representing a process which is spread across spatial scales—from the extremely local to the scale of global finance—and moving through a complex temporality in which its present is the least valued. The difference here from the problem of representing the city due to its spatial complexity that confronted Lynch in 1960, or the lack of a means for "cognitive mapping" due to the decentering effects of globalization that Jameson and then Žižek cite, is that the uneven process of the place—suspended between a predictable future of development with preserved heritage buildings and a slowly decaying present—is much more difficult to represent than the actual physical space. Industrial waterfront, even in transition, is easy to stabilize with photographs that catch the scale and textures of steel, concrete, and timber. Given this, the digital sounds bouncing off of the analogue parkade, as tug boats pulled log booms upriver, at least debanalized the *present* of the waterfront.

These three components of McNulty's Vancouver project can be framed within Lefebvre's shift, as Merrifield puts it, "from 'things in space' to 'the production of space.'"[18] The representation of 'things in space' is straight-forward—any number of representational strategies can show us the material *thingness* of things; artistic practices also metaleptically turn any commodity into a thing that has a depth and complexity beyond its surface.[19] The production of space, as I've argued, is much more difficult to represent as it is both temporal and spatial. McNulty's three tempo-ralities are all spatial and they are all attempts to represent the imagination and production of space at various moments. By bringing *one second* of Wells Coates' future—captured in the enduring emblem of futurity, the mono-rail—forward from the forgotten archive of city planning, McNulty chose a canny entry point to the various temporali-ties of Vancouver. Coates is an unknown urban futurist in Vancouver, yet his plan was echoed when the city was jumped-started into the imagined future of global capital by the mega-event Expo 86. In this way, McNulty's works get into the layered histories of the city through its planned, unplanned, and *unbuilt* possibilities. And, as I proposed earlier, with the complexities of urban territories understood as in excess of planning, and with the current crisis of planning in Vancouver (despite its marketability) where private developers have shunted aside public planners, an *artistic representation* of the city has the possibility of being a counter-representation. *One second of a possible future/monospan twin ride* and *the view from now/downtown parkade* enter the problem of representation in order to trouble three tempo-ralities, and how they haunt the production of space in Vancouver today.

[1]   Henri Lefebvre, *The Urban Revolution* (1970), trans. Robert Bononno, University of Minnesota Press, Minneapolis 2003, p. 156.

[2]   Ibid., p. 153.

[3]   Ibid.

[4]   Ibid., p. 154.

[5]   Kevin Lynch, *The Image of the City*, MIT Press, Cambridge, Massachusetts 1960, p. 1.

[6]   Ibid., p. 2.

[7]   Ibid., p. 10.

[8]   Ibid., p. 15.

[9]   Slavoj Žižek, "Some Politically Incorrect Reflections on Urban Violence in Paris and New Orleans and Related Matters," *Urban Politics Now: Re-Imagining Democracy in the Neoliberal City*, BAVO, NAi Publshers, Rotterdam 2007, p. 15.

[10] Peter Lang, "Over My Dead City," Kyong Park (ed.), *Urban Ecology: Detroit and Beyond*. Map Bok Publications, Hong Kong 2005, p. 11.

[11] Andy Merrifield, *Metromarxism: A Marxist Tale of the City*, Routledge, London 2002, p. 90.

[12] See Elizabeth Darling, "Wells Coates: Maker of a Modern British Architecture," *Architectural Review* (September 2008), p. 81–87. Anecdotally, while I was searching for the book that Coates' daughter, Laura Cohn, wrote—*The Door to a Secret Room: A Portrait of Wells Coates* (1999)—a local used bookstore owner told me that he had no material on Coates but that several architects in town were doing research on Coates and were hoarding research material on him.

[13] Lance Berelowitz, *Dream City: Vancouver and the Global Imagination*, Douglas & McIntyre, Vancouver 2005, p. 77.

[14] Gerald Creede, *Ambit*, Tsunami Press, Vancouver 1993.

[15] Berelowitz, *Dream City*.

[16] Ibid. p. 3.

[17] Another tension in the series of images is the car that also passes through the frame. Coates' design would not have been rejected, nor the interurban lines and the streetcars disassembled, if the private car had not become the king-pin of all planning.

[18] Merrifield, *Metromarxism*, p. 89.

[19] Here I am borrowing from Bill Brown when he writes: "above all, I am interested in the metaleptic effect whereby institutions don't preserve art but rather, through the act of institutional preservation, create art" ("Objects, Others, and Us: The Refabrication of Things," *Critical Inquiry* 36 [Winter 2010], p. 193). At a lower level than the institutional creation of the art object from objects the production of *things* that lay out their detailed surfaces is the strategy of many artists.

The Poetics of Bad History

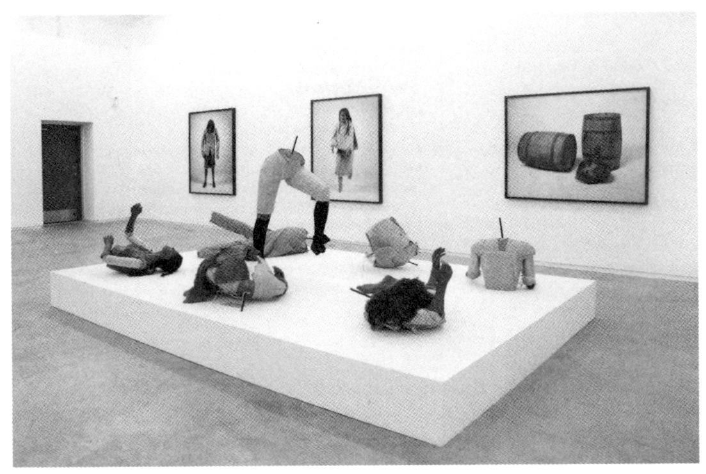

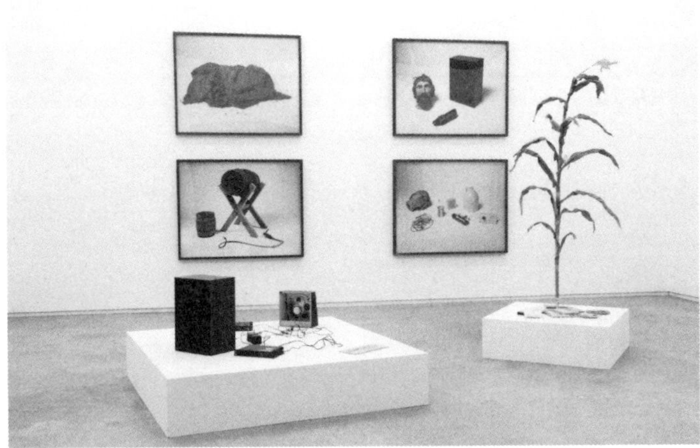

Sam Durant, *Scenes from the Pilgrim Story: Natural History*, 2007
Media and dimensions variable

History, as a form of knowledge, it seems, has been recently been drawn into new contestations as artists reflect upon particular moments and formations in the past in order to reopen the condition of the present. Why is art used increasingly to draw contour lines between contested moments from the past and the structural determinations of the present?
Why does the present—nestled between the turn to hardened national discourses after September 11, 2001, the financialization crisis of 2007, and the great shifts that will unfold as neoliberalism cracks into new forms of alliances and competition—call out via the past? But artists' historical turn, or a "historiographical turn" as Dieter Roelstraete defines it, in which

> [a] steadily growing number of contemporary art practices engage not only in storytelling, but more specifically in history-telling

in a "retrospective historiographic mode," has taken shape alongside a temporal turn that the cultural aspect of neoliberalism has been building slowly, solidfying unevenness into inevitability.[1]

The temporality that neoliberalism has crafted—how it told its own story through think tanks, the media, and cultural discourses—was necessary in order to live up to the claims its major figures, from Margaret Thatcher to Francis Fukuyama, called into being. Neoliberalism has incrementally shaped itself through a largely formal narrative in which the *story* of neoliberalism works toward a structural closing that imagines itself as its own conclusion. But the *plot* of neoliberalism involves a "disarrangement" of other social narratives.[2] In this foreclosure of history, neoliberalism did not anticipate any sequels and it worked hard to devise a story that halted modernist narratives of development, as well as utopian tales of social transformation, in favor of smaller ideological upgrades to itself. In the celebrated "end of history" that neoliberalism yearns to validate, the appearance of the future is blocked by the construction of a continuous present or absolute present.[3] This thesis of history is a dramatic symptom of the temporal thinking of our neoliberal moment: history is the timely development or "intelligent design" of that famously hidden hand of the market, freed by philosophy and ideology from the necessity of human actors or collective interventions.[4]

On the other hand, for contemporary artists invoking and investigating history, Walter Benjamin's philosophy of history has been a fertile (if not overused) ground. But, within the temporality of neoliberalism, Benjamin's conceptualization of history is thwarted, for the present cannot be a revolutionary now-time, nor the vanishing point of the past. Rather, the *present is the vanishing point of the future*, and the past is open for continual affective re-interpretation (as long as it leads to the present as it is!).

This turn to history by artists has been generalized by Mark Godfrey in "The Artist as Historian" as an archival impulse in which

> [t]hese varied research processes lead to works that invite the viewers to think about the past: to make connections between events, characters, and objects;

to join together in memory; and to reconsider the ways in which the past is represented in the wider culture.[5]

Deiter Roelstraete views this "mandate" of a historiographical tendency in art production as a structural inhibition for the art world to examine itself in the present, and by extension, to engage with the future:

> but there does seems to exist a connection, on the one hand, a reluctance to theorize the present moment in art (let alone its future), and, on the other, the massive amounts of art made today concerned with "yesterday": our inability to either "think" or simply imagine the future seems structurally linked with the enthusiasm shared by so many artists for digging up various obscure odds and ends dating from a more or less remote, unknowable past … [6]

This social and artistic historical turn, that is part historiography and part historicism, is not a simple intensification of the past, pulling it into a renewed relationship with the present. The poetics of history as a form of knowledge—that "attempts to define the mode of truth to which such knowledge is devoted"[7]—has fallen into two paradigms that are not in contradiction, but which can be toggled on and off, both serving the inevitability of the present. One tendency is a narrativization of a linear history that leads to the absolute present; the other is a similar model in which events and figures are cast as non-dialectical moments of stasis (events and people caught in time) that can be brought forward as eternal fixed ideas.[8] In this, the echoes of Lukács, arguing for the use of historical materialism and working within his own particular moment, bounce off of neoliberal temporality:

> Consequently history does not merely unfold *within* the terrain mapped out by these [social] institutions. It does not resolve itself into the evolution of *contents*, of men and situations, etc., while the *principles* of society remain eternally valid.[9]

Both of these models lose the push and pull of history, or, in another language, lose the dialectical aspect of history because they deny the bad side of history.

Marx deploys the concept of the bad side of history in *The Poverty of Philosophy* in order to complicate Proudhon's concept that the good side of history, which moves to advance the ideal of equality and evolves until economic contradictions end. Marx, however, does not accept the sterility of Proudhon's elimination of the bad side of history and instead makes it a central force: "It is the bad side that produces the movement which makes history, by providing a struggle."[10] As Étienne Balibar describes this force,

> history advances by the bad side, the side the theory had not foreseen, the side which challenges its representation of necessity and, ultimately, challenges the certainty … that history does indeed advance … [11]

Without this bad side of history—the events, people, and coalitions that were eliminated from the dialectic of history—there is no movement and a stasis, or "the end of history," is built. Does this not parallel the form of stasis we have found ourselves in, politically, today? Does not neoliberalism actually seek to use the bad side of history as an argument for the necessity to resist transformation? For instance, the financialization crisis provoked the promotion, in the USA, of the very economic architects who shaped and enabled the crisis? The bad side of history (even in the form of gross economic contradictions) is routinely made invisible or isolated as an abhorrence or a mistake that will be learnt from and is thus transformed into the good side of history that is held up as the engine of the eventual outcome, the equality to come (deferred even further after the market meltdown of 2008, deferred further for Greece!). Timeless and delusional ideals such as "We will be greeted as liberators!" "The market must not be interfered with," and "Liberal democracy is our universal desire!" all absorb the bad side of history and its unpredictable outcomes, or its outcomes that break the limited options that end in liberal democracy. But to break this, the temptation of "accelerationism," as Benjamin Noys calls it, needs to be resisted as well, and Noys argues the necessity to "problematize the radicalization of Marx's argument that suggests if history advances by the 'bad side' then the worse things get, the better the potential results."[12] But the spirit of neoliberalism also welcomes this acceleration for it provides an (often supranational) acceleration or "shock therapy" as Naomi Klein calls it, from above, even as on-the-ground reaction intensifies. And we know that the present has not been formed by the good side of history advancing equality, but has looped through time being both more brutal in its logic and more unpredictable in its outcome.

The absorption of the bad side of history as an unpredictability opens up a space within the cultural engagements of history as a form of knowledge: this can be contrasted with dips into *moments* as curiosities, the recirculation of cultural formations as a stable set of references which can be brought forward and magically changed from references to cultural capital within the value system of the museum and art market. In reentering the historical and kick-starting the dialectic of the present, artists, poets, and critics must strive to refigure rather than recover suppressed histories in order to enlarge the narrative of history alongside an impulse to create unexpected combinations of history that include the bad side, that ignite a more contested view of the present.

This tendency is striated through many of Sam Durant's projects. By linking, via its location, Robert Smithson's *Partially Buried Woodshed* to the murder of four protesting students by National Guardsman on the Kent State campus on May 4, 1970 (a narrative and imagistic moment of bad history that was instrumental in galvanizing opposition to the state's policies on the Vietnam War), the bad side of history is brought into a horizontal axis of association that leads, via Neil Young, to Kurt Cobain's futile death (another moment, but one which advances a myth of the individual).[13] This associational construction of time and event has a denseness that eludes less semiotically active constructions of history, creating instead a network of meanings in excess of the story.

In *Inversion, Proposal for the Five Dollar Bill (Huey Newton, Founder of the Black Panther Party for Self-Defense)* (2001), a drawing of Huey is above an inverted drawing of Abe Lincoln: a linking of the president who "ended slavery" and the radical figure who pointed to slavery's continued legacy. This is a monetary monument in some aspects, proposed for the US American five-dollar bill, but it is also an insertion of Huey and the history of the Black Panthers into official history as the classic bad history, whose goal was not an ideal of equality but a social and material equality. The perseverance of the figure of "Huey" is an anticoagulant in history's closure. Likewise, Durant's *Proposal for White and Indian Dead Monument Transpositions, Washington, D.C.* (2005) conceptually and spatially brings the bad side of history and official history together in order to represent

> the role of violence in the formation of the United
> States, and to raise questions about the function
> of monuments and memorials in that equation.[14]

In this case, the formation of the nation is troubled by history as a form of knowledge that must narrativize a founding history of the nation based on equality, while simultaneously burying the real destruction and inequality in its founding, a founding more properly based on creative destruction. Such unidirectional histories need to be "indigenized," argues Len Findlay who alters Fredric Jameson's call to "always historicize" to "always indigenize!" as a means to bring indigenous issues into the history of development and to derail "what counts as knowledge and who will benefit from its acquisition and exercise."[15] By troubling a founding history and opening it to another form of knowledge, the monument "indigenizes" a mythic history and thus returns it to politics.

In *Scenes From the Pilgrim Story, Natural History* (2006), Durant takes a waxen moment of historical stasis as the material for recirculation. Durant was able to obtain figures from the Plymouth National Wax Museum, in Massachusetts, as it was being decommissioned: the figures formed a natural history display of the establishment of Pilgrim settlements. The particular figures in Durant's exhibition are from the Merry Mount exhibition, a display in the museum that portrayed the free community headed by Thomas Morton, a community that was to live in concord with the Algonquins who had given them the land for their colony. This utopian project came down at the hands of the Puritans (or "those precise seperatists, that lived at new Plimmouth," as Morton describes them in the poem and narrative from his *New English Canaan* [1637] that commemorates and corrects the history of the May Day celebration of 1628 that ultimately turned the Puritans on Merry Mount). The canonical American author Nathanial Hawthorne has also produced a work that commemorates this radical social project: Hawthorne's short text, "The May-Pole of Merry Mount" sets up a utopian image of nature and light conquered by the dystopian grimness of the Puritan's unpleasurable toil and shadow-laden darkness. Durant's project, on the other hand, disassembles the frozen historical moment of the wax museum and reorganizes the pieces into sculptural platforms and photographic tableaus that inscribe a different semiotics into the poetics of history than the one built up by the national myth-building project of the Plymouth National Wax Museum. The clunky and battered wax figures and the historical reconstruction of the official Pilgrim time are the perfect figures of a narrative moment frozen as historical stasis. Despite stepping outside of the chronological framework of the majority of Durant's oeuvre, this project aligns with Durant's sculptural aesthetics: as he commented in an interview, "Formally my sculptures tend to be somewhere between models, props, and sculptures."[16] Models and props (including the infrastructure of the original display with reel to reel tapes and speaker boxes) turn a light on how the good side of history is narrated, which is also to turn a light toward the moment that we are living through, a use of history that denies both the materiality of history and its dialectical aspect: "we're making progress," "stay the course," all wartime denials of the bad side of history.

Durant's Merry Mount project breaks the narrative instantiation of the history of Plymouth Rock and the pilgrims and launches these graspable national moments back into a historical dialectic. In order to break the stasis of the foundational historical narrative, Durant treats each figure—now compellingly incomplete, missing their museum context, props, or legs, feet, and body—as a sign freed of its referent. This allows new comical, pathetic, or provocative assemblages of the partial figures: a pilgrim with a yoke carrying two wooden buckets, but with his red stockings ending in feet that are anything but "anatomically correct"; a "male colonist" also with curiously hoof-like endings to his legs and no head, just the fitting that would have fixed the wax head; an "Indian" figure on his knees, perhaps working but missing the tools from the original display so he appears to be prostrating himself before some invisible force; a colonist, in a stripped shirt, menacingly holding a piece of milled wood; a colonist head, lying carefully on its side beside a parallel barrel and an upright barrel; a colonist head, a pilgrim shoe, and a museum speaker box floating in a curious museological conundrum; and the torso and head of an "Indian" woman, her head turned plaintively, but missing one forearm and the wax-skin covering of her upper arms, with her 1970s-style fantasy breasts exposed to link "the Indian" with an earthier bodily connection, the perfect completion of the fully covered and alienated pilgrims.

These figures are historically charged merely through their representation of a foundational narrative of the nation, but they become even more so, devoid of their context and restaged as broken objects that hover in our current time. As Durant's *Proposal for White and Indian Dead Monument Transpositions, Washington, D.C.* asserts, the history of whites and Indians is the undone business of the nation and of social justice. On a larger scale, this history is the tragic recurring business of capital: the dispossession that begins in America is replayed across the globe in various scales today. These floating figures are both the frozen moment of a particular history—and its use—as well as the reminder of how the bad side of history is still one engine of the present.

Yet to make such a link between the past and the present is to at least partially accept that history naturally creates a linkage that is always, at best, partial and is always ideological, for history as a form of knowledge cannot move through time as easily as these figures appear to, landing in our present, battered but recognizable. *Scenes From the Pilgrim Story, Natural History* disassembles the poetics of history, not just by showing it to be a construction (materially and metaphorically played out by the figures and props in their careful arrangements) but also by making a movement from an artistic practice with an archival impulse to an artistic practice that enters into the poetics of history.[17] Here we have less of a return of the repressed and more of an investigation into the missing future—a future displaced by the continuous present, the end of history, and a static history that is having trouble upholding its myths. And, as Miranda Johnson explains, such indigenizing grasps a history that can be controlled through being "understood as expressing very local experiences" and can transform them "into kinds of texts and textual practices that can enable them to circulate publicly."[18] This making of public history based on nonconformist knowledge takes the public wax museum over to the bad side of history.

[1] Dieter Roelstraete, "The Role of the Shovel: On the Archaeological Imagination in Art," *e-flux journal* (March 2009), p. 1. See "After the Historiographic Turn: Current Findings," *e-flux journal* 6 (May 2009).

[2] Here, I am thinking of the difference between *story* and *plot* that the Russian Formalists distinguished, particularly Viktor Shklovsky in his analysis of *Tristram Shandy*. See *Russian Formalist Criticism: Four Essays*, trans. Lee T. Lemon and Marion J. Reis (eds.), University of Nebraska Press, Lincoln 1965.

[3] I'm referring to two powerful formations of the present here. One from Gertrude Stein, whose "continuous present" sought to overcome the temporality of reading and move to an avant-garde plane of temporally unlocked signifiers in a field. The second is Lenin's "absolute present" that has become itself a field of interpretation in the various recuperations/reuses of Lenin. For a good overview on the Lenin debate, see Michael Marder, "On Lenin's Usability," *Rethinking Marxism* 19/1 (January 2007). The phrase "the end of history" was initially popularized in Frances Fukuyama, *The End of History and the Last Man* (Free Press, New York 1992; introduction available at www.marxists. org/reference/subject/philosophy/works/us/fukuyama.htm [last accessed June 2013]).

[4] Even George W. Bush felt the heft of the past and took to reading historical biographies to correlate himself with a historical figure. The obvious analogy may seem to be Richard M. Nixon (unpopular imperial war, low public popularity, the continuance of Dick Cheney), but President Bush favored Churchill (war on fascism, statesman, war leader). The biography of Churchill that Bush read is *Troublesome Young Men: The Rebels Who Brought Churchill to Power and Helped Save England* by Lynne Olson. Yet even Olson has written in an op-ed that a comparison of Bush and Churchill is historically improbable. In Churchill's place she proposes Neville Chamberlain—in terms of his lack of experience of international diplomacy and tendency to unilateralism—as Bush's parallel. See "Why Winston Wouldn't Stand for W," *Washington Post*, July 1, 2007.

[5] Mark Godfrey, "The Artist as Historian," *October* 120 (Spring 2007), p. 143.

[6] Dieter Roelstraete, "After the Historiographic Turn: Current Findings," *e-flux journal* 6 (May 2009), p. 7.

[7] Jacques Rancière, *The Names of History: On The Poetics of Knowledge*, trans. Hassan Melehy, University of Minnesota Press, Minneapolis 1994, p. 8.

[8] In this second tendency, I'm merging Marx's critique of Proudhon's confusion of contradiction for the dialectic and Gayatri Spivak's critique of Marx's model of history in relation to India and the "Asiatic Mode of Production" where, she charges, he "runs the risk of restoration of the same hierarchy—philosophy (science) on top, being 'applied' to history (matter or *hyle*)—dialectical as well as historical materialism" (*A Critique of Postcolonial Reason: Toward a History of the Vanishing Present*, p. 90). But, on a more everyday level, I do think this is part of how the present feels so strange beyond contradiction, beyond classical formations of alienation.

[9] Georg Lukács, *History and Class Consciousness*, trans. Rodney Livingstone, MIT Press, Cambridge, Massachusetts 1971, p. 47.

[10] Karl Marx, *The Poverty of Philosophy*, International Publishers, New York 1963, p. 118.

[11] Étienne Balibar, *Philosophy of Marx*, trans. Chris Turner, Verso, London 1995, p. 97.

[12] Benjamin Noys, "Apocalypse, Tendency, Crisis," http:// www.eurozine.com/articles/2010-05-26-noys-en.html (last accessed June 2013).

[13] For the structuralists in the house, see Mary Leclere's application of Jakobson's vertical and horizontal axis to Durant's associational work in "Speaking of Others," *Afterall* 10 (Autumn/Winter 2004), p. 10.

[14] Sam Durant quoted in Rita Kersting, "Interview with Sam Durant," *Sam Durant*, Museum of Contemporary Art, Los Angeles/Kunstverein fur die Rheinlande und Westfalen, Düsseldorf 2003, p. 55–62.

[15] Len Findlay, "Always Indigenize! The Radical Humanities in the Postcolonial Canadian University," *Ariel* 31:1 & 2 (January–April 2000), p. 307–326.

[16] Kersting, "Interview with Sam Durant," p. 55–62.

[17] For an elaboration on the current archival impulse in visual practices, see Hal Foster, "An Archival Impulse," *October* 110 (Fall 2004), p. 3–22.

[18] Miranda Johnson, "Making Public History: Indigenous Claims to Settler States," *Public Culture* 20:1 (2008), p. 97–117.

After Big Failures

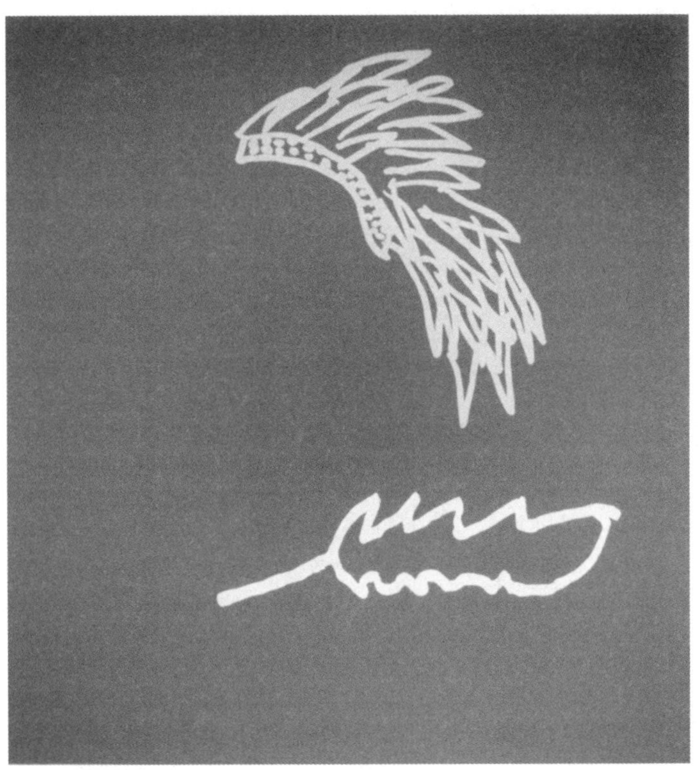

Brian Jungen, *Anonymous Drawings (Feathers)*, 1997
Latex paint on wall, 305 × 244 cm

The everyday is covered by a surface: that of modernity.
—Henri Lefebvre

Brian Jungen's first solo show, *Half Nelson* (Truck Gallery, Calgary, 1997), initiates Jungen's representational strategies through the appropriation of ethnographic modes of research and fieldwork. Based on large drawings rendered onto the gallery wall, *Half Nelson* used ethnographic methodology to hold up a mirror to cultural representations of "Indianness"[1] and is a stark engagement with classic ethnographic research as a device that constructs cultural differences rather than a tool that reflects or records them. With its ironic pairings of color—put into use by Jungen near the peak of the home buying and home renovating frenzy which continues to distort everyday life in boomtown Calgary even after the credit crash—this show laid crude fieldwork drawings in color combinations more usually found alongside polished granite countertops and stainless steel appliances. But *Half Nelson*, as do many of Jungen's works, grounds its criticality not so much in an artistic paradigm of combination and renewal, but in a reflexive ethnography that shows the limits of ethnography as a modernist science based on a politics of cultural recognition (a model carried forward into the Canadian public sphere as multiculturalism by philosopher Charles Taylor). The twist in *Half Nelson* (ironically named after a wrestling move) is that it is the dominant culture's idea of the Indian that is reflected in this fieldwork.

Half Nelson also points to a form of negative dialectics in Jungen's current work, and in fact I want to push an argument that the legacy of two big failures in Western developmental thought run throughout Jungen's work. The sculptural impulse that courses through his work is less an uncanny combinatorial method, gnarling binaries into dialectical vortexes, than it is a strain of speculation that points to potential and blockage, promise and actuality, use value and exchange value. Many of the sculptural works show a dry ideological humor—such as a black leather teepee made from Natuzzi leather sofas (*Furniture Sculpture*, 2006), mass-consumer commodities from the chain store The Brick (famous for its ads that shout out spectacular payment plans)—or an ironic reversal—such as the sculptures made from sporting goods (baseball gloves, bats, balls, golf bags, etc.) which slyly turn these coveted objects of sports into signs of "Indianness." Instead of the timeless Indian lifted out of history to become a sports symbol or team name, unused sports equipment (thus kept free of signs of use value and holding the oily aura of mass production and personal dream) are "indigenized" into signs of "Indianness" that circulate in popular culture.

Representation becomes the site of Jungen's critique—and these sites are complexly scaled for the local to the global as well as the very spaces of representation themselves—rather than a corrective politics of recognition. But to frame Jungen's work through developmental discourses, I first want to suspend globalization and a politics of the local as the primary frame for reading Jungen's work. Jungen's best-known sculptural works that take Nike Air Jordan's as their basic material, *Prototypes for a New*

Understanding (1998–2003), can and have been written about in relation to globalization and, starting from a global brand, a global sports figure, and a global dream commodity, these sculptures do beckon a dive into the global flows of commodities as well as the impulse to root First Nations culture in the local. But Jungen's work does not slide into an understanding of globalization that erases its own geography and the circuits of capitalism that such a spectacular language of flows can create. Instead, to approach Jungen's work, globalization has to be attached to a different history and discordant temporalities. Such a rereading is possible when, as Arif Dirlik asserts, "Globalization as a discourse … [is] understood as both a continuation of and a disavowal of an earlier modernization discourse."[2] With globalization suspended in this manner, a language of development forces a return to the project of modernity and its tougher side, modernization.

Globalization debates have pushed stage theories of modernity to the foreground once again, and alternative modernities have proved to be laden digs of artistic and architectural investigation. However, modernization has not grabbed the same critical attention as its more philosophical half, despite the uneven building up and tearing down of the productive capacities in globalization brought about by the intensification of modernization. At the same time as cities such as Buffalo, New York, or Windsor, Ontario, stand in rusty contrast to the (now faltering) build up of production in China, and the scattering of flexible production globally, the developmental dreams of a modernist economy of resource extraction in places such as Tofino, BC, give way to the globality of tourism and real-estate development. Whether this represents a second modernity, or whether this is the lurching from expansion to crisis in global capital is also being refigured at this moment: the language of crisis has seamlessly reemerged into everyday speech, twisting developmental narratives of *any* modernity into a tailspin.

But the aesthetic and social aspects of modernity and the economic base of modernization should not be prized apart, nor should they be located in previous moments of capitalist development. In fact, it is possible to propose that if modernization theory failed in its promised mission (economic and social) and caught globalization in

the wake of its own failure, neoliberal globalization has
dropped the proactive language of modernization for
a naturalized stridency of privatization and the market.[3] Yet
the local voices and global institutions of neoliberalism have
done so while also holding gleaming promises of modernity
as the future, as the gold at the end of the narrative. And
this emerged even as actually existing neoliberalism drove
the goals of social and economic equity and liberal
democracy for all further into the imagined future. Other
forms of social and economic organization—local community development, regional cooperatives, national currency
control, international unions, world social justice politics—
are eschewed by neoliberalism as rusted sites of the past.
Instead, ideologies of free trade, competition, flexible labor,
"active individualism," and self-responsibility are its social
imaginary. In this, contemporary forms of the spectacle
(for instance, the centrality of democracy as an interpassive
spectacle) and a particular mode of alienation *as proximity*
become the aesthetic fusion of neoliberalism and everyday
life.

A temporally uneven modernity joins the developmental language of modernization with the various forces of
neoliberalism that swirl in the present. Modernity continues
its status as the great unfinished project that Habermas
defined precisely because it has simultaneously already failed
and has yet to be fully realized. The rolling back and rolling
out of neoliberalism holds out the earlier promises of
modernity as it enacts a modernization as dark as the one
Friedrich Engels caught with his own ethnographic descriptions of "The Great Towns" in *The Condition of the Working-
Class in England in 1844*.[4]

Tellingly, this deepening of uneven geographical
development cuts against the grain of cultural globalization,
whose more optimistic language stresses connectivity,
linked flows, networks, and local knowledge's inflected with
globality. A golden landscape takes shape, formed by
the mass output of the US culture industry, yet modified
by Bollywood, Iranian, or Punjabi pop, Japanese anime,
Canadian rock collectives, Gameboy music clubs in Vienna,
and other hybridized and hypermobile cultural forms
that mark moments of affective consumption. Counter
to this language of cultural connectedness, inclusion, and

transformation, the totalization of the global economy is just as much about expulsion and exclusion as it is about inclusion and uplift. From this fragmented relaunch of aspects of modernity, Jungen's work enters into an investigation of the failure of the project of modernity in the form of global modernity. Dirlik usefully builds a larger definition of this complex:

> Globalization may be viewed as the process whereby modernity—capitalist modernity—has gone global, universalizing not only the material and ideological practices but also the contradictions of modernity, including the very negation of its claims to universality. Global modernity may promise liberation from the past globally, including from the past of modernity itself, but it also bears the stamp of the colonial economically, politically, socially, and culturally, perpetuating past inequities while adding to them new ones of its own.[5]

This global modernity carries both its contradictions and histories forward.

To catch the manner in which global modernity is a continuation, a promise, and a smashing disaster, Jungen's work spatializes the debate of modernization by a reworking of the social promises of modernist architecture. I don't mean that Jungen's project points to the utopian moment that modernist architecture held out (a moment woefully lost today as architecture is economic or formal but rarely *productive*), but rather that he gestures to a modernity that *was to come* from modernization and the democratization of production. This form of modernization intersects with craft practices (as a form of labor) as well as mass production, and this is both a theme examined in Jungen's work as well as a poetics—that is, a working principle. This troubled trajectory bounces from Russian Productivism to Arne Jacobsen to Buckminster Fuller and to Moshe Safdie, yet it also cuts through more collective formations such as Archigram and Archizoom. This poetics of making is in contrast to global modernity and the invisible production of companies such as Nike, Ikea, Canadian Tire, and The Brick (all places that Jungen has drawn material from for his transformative sculptural works). Other subtle signs of these productive relationships exist in Jungen's work—the worn sewing machine tabletops that combined into a scaled-down basketball court in his installation in the Triple Candie gallery space (untitled, 2004), and the "talking stick" baseball bat with the labor slogan "work to rule" carved into its barrel (here the strikebreaker's tool is discursively flipped). Part of the uncanniness of Jungen's objects or *things* is that they hold the aura of the commodity without being fetishized as objects that hold no trace of the forms of labor that they sprang from—and that the labor of art production is often alongside the craft labor or the mechanical production of the original object.[6]

But failures are only fertile for further investigation if they are the remnants of an idea that actually promised something. In the gap between the promise and the failure is where a negative dialectics—a process that illuminates that promise as it simultaneously points to its loss—resides. The second failure that Jungen builds from is ethnography, which as a methodology promises cultural readability, cultural translation, and cultural understanding. Rather self-servingly, in the hands of artists, Hal Foster argues, ethnography "promises a reflexivity of the ethnographic at the center even as it preserves a romanticism of the other at the margins."[7] Dirlik tackles this form of romanticism (that is both temporal and spatial—imagining pasts and spaces outside of modernity) cautioning:

> Native pasts may serve as sources for claims to alternative cultures and knowledges. But these are pasts that are themselves inventions of modernity, that already have been imagined in the face of hegemonic Eurocentrism as well as more than a century of social and political transformation.[8]

Jungen's dialectical ethnography in *Half Nelson* (1997)—or what we could call a reverse ethnography—began with the artist as the ethnographer sending out non-native field reporters to gather cultural information through the classic mode of a survey of the consuming public in one of Calgary's megastructural mall spaces: the ethnographic subjects were asked to draw a visual representation of the referent *Indian*.

The ironies are apparent. European ethnographic methods are deployed in a Canadian urban area just as they were once sent out to urgently gather information of cultures that were constructed as disappearing under the pressure of modernity—cultures that were imagined not to provide alternative modernities (or another narrative of development), but cultures too primitive or brittle to survive. The flip in *Half Nelson* is that, even though the same *idea* is researched by Jungen or Franz Boas (the idea of the *Indian*) what will be revealed by the research is a *representation of the representation of the idea*. This is not simply reflexive postmodernism, nor is it an ethnographic trick based on center and periphery as Foster suggests, a trick that ultimately holds up a mirror to a dominant culture through its drawings so that its racism will be apparent. Instead we can see the discourse of critical ethnography and the artist as ethnographer merge to take apart the surety of ethnography and to destabilize the fetish of representation of First Nations culture. *Half Nelson* is neither a counter nor corrective representation, nor is it an ethnography of white culture. Instead the drawings that make it up on the wall via the artist as ethnographer show ethnography as a failure in its study of culture and in its social pedagogy. The drawings of what Foster calls "popular primitivisms" illuminate a crude lack of cultural understanding and merely reproduce abject images of First Nations culture.

Of course, the solicited drawings do actually show the longevity of the circulation of abject images: that is, the drawings reflect the referent of "Indian" in Canadian society rather than any actually existing sign. But rather than a reduction of the social and the economic to a cultural image, it is a failed social semiotics with jagged material effects. The social conditions of First Nations people are so uneven and unjust that the Human Rights Commission of United Nations reviewed Canada's compliance with their Covenant on Civil and Human Rights, and correspondingly Canada was one of only four nations in the UN to vote against the United Nations Declaration on the Rights of Indigenous Peoples in 2007.[9] The promise of ethnography as a form of cultural understanding is crumpled (reemerging as complaints to the UN!) and Jungen's drawings comfortably render the dystopian lack of cultural communication in crude signs and adept color combinations. Lingering below this surface is the deflected social and political promise that Canada's multiculturalism—based on a politics of recognition and "understanding"—has voided: when social justice is asked for, the response is cultural recognition. No justice, just museums.

Social and economic justice and universal human rights, all supposedly arriving in the wake of development, were the promise that modernity extended to the nations pulled into the world system—modernization was to relaunch postcolonial nations into globalization and level the playing field. In the 1970s, with the restructuring of the architecture of the global market, modernization was "reinvented as globalization,"[10] and uneven development has deepened the very gap modernization, and its tag-along cultural project of modernity, was to have alleviated. Modernity may have promised development—then the "second modernity" that Ulrich Beck identified promises flexibility and movement—but what has been delivered is a dramatically uneven development between nations, within nations, and even within cities. Rather than a global cosmo-politanism, mobility intensifies into the forced movement of people (reflected in the increase of refugees and the global migrant labor force). At an urban scale and architecturally, the modernist dream of functional spaces and the social engineering of urban planning have given way to housing as real estate attuned to a mercurial market.

Like the "ethnographic turn" that Foster describes, a spatial turn in art production has allowed artists to spatialize the promise of modernity in site-specific art and in investigations of modernist architecture. Jungen joins in this trajectory through his use of iconic modernist architecture—Buckminster Fuller's geodesic dome and Moshe Safdie's Habitat, both of which came to international fame at Montreal's Expo 67. These two forms of architecture carry the futuristic optimism of a modernism that aimed to wed design with function, but importantly both of these architectural prototypes were *productivist* at their base. Instructions of how to make Fuller's domes show up in architectural magazines in the 1960s as well as in handicraft books now discarded in thrift stores alongside macramé books and other crafts that sprang up in reaction to the increasingly spectacular nature of daily life. From a military beginning (for Distant Early Warning [DEW] Line shelters in the arctic) to a hippy back-to-the-land movement in the 1960s, the domes have been remarkably flexible in their use due to their ease of production. They turn up in Jungen's work as the sculptures *Bush Capsule* (2000) and *Little Habitat* (2003/2004). *Bush Capsule* reworks plastic chairs (a truly global product) into a jerry-rigged geodesic dome sheathed in opaque, heat-shrunk polyurethane. These sculptures were to have a use value beyond art as Jungen designed them to be portable dwelling pods that could be used in the bush (and, in this sense, they are part hippy-pods and fixtures that challenge the relationship between ownership and dwelling, and between ownership and fixity).[11] *Little Habitat* (there are two versions) reworks a Nike Air Jordan shoebox into a mini-dome by scoring the cardboard into the pattern for the folds necessary to make the geodesic shape. Moshe Safdie's 1967 housing project also began as an experiment in production as it was the first form-cast concrete building that would use the cast pod as a structural element of the building. Safdie's metabolist aim was to have an expandable building form that could be stacked to add housing when it was needed. Jungen used this productivist model to build a sprawling shelter and adoption centre for cats, *Habitat 04, Cats Radiant City* (2004), in Darling Foundry in Montreal—applying Safdie's modular stacking to carpet-covered cubes to build a cat city not unlike the sad, shag carpet-covered cat architectural *things* that stack up in thrift stores (the burial ground for craft dreams).

But what are the social referents for these formalist gestures? Both sculptures foreground the ease of production of the dome and the form-cast modular structure (despite the actual difficulties Safdie ran into) and both point to a strain within architecture that was about seriality, about multiples, and about a democracy or accessibility of design based on mass production.[12] This *dream*, in some sense, is about the intersection of quality (as materiality, thought, and labor) and quantity. But these works also point to the failure of these modernist promises of development in relation to built space, on one hand, and to modernist city planning that had a goal of housing the working class—a goal that often was deflecting into warehousing, containment, and, in

Vancouver, dramatic homelessness, on the other hand. So while Jungen's domes are diminished in scale to become nonfunctional and somewhat comical sculptures, the scalar play with modular housing is tragic, and ends at accommodation for cats, rather than people. The negative dialectical aspect of Jungen's engagement with these forms is that this promise of architecture—and the critique of it—now resides in art rather than reaching realization in the social.

To return to globalization and to the discordant temporalities of the present, Cuauhtémoc Medina writes that "[Jungen's] works are games that mobilize aesthetic and cultural misunderstandings to explore ways to politicize cultural stereotypes in the age of global capitalism."[13] But Medina also frames Jungen's work within a history of globalization other than the flash and flow of commodities, by rerouting contemporary globalization through colonialism. For Medina, it is the colonialism that generates the stereotypes that *Half Nelson* and other works seek to disturb and redistribute, and to hold the mirror of production up to the source culture of the stereotypes. *Half Nelson* then begins a practice that strikes off of the temporalities of global modernity so that we can see how both the economic and political past of modernization, and the future cultural and social promises of modernity are stamped into the global present. This dialectic is also a deferral, a lag time in which possibilities are held suspended.

[1] See Maria Crosby, "The Construction of an Imaginary Indian," *The Vancouver Anthology: The Institutional Politics of Art*, Stan Douglas (ed.), Talonbooks, Vancouver 1991; and Daniel Francis, *The Imaginary Indian: The Image of the Indian in Canadian Culture*, Arsenal Pulp Press, Vancouver 1992.

[2] Arif Dirlik, *Global Modernity: Modernity in the Age of Global Capital*, Paradigm Publishers, Boulder/London 2007, p. 6.

[3] See Neil Smith, "The Satanic Geographies of Globalization: Uneven Development in the 1990s," *Public Culture* 10/1 (1997), p. 169–189.

[4] Friedrich Engels, *The Condition of the Working Class in England in 1844*, trans. F. Wischnewtzky, Allen and Unwin, London 1952.

[5] Dirlik, *Global Modernity*, p. 7.

[6] Here, I would extend an argument that Jungen's work also infuses the class relations of objects into his sculptural work. The plastic patio chairs and leather sofas from the Brick are complex class-saturated signs. Within the frame of the fiery debates of identity politics, the easy binary of race and class is not possible in Jungen's work (even as the work circulates in global commodity flows of art, a flow itself unanchored from the recognition of class).

[7] Hal Foster, *The Return of the Real*, MIT Press, Cambridge, Massachusetts 1996, p. 182.

[8] Dirlik, *Global Modernity*, p. 48.

[9] As Candice Hopkins reminded me in correspondence, all the nations who blocked the declaration—Australia, Canada, New Zealand, and the United States—have active indigenous movements, so the refusal to get on board the agreement is not merely symbolic or ideological, but is a wing of a politics that asserts colonialism in our present moment. Within a left discourse, First Nations have often been tied into new social movements—but this chronology is off, for they are, in some ways, the first social movements whose methods cover the range of legal, para-legal, activist, and guerrilla tactics.

[10] Neil Smith, "The Satanic Geographies of Globalization: Uneven Development in the 1990s," *Public Culture* 10/1 (1997), p. 169–189.

[11] Correspondence with Candice Hopkins, and conversation with the artist.

[12] Although, following Barret Watten's use of "constructivist aesthetics" as "broadly put, the imperative in radical literature and art to foreground their formal construction …" (*The Constructivist Moment: From Material text to Cultural Poetics*, Wesleyan University Press, Middletown 2003, p. XV), Jungen's work would be seen as constructivist. The relation of craft and labor to mass production and seriality in Jungen's work links construction with production so his work can be seen as simultaneously holding a constructivist and productivist imperative. Here I am using productivist broadly as well, in the sense that it is an imperative in that reveals the modes of production in art and everyday objects.

[13] Cuauhtémoc Medina, "High Curios," Lucy Kenward, Monika Szewczyk (eds.), *Brian Jungen*, Vancouver Art Gallery/Douglas & McIntyre, Vancouver 2005, p. 27–37.

A Geography of the Difficult
Jeff Derksen and Neil Smith

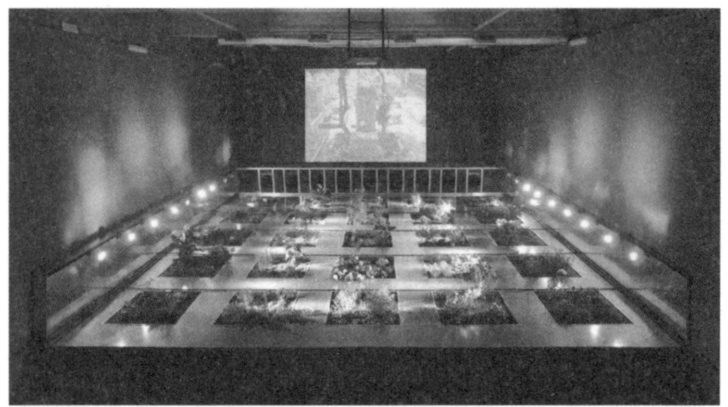

Alfredo Jaar, *Let One Hundred Flowers Bloom*, 2005
Multi-media installation

The struggle for hegemony was
not merely the disciplining of
the docile/useful bodies, nor was
it simply the cheap bread and
circuses … rather it depended on
the world of representation,
and on the summoning up of
ghosts and costumes of the past
to revolutionize the present.
—Michael Denning, *Culture in the
Age of Three Worlds*

What strange production of nature
animates the scene in Alfredo Jaar's
Let One Hundred Flowers Bloom
(2004), in which one hundred flowers in a ten by ten meter square,
kept alive through a complex
hydration system, are bent to the
edge of death by industrial winds
and freon-cooled air? And what
provocative cultural politics posits
this survival test, recalling Mao's
tragic One Hundred Flowers
campaign, while being watched
from afar by the specter of Antonio
Gramsci? Projected into the
gallery, the real-time image of

Gramsci's grave fills the room with the conscience of the organic intellectual. What "ghosts and costumes of the past" are being summoned and reanimated to revolutionize the present?

Jaar's work over the last quarter century inhabits the creative nexus of three movements: the malleable geography of capitalism and anti-capitalism; the cultural politics opened up after conceptualism and the expansion of the art object into the public sphere; and as well as the projections of culture and especially art production as both body and anti-body of a highly uneven globalization. The intersection of these three movements also entangles with two crucial shifts in the theorization of culture: from a theoretical emphasis on consumption as the engine of cultural meaning, to the possibilities of cultural production as a window on the social; and from a politics of culture to a cultural politics contained in, yet bursting out from, the ventricles of the global.

Gramsci's Ghost and Specters of the Intellectual

The interest in the rediscovery of Gramsci in the 1960s and 1970s by the multinational Left may now have faded, but he has remained a powerful inspiration for a broad range of theoretical endeavors. His versatility is no doubt due to the heterodoxy of his writing, but also in no small part to the necessary code in which his more reflective prison writings were presented and their consequent ambiguity of meaning. In English-language cultural studies, the Gramscian moment, beginning with the Birmingham Centre for Contemporary Cultural Studies (CCCS), regenerated debate on Gramsci's notions of the national-popular, the organic intellectual, the subaltern, and especially the concept of hegemony. Stuart Hall describes the "'detour' via Gramsci" as a displacement that challenged the institutional practice of cultural studies to create the conditions for generating organic intellectuals." Hall recognizes that this return is also a displacement across history and that the intellectuals at the CCCS "were organic intellectuals without any organic point of reference because of the difficulty in locating an emergent historical movement."[1] Rather, Hall draws on Gramsci's gripping phrase, "pessimism of the intellect, optimism of the will," to propose that cultural studies were at least preparing "organic intellectuals with a nostalgia or will or hope."[2]

More optimistically, Hall identified two fronts to focus the work of the organic intellectual. First, the Left had to capture the cutting edge of theoretical work because "if you are in the game of hegemony you have to be smarter than 'them.'"[3] Second, Hall sketches out a larger, more social and less institutional role: the organic intellectual in waiting

> cannot absolve himself or herself from the responsibility of transmitting those ideas, that knowledge, through the intellectual function, to those who do not belong, professionally, in the intellectual class.[4]

This is not a process of bringing enlightenment to the workers, a presumptuous paternalism Gramsci would have abhorred. Hall's work on the rise of Margaret Thatcher, the blows to the New Left in Britain, and the formation of an exportable neo-conservative Thatcherite doctrine pushed this responsibility productively, examining the cultural aspects of this new social order, and it developed that phase of cultural studies as a robust social tool. Gramsci in the meantime also became a sometime theoretical cipher for postcolonialism and subaltern studies.

Gramsci has also been appropriated by less likely suspects. In the hours after the September 11, 2001, attacks, as American news readers and executives scrambled to report without a script—naked and face to face with the horrors of global truth—one National Public Radio commentator blurted out that perhaps the attacks proved Gramsci's notion of hegemony correct and confirmed the necessity of social revolution. More astonishing, Gramsci has been adopted by American neo-conservatives. The website of American Vision, a group whose motto is "Equipping and Empowering Christians to Restore America's Biblical Foundation," includes an article simply titled "The Ghost of Antonio Gramsci" which claims that "America is haunted by the ghost of Antonio Gramsci" because his "antipathy and positive opposition to Christian ideals" dominate American culture today.[5] The right wing reactionary

talk show host Rush Limbaugh invokes Gramsci in his
bestselling book, *See, I Told You So* (1993), arguing that
conservative American hegemony depends on taking control
of cultural institutions, winning the country's "Culture War,"
and pursuing the larger imperial project of the American
ruling class.[6]

Alfredo Jaar enlists Gramsci too, but for what
purpose? What questions does he unleash about the role
of public intellectuals, cultural institutions, space and place,
art production? Gramsci is versatile, yet Jaar's harnessing
of Mao's flower fancy to Gramsci's grave is strikingly original:
Gramsci's appeal, after all, lay precisely in his perceived
challenge to various orthodoxies, of which Maoism (albeit
after Gramsci's time) is surely one. Mao's campaign,
encouraging first a hundred then a thousand intellectual
flowers to bloom, was just as surely followed by the "cultural
revolution" which uprooted the same flowers and discharged
them to the compost of hard peasant labor, thus remaking
nature.

Liberal intellectuals rarely ever were organic. From
fascism to McCarthyism, the connection of intellectuals
with the working class was largely if unevenly severed, and
throughout the 20th-century, however grand their progressive rhetoric, liberals functioned as the prophylactic of
empire designed to protect against popular impregnation by
subversive ideas. The rise of free market neoliberalism in the
1980s and the defeat of official communism have exposed
the conservatism of the liberal tradition. The original
neoliberals dating to the mid-20th-century, organized against
social liberalism of a Keynesian sort, lived out the welfare
state in relative banishment, but are now back with a
vengeance. They are at least honest about their conservatism.
Among their standard bearers is Chicago economist Milton
Friedman, who quite undemocratically helped bring free
market economics to Chile. The coup, backed and fomented
by the CIA, against democratically elected Salvador Allende,
brought Generalissimo Augusto Pinochet to power on
September 11, 1973. Jaar, born in Chile, has referred to this
event as "our own little September 11," and it led to a reign
of official (US supported) state terrorism that murdered
more people than perished in the "larger" September 11,
28 years later. Chickens do come home to roost.

Where liberalism clogs the potentially searing political power of art by dispatching most, if not all, political positioning to the dreary doldrums of didacticism, Jaar's work asks questions that punch through such an easy dismissal. Mao's garden meets Gramsci's grave, but only under the harshest of conditions. The "lament" of this piece for Alfredo Jaar is certainly about a lost political opportunity, but equally it evokes the near-loss of a cultural politics of art and the ability of art to be part of a "revolutionary" debate. A certain lost geography plays a central role here.

Lost Geographies, Lost Politics

French geographer Yves Lacoste famously indicted academic geography as an exercise in war: "La géographie, ça sert, d'abord, à faire la guerre" [Geography serves firstly for war]. Alfredo Jaar made a similar point in his 1990 exhibition, *Geography = War*. In this installation he mapped the movement of toxic waste from Italy to a small town in Nigeria where it eventually contaminated and killed many local people. *Geography = War* in fact provided a perfect pre-critique to the subsequent claim of neoliberal economist Larry Summers, now President of Harvard University, who argued while officiating at the World Bank, that Africa was "underpolluted" because low wages there meant a low value of life and it was therefore economically inefficient to pollute in higher wage locations such as Europe, North America, or Japan where subsequent pollution-caused deaths were more costly. *Geography = War* caught the emerging neoliberal moment in its ascendancy, and many other of Jaar's projects use the same geographical sensibility as a lens into world politics: *A Logo for America* (1987), *The Rwanda Project 1994–2000* (1994–2000), *Emergencia* (1998), and *The Cloud* (2000), for example. Jaar's geography *is* politics.

The geography of *Let One Hundred Flowers Bloom* is simultaneously apparent and opaque. Geographical processes both give life and threaten it, the work of climatic elements and geography separates yet connects the demise of Gramsci, videoed from his gravesite, and the dream of Mao installed in the gallery. It is tempting to see here Mao's defeat—the natural elements against the hundred blooms—in the grave of Gramsci, but that would get history

the wrong way round. So how does Gramsci's 1937 death
at the hands of Mussolini connect to the terse survival of
Mao's flowers, planted 20 years later and now on view in
the gallery? Geography may still equal war here—between
Maoist and Gramscian lenses on revolution and its much
more difficult aftermath.

A central conceit of neoliberalism is that its
globalization strategy will "create a level playing field,"
collapse time and space, take us beyond geography. Instanta-
neity and utopia become one; with time and space collapsed nothing remains to be decided. Such wishful thinking
betrays the fact that concealed within the control of time
and space is incredible political power, and that if the
populace can be convinced that time and space have in fact
collapsed, the sources of power themselves become invisible. Power resides nowhere yet everywhere. Hardt and
Negri's *Empire* (2000), arguing the nowhereness of global
power, becomes an adjunct of the globalization it would
oppose. The ideological drive of American power in the
20th-century took precisely this course, hiding the emergent
American Empire as an "American Century" and consigning
its opponents to the King Canute asylum for those
who would oppose the inevitable tide of history. The "lost
geography" of the 20th-century is not simply a case of
passive ignorance, but of political strategy. Jaar takes exception. If despatializing the world in practice and imagination
depoliticizes it too, then respatializing the world raises the
possibility of repoliticizing it. By revealing the geography,
Jaar shows us, we reveal the politics too.

Poetics & Politics of the Image

Pier Pasolini's poem, "The Ashes of Gramsci," published
in 1954, mediates Mao and Gramsci in *Let One Hundred
Flowers Bloom*. Pasolini speculates over the silence of the
"humid garden" of Gramsci's grave in an "autumnal May."
It is a poetic lament, stacking up darkened adjectives,
but it is hardly an elegy for Gramsci himself, nor an eager
expectation of social transformation. The universalist
ambition of the vision of social change is run through the
historical particulars of Pasolini's own existence and
the possibilities exuded by Gramsci. Written in the "non-will

of the postwar years," *The Ashes of Gramsci* (2005) pushes
a disgust for a world divided by class ("… doesn't the
world—or at least // that part that holds power—seem
worthy only / of rancor and an almost mythical contempt?"),
and it carries a desolate distrust of agency and historical
consciousness ("But while I possess history, it possesses me.
I'm illuminated by it: but what's the use of such light?").

Pasolini's lines also tellingly illuminate Jaar's uncanny
and effective project for Documenta 11, *Lament of the Images*
(2002), which forcefully and with a similar elegiac tone yet
analytic edge, materialized the political economic power
driving images in the global mediascape. Jaar pulls Pasolini's
despairing dialectic forward to today. The poetics of *Lament
of the Images* takes the introspection of the public elegy and
melds it with an auto-critique associated with the avant-
garde in order to link image-production and circulation with
key social moments that are themselves extremely visual—
Nelson Mandela's release from prison, the US Department of
Defense's monopoly purchase of satellite images of the 2001
bombing of Afghanistan, and Bill Gates' privatization of the
17 million plus images of the United Press International
archives. In visualizing a global political economy of such
immaterial material—images—Jaar catapults critiques in the
field of cultural production into the global heart of US
cultural imperialism.

Jaar's lament of images informs the present project
too. Associating an auto-critique of the image with the
avant-garde, he links image-production with political
economies that interlace the cultural field, including the
international art market. The politics of the image has been
a struggle in poetics as much as it has been in visual art,
and these different cultural realms have often fused at
crucial moments, igniting disruptions against the barrier of
art forms. Jaar has structured works around the relationship
of image and text, "displacing the image for text" (as
Michael Corris has written),[7] but in Jaar's case this is not a
displacement in which text trumps the image, or a substitu-
tion of one signifying practice for another, but rather it
is a device that puts the reader/viewer into a different
relationship with the image. As Walter Benjamin argued,
in another context,

> only by transcending the specialization in the process
> of production that, in the bourgeois view, constitutes
> its order, can one make this production politically
> useful; and the barriers imposed by specialization
> must be breached jointly by the productive forces
> they were meant to divide.[8]

Jaar's use of text breaches the separation of image and text, a poetics aimed at making the production of meaning politically charged and opaque rather than portraying it as neutral and transparent. This emphasis on production of meaning rather than the reception of a decontextualized image is similar to the goal of the "productive reader," a project sought by various poetic formations over the last 30 years. Specialization, whether it is the isolation of the cultural field to its own economy of meaning production, or the intensification of the commoditization of the international art market (which became a "bull" market following September 11, 2001) is "transcended" by an exterior imperative in Jaar's projects, namely the necessity to address social and political crisis. This impulse circulates in Jaar's work with the recurring reference to the great Imagist poet, William Carlos Williams:

> It is difficult
> to get the news from poems
> yet men die miserably every day
> for lack
> of what is found there.[9]

For Jaar, it is difficult to get the news from art, and people do die daily for want of it, but art can be made the news.

Art After the Global, and After

Cultural critic Michael Denning speculates that, despite the logic of homogenization or hybridization that has framed the debate of a global culture,

> perhaps there is not one global culture in this period
> [post-World War II] but two overlapping ones, both
> to a large degree conscious of their global ambitions.

The first—figured by Nike—is commodity aesthetics, the culture of the transnational corporations

which is centered on "supplying (for a profit) the means for
everyday subsistence."[10] The second global culture "is not
a single text, but a move in a long and powerful history" that
moves out from the mass migration from the rural Third
World to the "global slums"(as Mike Davis calls them)—this
culture is prefigured by Bob Marley. To draw a radical
history of this alternative global culture, Denning traces its
beginnings to earlier forms of internationalism as it "inter-
sected with the national-popular hopes of the anti-colonial
movements … "[11] Aimed at bringing forward this lost history
of the intersection of proletarian culture, internationalism,
and the global cultural effect of anti-colonial movements,
this alternative posits culture as the body and anti-body of
a highly uneven globalization. Art production also represents
this contained body and potentially bursting anti-body.

A stripped-down trajectory of conceptual art that
agitated a "new paradigm of production"[12] illuminates the
tension of containment and rupture in art production since
the 1960s. The challenges that conceptual art and photocon-
ceptualism mounted to this dilemma frame Jaar's work.
Andrea Fraser narrates a movement from the critique of the
autonomy of art and artistic production, through a challenge
to the commodity status of the work of art, to, finally,

> the critique of the autonomy of art institutions and
> their instrumentalization by social, political and
> economic interests [which] resulted in (self) instru-
> mentalized political documentary practices.[13]

In different language, this can be narrated as a movement
for art to engage intellectually and productively with the
social movements of the 1960s and 1970s and with
the critiques of commodification. As Peter Wollen has
commented (paraphrasing Joseph Kosuth):

> the function of art is to question the cultural codes
> within which it operates, is institutionalized and
> received, the codes that give art its political power
> and meaning.[14]

Yet even this assessment of a politics of art and a "global conceptualism" needs to go further: rather than examine the social and political codes of art in itself, it could link art into the alternative global culture that Denning identifies.

In its mimetic yet critical relationship to the social, these challenges to the category of art opened up the methods, medias, and practices that now circulate in the international art world. But this trajectory of imminent critique, institutional critique, and the movement beyond the gallery space into differently imagined public spheres opens other questions to the roles and potentials of cultural production within global capitalism—a capitalism without an outside. Like every *thing*, every commodity, art can *be* anything or anywhere, but can it use this plasticity to take on a new or different utility? The model of overlapping global cultures with radically different projects opens a path beyond the endgame of artistic strategies that dead-end at the impossibility of bursting out of art itself as a category, the cultural institutions that contain it, or the circuits of capital that that relentlessly commodify it. Artistic production's political utility is strengthened when it helps sculpt a cultural front.

In a recent interview, Jaar has volunteered:

> I still believe images are more necessary than ever. But I also believe that the political and corporate landscape of our times is full of control mechanisms that will not allow certain images to exist in their proper context. As artists are producers of meaning, we need to contextualize images properly. We must create a framework for their political efficiency.[15]

Jaar is a critical poet of the politics of the image who insists on "contextualizing the images properly." For him this means a reflexive embeddedness: art living an arch refusal of any simple binary between art and the global, art and politics. His art *is* global anger. The tightrope he walks—between Mao and Gramsci (two of the most imaged revolutionary figures), between propriety and truth, between the present and the possible—is far thinner, far higher, and far more ambitious than most of us would dare traverse. If the best of Mao survives in the ominous and authoritative shadow of

Gramsci's grave, Jaar should be trusted to map the political geography that connects them for us, into a better future.

[1] Stuart Hall, "Cultural Studies and Its Theoretical Legacies," Lawrence Grossberg, Cary Nelson, Paula Treichler (eds.), *Cultural Studies*, Routledge, London/New York 1992, p. 277–285.

[2] Ibid., p. 281.

[3] Ibid.

[4] Ibid.

[5] Gary DeMar, "The Ghost of Antonio Gramsci" http://americanvision.org/1419/ghost-of-antonio-gramsci/ (laccessed July 2013). Demar also seems to be haunted by Gramsci's ghost as he has a more recent article on the same website, "Has the Ghost of Antonio Gramsci Returned? http://americanvision.org/1417/has-ghost-of-antonio-gramsci-returned/ (last accessed July 2013).

[6] Charlie Bertsch, "Gramsci Rush: Limbaugh on the 'Culture War,'" Bad Subjects Collective website: bad.eserver.org/issues/1994/12/bertsch.html/view?searchterm=charlie%20%20bertsch%20limbaugh (last accessed June 2013).

[7] Michael Corris, "White Out: Alfredo Jaar's Lament for Lost Images," *Art Monthly* 260 (October 2002), p. 6–10.

[8] Walter Benjamin, *Reflections*, trans. Edmund Jephcott, Schocken, New York 1986, p. 230.

[9] William Carlos Williams, "Asphodel, That Greeny Flower," first published in 1955 and collected in *Picutres from Brueghel and Other Poems*, New Directions Books, New York 1962

[10] Michael Denning, *Culture in the Age of Three Worlds*, Verso, London 2004, p. 31.

[11] Ibid., p. 32.

[12] I have lifted this phrase from Sabeth Buchmann's essay "Eyes On the World," in *Dorit Margeiter*, 10104 Angelo Drive, MUMOK, Vienna, 2005.

[13] Andrea Fraser, "What's Intangible, Transitory, Immediate, Participatory and Rendered in the Public Sphere? Part 2" *Museum Highlights: The Writings of Andrea Fraser*, ed. Alexander Alberro, MIT Press, Cambridge, Massachusetts 2005, p. 77.

[14] Peter Wollen, "Global Conceptualism and North American Conceptual Art," *Global Conceptualism: Points of Origin, 1950s–1980s*, Queens Museum of Art, New York, 1999, p. 73–86.

[15] Alfredo Jaar, Wolfgang Bruckle, Rachel Mader. "Alfredo Jaar: The Mise-en-Scene is Fundamental," *Camera Austria* 86 (2004).

A Private Riot Going On?
Jeff Derksen and Christian Parenti

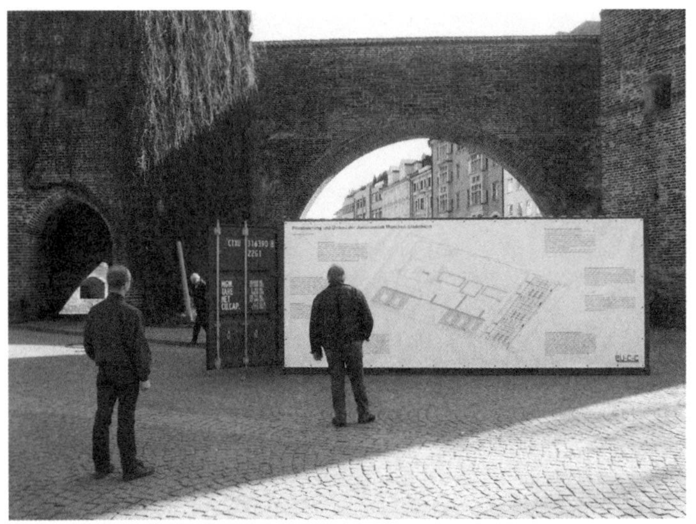

Oliver Ressler & Martin Krenn, *European Corrections Corporation*, 2004
Container installation, Munich

The link between culture, society, and prisons is not easily envisioned through definitions of culture as either the coherent core of a national or ethnic identity or as the liberating humanistic project of historically built social imaginations—that is, as cultural production. The positive and instrumental aspects of culture, as aesthetic production or social progress and collective knowledge, would seem to clash with the prison's discourse of containment, discipline, rehabilitation, and punishment.

Yet the frightening thing is that cultural "progress" like prisoner "rehabilitation" is, historically speaking, an easy fit with the political projects of racism and class exploitation. In part, this tension and weird compatibility arises from the silence that surrounds the everyday details of prison: What goes on in there? Who really goes to prison? How exactly are we on the outside connected by ties of blood, treasure, and fear to the world of the big house?

To culturalize prison is also to naturalize its social role and to occlude its place within a larger political economy of capital accumulation based on exploitation, social exclusion, and an inevitable degree of poverty. Although the terms "culture industry" (to describe the instrumental role of culture as an apparatus of the capitalist state) and prison industrial complex (to draw a comparison to the military industrial complex in the US) miss each other by decades, the overlap in the terminology points to a parallel in the transformation of these two complexes. Both culture and prisons are spaces of neoliberalism, having had deeper layers of the ethos of deregulation (an actual reregulation) of production combined with new technologies of surveillance embedded into them. This is seen in the on-going attempt of the Federal Communication Commission in the US to allow for mega-media corporations to own and control a greater percentage of radio, television, and cable outlets, and in the increased privatization of prisons during a time of massive industry expansion.

By building a small walk-in container in the commercial and pedestrian center of Graz, Martin Krenn and Oliver Ressler emphasize and warn, in *European Corrections Corporation* (2003, 2004), of the movement in Europe from state-run prisons to "partially privatized" prisons run by corporations such as Wachkenhut and Corrections Corporation of America. The tarpaulin that covers this container is printed with an architectural representation of an imagined refurbishing and expansion of the nearby Graz-Karlau corrections facility. The fictional corrections corporation that Krenn and Ressler devise to run the prison is EUCC (European Corrections Corporation) and it comes complete with a detourned website. Along with pointing to the EU as a newly spatialized economic (and therefore disciplinary) territory, the name projects the founding of pan-European private corrections companies as the industrial and economic strategy wafts over from America. Although, private prisons are, politically speaking, less important than the more general critique of the over-use of incarceration by Western states, the imagined plans for the retooled Graz-Karlau prison show a space doubled in size to incarcerate more prisoners, but also to include production space that will use the prisoners' labor power to generate surplus capital for the fictional EUCC.

Coupled with this installation is a video derived from interviews with British prison activist Mark Barnsley. Barnsley's interview tells the tale, in part, of his own struggle to resist the prison as a production site in which the prisoners are forced to work for low wages and without the usual or even minimum health and safety regulations or employment rights. Barnsley's narrative highlights, in one sense, the transition from a provisionally social discourse of prisons as the site of rehabilitation and the production of fit citizens to sites that generate surplus value for private corporations as the labor power of prison is seized. For Barnsley, private prisons are a microcosm of the ideal neoliberal capitalist economy because the corporation owns the prison receiving state funds for keeping the prisoners there, the workshops where the prisoners produce goods for the corporation and the store where the prisoners can spend their money. This no-leak machine for capital accumulation also keeps its "workers" in the ideal capitalist situation, Barnsley proposes—either locked up or working. Yet, despite the microcosm of the perfect capitalist machine, the cost of running prisons is excessive, and this cost is spread to the state in the public-private partnership in which the private companies cream off the surplus created through state subsidy.

But Barnsley also redefines the prison as a site of resistance to the neoliberalization of production that has accelerated with globalization. In a sense, Barnsley folds prisons back into a larger social discourse of struggle rather than having them set off in a liminal space, or "secret world" as he designates it, cloaked by the secrecy provided by prison architecture and the general social sense that prisons are on the outskirts of the social, filled with those who did not hold up their end of the social contract and therefore forfeited or suspended their rights of citizenship.

Krenn and Ressler bring this representation of a prison cell and of prison in its entirety back into the public sphere in Graz at a moment when prisons are moving more into the shadowy and increasingly corrupt world of privatization as part of the general trend toward privatization—a trend that has progressed unevenly yet steadily. This gesture

is not to propose that public prisons are more desirable
(as Richard Vogel asserts "all prison reform must always be
revolutionary"), but to avoid the turning away of a public
gaze on the shape, materiality, and function of prisons—
as well as the economic role that privatized prisons play in
capitalist accumulation and the manner that prisoners are
used in that accumulation. In *Are Prisons Obsolete?* Angela
Davis identifies how prisons, and their functions, have been
naturalized and taken for granted as a part of our society:
"Thus, the prison is present in our lives and, at the same
time, it is absent from our lives. To think about this simultaneous presence and absence is to begin to acknowledge
the part played by ideology in shaping the way we interact
with our social surroundings. We take prisons for granted
because of the realities they produce."[1]

By moving the model of the prison cell into
a public square, Krenn and Ressler make this turning away
or absence all the more difficult by interlacing and
complicating the *private* corporate function of the prison
with issues of public space. There is a movement of
the privatization of public space, and the creation of hybrid
public-private spaces such as malls and sidewalks, that
structurally parallels the privatization of state companies
and state functions (from prisons to medical services
to pensions). With prisons, this movement is more obscure
in that both the privatization process and the role of
these newly private-public prisons is exceedingly well
cloaked.

While *European Corrections Corporation* casts prison
growth as caused by prison interests (that is, prison
as an industry) there linger deeper critiques of state power
in the installation and video that can be brought forward,
critiques which have an impact both on North America
and Europe. Ultimately, the whole of capitalist society
is greater than the sum of its corporate and non-corporate
parts. To understand the complexity of the West's current
incarceration binge and criminal justice crackdown, we
must move to a holistic class analysis that looks at the needs
of the class system and class-based society in general
and not just at the needs of prison firms and their methods
of generating profit. Prison corporations can be seen as
articulated into the class system as a whole.

Capitalism needs the "surplus population" that the prison system, and other mechanisms of social exclusion, creates. Capitalist production requires and reproduces poverty, but it is also threatened by the poor that it produces. Prison and criminal justice not only creates political obedience and controls the poor and excluded citizens that it needs, it also regulates the price of labor. That is what the repression of the capitalist state has historically been about, from clearances and enclosures, the Atlantic slave trade, the many bloody wars against organized labor, to the militarized ghetto of today in North America. Capitalism was born of state violence, and repression will always be part of its genetic code as well as a mechanism for expansion.

To understand the wider political effects of state violence it is worth contemplating the opposite: state assistance for poor and working people. As Frances Fox Piven and Richard Cloward wrote in the *New Class War*, "the connection between the income-maintenance programs, the labor market, and profits is indirect, but not complicated."[2] Too much social democracy, they imply, and people stop being grateful for poorly paid, dangerous work. So too with the converse, the link between state repression, labor markets, and profits is indirect but not complicated. Repression manages poverty. Poverty depresses wages. Low wages increase the rate of exploitation and that creates surplus value that, at one level, is what all forms of capitalist accumulation is all about.

This dynamic works at a macro-scale upon the society and economy as a whole. Policing and incarceration—directly profitable, or more likely not—are thus part of a larger circuitry of social control. Incarceration is the motherboard, but other components—jails, immigrant detention centers, the militarized border, psych wards, halfway houses, hospital emergency rooms, homeless shelters, skid row, and the ghetto—are all wired into the circuitry. All of these locations share populations, and all serve to contain and manage the social impacts of poverty.

But a question still remains: If capitalism always creates a surplus population, why did it not use criminal justice to absorb, contain, and isolate these groups in the past?[3] To some extent it did. But in each epoch and place, capitalist societies have developed specific and unique

combinations of co-optation, amelioration, and repression
to reproduce the class structure and deal with the contradictions of inevitable poverty. But over the last three
decades an international crisis of over-production and
declining profits has lead to a stead erosion of the social
democratic method of class containment, and a move
toward great poverty (as an instrument to lower wages), and
with great poverty a turn toward a more and more aggressive
politics of repression. In the current epoch, this shift has
been from coercion to the other pole of hegemony—
brute force. To restore sagging profit margins, capital also
launched a multifaceted domestic and international
campaign of restructuring. Though the cause of the profit
plunge was multifaceted—the rising organic composition
of capital, and general over-production and saturation of
global markets—*class struggle was a key part of the equation.*

And finally, the political discourse of criminal
justice helps to reproduce racism in a fashion that is suffi-
ciently coded and thus ideologically palatable enough
to be mass marketed in the present day and age as part of
a social necessity. The acceptance of prisons in the social
landscape is also the acceptance of racism in that landscape
as well—but it is ideologically cloaked in terms of safety for
society in general and in the rhetoric of rehabilitation and
repayment of one's debt to society (and appeasing the quest
for retribution by victims or families of victims). It is no
coincidence that people of color are the most likely to be
incarcerated in the UK and the USA. As Angela Davis notes,
in California in 2002, the racial composition of those
in prisons cut against the demographics of the state, with
35.2% Latinos, 32% African-Americans, and 29.2 white
prisoners.[4] The modern class system in the West is imbri-
cated with the traditional racism born of mercantilist slavery
and colonial conquest.

One must also remember that prison spreads its
surveillance and fear out beyond the walls into the social
landscape as a whole. In California, the bureaucrats at
the Department of Corrections (CDC) describe a strange
geography of power. Rather than focusing solely on prisons
and prisoners, officialdom speaks of "the system" containing
a "total CDC population" of nearly 290,000. About 60
percent of this population is "under the custodial control

of the Department." The remainder are "serving the rest
of their sentences in the community" as parolees—
members of a semi-free sub-caste. In the mind of the prison
bureaucrat the prison regime does not stop at the gate; "the
system" extends into the streets where the line between
the convict inside and civilian outside becomes blurry.

An estimated 6.6 million Americans live under the
control of the criminal justice system: in jail or prison, on
parole or probation (which is usually a county-level program
used for low-level offenders in lieu of incarceration). The
majority of this population, oscillating back and forth
between courts, jails, prison, and parole, are poor and dark
skinned. The massive fourfold increase in incarceration
over the last two and a half decades has translated into
an increased flow of politically marked, criminalized bodies
through the circuitry of social control. One frequently
overlooked space in this circuitry of social control is "the
community," where parolee and probationer serve "street
time" as the "unjailed" legal zombies of the court system.

Parole and probation are not just simple functions of
prison; instead each component in the system amplifies and
feeds the others. As criminal law becomes more punitive,
the surveillance and policing mechanisms of parole have
grown more intense. Just as the total number of ex-cons
hitting the streets has increased, so has the proportion of
that group who are sent back to prison. And within the
subset of those who "fail" parole, a greater proportion than
ever are sent back to the joint for simple "technical viola-
tions" like missing a meeting with a parole agent or failing
a "whiz quiz"—that is, showing traces of drugs in their urine.

Thus we see prison as increasingly self-sufficient,
self-generating its own population. The propellant in this
process is the continually expanding infrastructure of
routine identification and surveillance. By this means,
prison extends its social power outward into the free world,
feeding itself and creating a sub caste of permanent convicts.
As Barnsley says in the video regarding the UK, the emergence of private prisons also saw a rise in the per capita
number of people jailed—as more and more people were
fed into them to help generate the profits (aided by state
funding) for those corporations. Alongside this, as Richard
Vogel notes, the rise in prison population is tied to that

silent partner of production—deindustrialization. And deindustrialization has a greater effect on minority groups.[5]

Looked at holistically, the incarceration binge and criminal justice acceleration has an economic, class, racial, and social angle. Along with these, it has the ideological effect of obscuring its own nature by appearing to be natural and of necessity for society. Here the ideological role and effect of prisons reveals the ideological and social role for cultural production. Cultural production, especially under global capitalism, should reveal and seriously engage with the structure of our society and how that structure is being reproduced globally. *European Corrections Corporation* is positioned as an unambivalent warning of the effects of accumulation strategies that continuously create new territories for exploitation—from DNA, to biodiversity, to water, and it warns, perhaps indirectly, about the role of state violence in all of this. It also serves to warn of the dangers of global flows bringing new and reprehensible strategies crossing from North America.

[1] Angela Y. Davis, *Are Prisons Obsolete?* Seven Stories Press, New York 2003, p. 15.

[2] Frances Fox Piven and Richard Cloward, *New Class War*, Pantheon, New York 1983.

[3] Christian Parenti, *Lockdown America: Police and Prison in the Age of Crisis*, Verso, New York 2000.

[4] Davis, *Are Prisons Obsolete?*

[5] Richard D. Vogel, "Capitalism and Incarceration Revisited," *Monthly Review*, vol. 55, issue 04 (September) 2003, http://monthlyreview.org/2003/09/01/capitalism-and-incarceration-revisited (last accessed July 2013).

National, Global, or Neoliberal Suburb?

The golden cultural promise of globalization, back when promises were cultural and not merely economic, was that the dynamics of cultural flows and interchange would propagate hybrid cultures and multicultural robustness strong enough to interlace the local into the global without a homogenization of local cultures, and strong enough to push the approaching global culture toward heterogeneity. What was identified as the central struggle of globalization—of heterogeneity and homogenization—would be a struggle fought out through the flows of people, ideas, images, information, finances, and ideologies, and then materialized in globalized locals, a network of global cities, in pressurized liminal zones, and at the permeable borders of nations. Suburbs were not immediately embedded into this global spatiality. The Anglo-American suburb, "the peripheral suburb" as Robert Fishman designates it, is seen as attached to the urban scale, transforming the nature of the city by its activity on the edge. Yet, even while the city has been rescaled as global, unmoored from its national anchors, as Saskia Sassen puts it, the suburb has remained decidedly national or regional, reflecting a space of national identity and regional planning. Globalization has certainly altered suburbs, animating them beyond the serial sameness that they were born from in the postwar period, pushing them to zones of intense real-estate speculation paralleling the gentrification of city centers, to areas of thick multiculturalism as ethnic and racialized communities settle where housing prices are somewhat lower, to a model of the global transportation of taste, such as the model of Orange County, California, erected outside Beijing.

While the uniformity or sameness of the suburbs is tied to its mode of production and its modernist seriality—where a limited range of architectural forms were repeated—their sameness globally is not necessarily architectural (as this can be regionally or nationally inflected), but can be traced back to both the suburb's origins and to the ideological influence of neoliberalism today. Robert Fishman, by returning to the late-18th-century origins of suburbia as "a tightly restricted environment of privilege that protected its residents from the dual impacts of industrialization and overwhelming immigration from overpopulated rural districts,"[1] is able to vault suburbs into a global phenomenon by reiterating their class nature. These bourgeois utopias have sprung up around the globe—from gated communities on the edges of cities and close to leisure spaces to American-style suburbs outside of megacities—but rather than their proliferation, Fishman points out that what is global about these suburbs is that "they reproduce in the megacity the relations of economic and cultural domination that characterize the global economy as a whole,"[2] and "imitate the spatial patterns of privilege in the dominant global society, the United States."[3] The spatiality of class privilege, writ large in the geography of production and consumption globally, is exported in the model of the Anglo-American suburb to the edges of globalized cities.

The discourse of suburbia has emphasized sameness and repetition as a result of its mode of production, but the global suburb may be reproducing itself through neoliberal governmentality. Neoliberalism has usefully been defined as "ideological software for global competitiveness"[4] that turns up competition between regions and localities becoming the interface between regions and places. While neoliberalism is localized (and takes particular forms in these localities in negotiation with residual Kenyensian forces and "postnational solutions") dropping down from supranational institutions, Jamie Peck and Adam Tickell argue that, from the early 1990s, "the very social and spatial relations in which ... regions were embedded had *themselves* become deeply neoliberalized. Neoliberalism was therefore qualitatively different because it inhabited not only institutions and places, but *also spaces in-between*. In other words, neoliberalism was playing a decisive role in constructing the rules of interlocal competition by shaping the very metrics by which " ... regional competitiveness, public policy, corporate performance, or social productivity are measured—value for money, the bottom line, flexibility, shareholder value, performance rating, social capital, and so on."[5] This software of competition complicates the global cultural paradigm of homogeneity versus heterogeneity by narrowing the poles between heterogeneity and homogeneity: combining "from above" neoliberalism, with its one size fits all approach to crisis management or policy development, with a more localized or national "from below" process, neoliberalism promotes competition, diversity, flexibility, and "creative options," while demanding a rather rigid bottom line of high profitability, individual (not collective) freedom, rights, and resources, minimal state intervention to the market, risk and debt downloaded to regions and cities, and the agreement that social problems (even if they were created by neoliberal economic policies) be addressed through neoliberal economic policies rather than provisionally stabilizing social policies. Through this scaled set of contradictions— the contradiction of a system that proposes one-size-fits-all solutions and asserts "there is no other way," yet at the same time offloads problems to localized solutions—neoliberalism facilitates a complex sameness.

Given the scope of the penetration of neoliberalism into policies and governance, from the supranational, through the national, to the urban, and given its uneven geographical spread, the neoliberalizing of relations (economic, social, spatial, cultural and personal) can seem to be everywhere, even in suburbs that may at first appear regional or national. Given the central contradiction within neoliberalism—the advocacy of minimal government interference in the market, yet a high degree of governmentality to initiate neoliberal policies—both the highly planned regional suburb and the "unplanned" peripheral suburb can be a product of the ideological software of neoliberalism.

For instance, the city of Almere in the Netherlands, which functions as a suburb of Amsterdam, followed in the tradition of Dutch planned cities and was planned by a state development authority under the Ministry of Transport and Public Works. As Petra Brouwer describes it, Almere was devised as a process in spatial structuring,

> a process driven by long-term objectives … that were continually monitored as to their validity and method of implementation. The spatial design was left until last so that it could incorporate the latest research data.[6]

Despite its links to the total planning of modernist urbanization, Almere is a consumption-side plan, giving the residents the "lifestyle" that they want, gathered from extensive research. Architectural critic Bart Lootsma explains how this plan functions:

> There may be shopping centers, cultural centers, schools, sports clubs, and community centers in Almere, but the only real centers are the dwellings themselves. Each dwelling is an individual center.[7]

This form of individualization troublingly parallels both neoliberalism's distrust of common goods, collective structures, and public spaces open to practices less regulated than consumption and leisure, *and* the Anglo-American suburban dream of bourgeois utopias (yet scaled to an individual dwelling). And its spatial relationship to Amsterdam falls along the classic Anglo-American model— the model being exported globally—as Almere is attached, through patterns of everyday reproduction, yet peripheral to Amsterdam and is distanced from the problems of space, race, and class associated with Amsterdam (and famously by its large-scale social housing project, the Bijlmer). Rem Koolhaas has proposed that

> the Biljmer presents a potential reversal of the Oedipal formula, in which the father threatens the son. Instead of Team X attaching the mechanistic attitudes of CIAM for a fetishistic obsession with the objective and quantifiable—from the grave, as it were—the equally fetishistic concern with the ineffable and the qualitative that characterizes its allegedly humanistic replacement.[8]

Is neoliberalism so prevalent as a software that creates the relationship between places, that neoliberal suburbs have become the replacement of the "humanistic replacement" to modernist urbanizations?

The individualization and the neoliberalization of space in the exhaustively planned town of Almere is not unlike the forms of individualization found in North American suburbs: thick social planning and the unplanned merge within neoliberalism. For instance, the city of Calgary, located in the oil-rich province of Alberta, is spatially one of the largest cities in North America—the flat prairies to the east and the rolling foothills of the Rocky Mountains to the west do not block the expansion of the city. Neither is the city's peripheral expansion halted by the kind of time-consuming urban planning that shaped Almere. The City of Calgary's website has a useful section that walks developers through the process of buying farmland on the edge of the city, laying out housing lots, and developing a suburb. Nowhere in the process is it suggested that community meetings must be held to discuss the affect of the new development, nor are there lengthy city ordnances to follow.[9] This stripped-down govermentality—ruled by the housing market as Calgary booms in the period of record high oil prices—is the neoliberal utopia of noninterference. Yet the serial suburbs of Calgary, monochromatic in the landscape, look and feel very much like the highly planned city of Almere. Both share polynuclear centres attached by roadways, trails (and in the smaller-scale Almere, bike paths) that atomizes areas, and both share the dwelling as the space of individualization.

To resist the idea of suburbs as a form of global sameness or as a form of regional or national particularism—that Almere and the suburbs of Calgary appear similar or that each is distinct—is to move away from the idea of suburban sameness as a product of their particular regional and national functions and planning histories, and to speculate on the way in which neoliberalism produces patterns of *sameness* within a global rhetoric of differentiation. Global suburbs may not be global in the sense of the global being a varied nexus of global forces and flows, rather they may be neoliberal in their reproduction of the economic and social relations of the global economy and in their spatialization of an individualized neoliberal subject.

[1] Robert Fishman, "Global Suburbs," *Urban and regional Research Collaborative, Working Papers Series*, University of Michigan. http://sitemaker.umich.edu/urrcworkingpapers/all_urrc_working_papers/da.data/00000000000000000000000000000000000000308464/Paper/urrc_2003-01.pdf (last accessed July 2013), p. 2.

[2] Ibid., p. 6.

[3] Ibid.

[4] Jamie Peck and Adam Tickell, "Neoliberalizing Space," *Antipode* 34 (3), p. 380–403.

[5] Ibid., p. 387.

[6] Petra Brouwer, "Boomtown Almere," *Archis* 11, (1999), p. 10–20.

[7] Bart Lootsma, "Almere, City of Longing," *Archis* 11, (1999), p. 34–39.

[8] Rem Koolhaas, "Generic City," Jennifer Siegler (ed.), *S,M,L,XL*, 010 Publishers, Rotterdam 1995, p. 867.

[9] Unfortunately, this item is no longer on the City of Calgary website.

Frontiers of Use
(On the Work of Bas Princen)

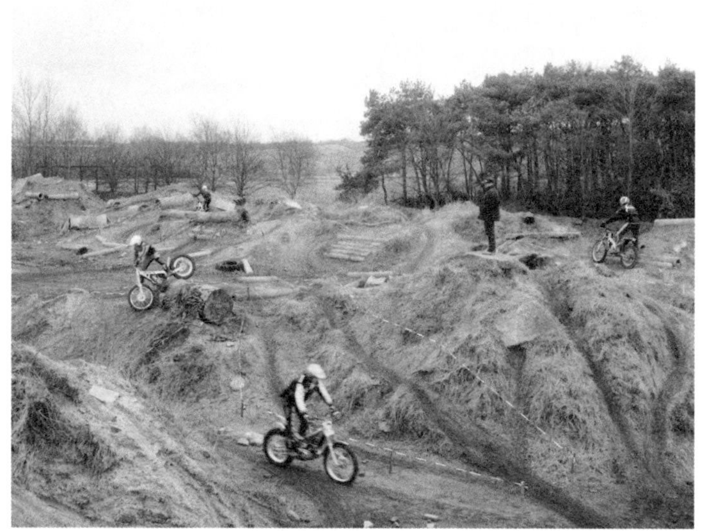

Bas Princen, *Rubble Dump*, 2000
C-print, 125 × 155 cm

Mary Louise Pratt points to
the "reinvention" of America in
the writings of commentators
who traveled to South America
on the heels of Alexander von
Humboldt. Von Humboldt's writing
itself produced this terrain again
as a "new continent" through a
prose that utilized both emotive
and technical languages to capture
the spectacle of nature, a spectacle
overwhelming human comprehen-
sion. But the travelers, soldiers,
and speculators who followed him
in the 1820s and 1830s dropped
the emotive and aesthetic aspects
of Von Humboldt's accounts,
and instead introduced "pragmatic
and economistic rhetorics." As
Pratt notes,

> In direct contrast with Von
> Humboldt, unexploited nature
> tends to be seen in this litera-
> ture as troubling or ugly, its
> very primalness a sign of the
> failure of human enterprise.[1]

This global capitalist vanguard into South America viewed the landscape as an uncultured terrain and a "dormant machine waiting to be cranked into activity."[2] This shift in viewing the landscape is paradigmatic, illustrating not so much the technology of viewing nor the scopic regime of European travelers, but a conception of the world in which nature exists to satisfy the wants and needs of humans. These wants and needs, however, are themselves as unnatural as landscapes whose value will be realized through exploitation. In this inscription, the landscape gains its value only in its economic exploitation.

The exuberant tone and the endless possibilities seen in the writing that reinvented America is there in part because the borders of nature, and of the world, were not visible or imagined. But today even the rhetorics of globalization point to the finite quality of the globe rather than the infinite quantity of nature. Globalization's reach, having extended its fingers through the world for over five-hundred years, has felt its limits. This has generated new strategies of expansion and accumulation. The continual dividing and subdividing of the world has been so thorough (yet not exhaustive) that commentators speak of a "space-time compression,"[3] and propose that: "The time-space of nature has changed irrevocably."[4] This change occurred as part of a process in which, "faced with the loss of extensive nature, capital regrouped to plumb an everyday more intensive nature."[5] The compression of space, and the compression of nature lead to new spatial practices that produce space in more intensive ways. Like capitalist expansion, spatial practices have brushed against the limits of space and have regrouped to find new uses and values for a variety of landscapes. The compressed spatiality of nature and its intensive use have developed new frontiers of use.

So far I have outlined a relatively basic Marxian view of nature—that it exists to be appropriated for the fulfillment of human beings. In this formulation, nature is transformed essentially into a commodity—a commodity that is the materialization of both use value and exchange value. Its use value is derived from the manner in which nature can satisfy human needs and desires, but these needs are beyond the biological basics and are formed through the capitalist mode of production (see Harvey *Limits to Capital*[6] and Michael Lebowitz *Beyond Capital*[7]).In other words, those troubled yearnings or exciting and satisfying buys we all experience are products of the capitalist mode of production's intensification of consumption and its pleasures, to avert a crisis of overproduction. Yet these yearnings continue! We produce them at the same time as they produce us.

We consume nature in this relationship, wringing both use value and exchange value out of it and aiming at surplus value—even when the landscape is seemingly set aside, preserved, or "underused." Cindi Katz has argued compellingly that nature has become an "accumulation strategy" through both the preservation and privatization of nature. The limits of capital may have been reached in some senses, but its ability for "creative destruction" produces new strategies of accumulation even in nature as "nature," and in the seemingly used-up terrain of the globe.[8] But universal claims about the domination of nature ignore, as Levins and Lewontin point out in *The Dialectical Biologist*, that the attempts to transform nature have been greatly varied, and some have been more successful, lucrative, or damaging than others.[9]

The human relationship with nature and with various landscapes is not only processed through nature as a commodity, but is also transformed by spatial practices and the textures of everyday life. Space is, both "pulverized" (Lefebvre), atomized, and controlled by its commodity form and through its reorganization by social power. Yet, at the same time, space is also produced anew, and coheres through the spatial practices of individuals and groups in particular places. In its form as a commodity, nature (and the landscape) is reorganized, redeployed, and redefined through the "discovery" of new use values generated by spatial practices. And like desires and wants, this process takes place within the capitalist mode of production. Nature is simultaneously a commodity (with use and exchange value) and a set of spatial practices that take shape in particular places and accrue meaning within particular groups. The continual reinvention of nature involves work—this is the basis of Marx's definition of nature—and, as Noel Castree and Bruce Braun argue, "nature's construction involves more than just capital and commodities conventionally understood" and that "nature's remaking occur[s] within networks that include social, technical, discursive, and organic elements simultaneously."[10]

Leisure is not the flip side of work, just as consumption is not the flip side of production, but is in a dialectical relationship to it. And the relationship between work and leisure is mediated by nature. Nature is not only a space where work takes place, but it is also the terrain of leisure, and of the spatial practices of leisure. The plumbing of intensive nature after the transformation of extensive nature that Katz observes also changes the characteristics of the spatial practices of leisure, as well as where they take place. Indeed, leisure often steps in where labor has vacated a spent landscape or been pushed out as greater profits are sought elsewhere. The liminal spaces left behind in the capitalist landscape are remade as new use values are found in the landscape. Hollowed rock quarries become swimming holes, service roads near airports become viewing platforms for plane watchers, bridges on logging roads that are no longer used because the hillsides have been clear-cut become bungee-jumping sites, fishless rivers give way to white-water rafting, obsolete airstrips become late-night drag strips, urban nature sites become tent villages for a city's dispossessed, trails through and around suburban areas become radio-controlled car tracks, mountain-bike courses, or 4×4 challenges. Layers of use build up on one another and new frontiers of use are created in the compressed and fragmented space of intensive nature. Use values, wrung out by gear—the technology of spatial transformation—produces the landscape again and again in the spatio-temporality of capital. But these sites are never outside of, or are merely paused within, this spatio-temporality: space, in capital, is always busy. Long-term fixed investments—such as urban real-estate speculation or resources awaiting extraction—may create the view that landscape and nature are somehow outside of production, but in the uneven temporality of global capital, the slow use of the landscape is inevitably productive.

In the meantime, in the between time, spatial practices of leisure step in and open additional opportunities for consumption: synthetic clothes that wick off sweat, shoes that absorb the pressure of body weight, 250cc trials bikes that can jump from rock to rock like goats, fully-suspended mountain bikes geared like tractors, Ski-Doos for frozen landscapes, Sea-Doos for water, jet-skis for the beach, and an SUV and trailer to haul them all. This rapid turnover and layering of use values is now part of a mode of life that is produced within and through the mode of production. In secret, symbolic, and public places, this expressive aspect affectively combines contained pleasures and use value (for use value is a kind of pleasure).

The urban landscape is also transformed by frontiers of use that produce the terrain of cities. As Neil Smith has so fluidly argued, the frontier myth "which was originally engendered as an historicization of nature … is now reapplied as a naturalization of urban history."[11] The myth and process of the urban frontier is now integral to gentrification in the urban landscape, and gentrification has been extended to a global policy. Frontiers of use in the urban landscape bring spatial practices that both speed up and slow down gentrification. Artists may move into a former industrial section of town and "regenerate" warehouse and former production sites into live-work studios, and subsequently coffee shops, galleries, and bars may spring up as part of this transformation; these spatial practices may drive out existing residents through higher rents and the area will begin to appear "cleaner" and "brighter" and accumulate the kind of cultural capital that hastens gentrification. On the other side, at another speed, the spatial practices of the homeless, or of the sex and drug trade that are often pushed into zones of containment near industrial areas, can slow gentrification. This territory can be regained for the bourgeoisie by fragmenting it into frontiers and taking it step by step in the spatial practices of recolonization. But this is neither natural nor inevitable: artists may also retard gentrification and the disenfranchised can struggle for greater local control through social apparatuses. But this can occur only after the class nature of the frontier myth, gentrification, and use values are understood.

Spatial practices and the frontiers of use in intensive nature and in the intensive urban landscape also create what Lawrence Grossberg has called "affective alliances." As cultural formations, affective alliances are a "configuration of texts [in the broadest sense], practices and people."[12] The formations are not "merely cultural" nor merely discursive, but are powerful affective formations that articulate people, and cultural and spatial practices into alliances that produce space in combination with a mode of life. Grossberg is careful to spatialize both "affect" ("the energy invested in particular sites") and everyday life: "Everyday life is itself organized by the rhythms of places and spaces, and by the specific configurations of places."[13] Grossberg provides a framework where the intensity of everyday spatial practices can merge in a more collective formation to challenge the territorialization of a mode of life. As I suggested earlier, desires and use values are in a relationship mediated by the mode of production; but nonetheless both grow out of an intensity of everyday life and the struggles with the limits of choices and freedoms and with the deeply felt, and sometimes deeply strange, *things that we do*. These things that we do gain energy from affective alliances to become productive of space and of identities and larger social relations. The possibilities of the alliances are not limitless, but they can be transformative.

Frontiers of use arise from the combination of use value, the production of a mode of life, and spatial practices within the spatio-temporality of intensive nature. No space is unused, but the strangeness of use values generated in the compression and contradictions of fast and slow accumulation strategies open spaces to uses. The production of micro-locales whispers the names of secret places where we meet.

[1] Mary Louise Pratt, *Imperial Eyes: Travel Writing and Transculturation*, Routledge, New York & London 1992, p. 149.

[2] Ibid.

[3] David Harvey, *The Condition of Postmoderity*, Blackwell, Cambridge 1990.

[4] Cindi Katz, "Whose Nature, Whose Culture," Noel Castree, Bruce Braun (eds.), *Remaking Reality: Nature at the Millennium*, Routledge, New York and London 1998, p. 46.

[5] Ibid., p. 47.

[6] David Harvey, *The Limits to Capital*, Verso, London 1999.

[7] Michael Lebowitz, *Beyond Capital: Marx's Political Economy of the Working Class*, Palgrave MacMillan, Houndsmill 1992, 2003.

[8] Katz, "Whose Nature, Whose Culture."

[9] Richard Levins and Richard Lewontin, *The Dialectical Biologist*, Harvard University Press, Cambridge 1985.

[10] Noel Castree and Bruce Braun, "The Construction of Nature and the Nature of Construction," Castree, Braun (eds.), *Remaking Reality: Nature at the* Millennium.

[11] Neil Smith, *The New Urban Frontier: Gentrification and the Revanchist City*, Routledge, New York and London 1996, p. 16–17.

[12] Lawrence Grossberg, *We Gotta Get Out of This Place: Popular Conservatism and Postmodern Culture*, Routledge, London and New York, 1992, p. 397.

[13] Ibid., p. 154.

Fugitive Spaces

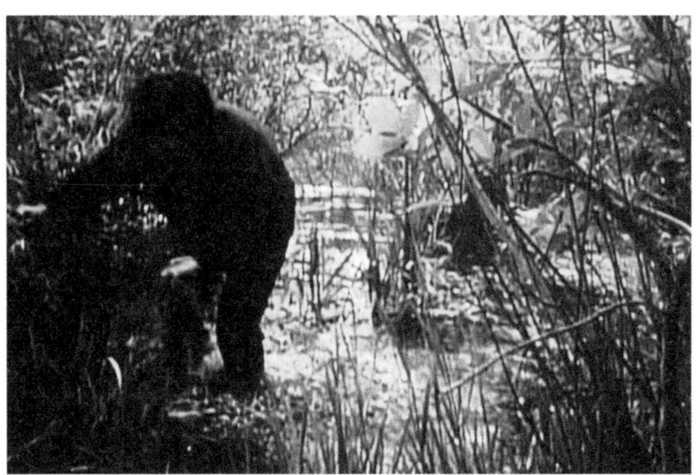

Jin Me Yoon, *Unbidden: Jungle-Swamp*, 2003
Single-channel video installation, dimensions variable, 8-minute 46-second loop

In works such as *Souvenirs of the Self* (1991), *A Group of Sixty-Seven* (1997), and *Welcome Stranger Welcome Home* (2002), Jin Me Yoon builds deeply reflexive and social cultural narratives that strike the problematic of national history and instrumental landscapes against the claims of identities pitched through a world system that relocates bodies as easily as capital. While these works take place in a transnational debate sprung loose from the geographical narratives of center and periphery and First World cosmopolitanism, they also confront attachments of belonging and displacement refracted through national spaces made material through imagination and the state, yet rendered vulnerable by a world order increasingly competitive, coercive, and corrupt. With a critical glance back, these works are as much speculations on an emergent global geography of production and consumption as they are pointed interventions into

Canadian narratives of citizenship, identity, inclusion, and space. Yet Yoon's work cannot be contained within static conceptualizations of the space of the nation state, for her work has consistently torqued the spatial and the temporal, the national and the transnational, and the geographic and the epistemological.

I want to follow Susan Edelstein's proposition that "[w]ith the *Unbidden* project (2006), [Yoon] turns her attention to the active exchange between the psychic and the physical," and that the "subject is no longer primarily about surface exteriority, but is, instead, more akin to embodied consciousness"[1]; but I want turn attention to the dialectical sense of space and spatialization that *Unbidden* amplifies. While it is tempting to identify a turn in an artist's work, I do propose that *Unbidden* approaches space with different devices than Yoon's earlier work—not a rupture in a project, but a sharpening of the ways that space is produced at this moment, and how it is produced at a number of scales and through various cultural representations.

Irit Rogoff, in *Terra Infirma: Geography's Visual Culture*, builds an argument that interlaces an active model of geography and space with the representational possibilities of visual cultural and artistic production, and her insistence on the dialectical nature of space is useful for *Unbidden*:

> [A]n active process of "spatialization" replaces
> a static notion of named spaces and in this process
> it is possible to bring into relation the designated
> activities and the physical properties of the named
> space with structures of psychic subjectivities such
> as anxiety or desire or compulsion.[2]

The deeply historical and contested landscapes (and their representations) that served as "named spaces," and the site of intervention in *Souvenirs of the Self* and *Group of Sixty-Seven* do not present the same process of spatialization as the unnamed spaces of *Unbidden*. The dialectical aspect of space and the body in Yoon's work is made more constructive in *Unbidden*. To grasp this dynamic, we have to invert Rogoff's fundamental question of "How can we read bodies as 'geographically' marked?"[3] to, how can we read geography as marked by the body?

The geographic sites where *Unbidden*'s videos and photographs were shot are dramatically altered by the body and its actions—the active process of spatial production marks these sites by setting cultural references and representations in motion alongside a discourse that has recently become dominant in producing space, particularly national and urban space. *Fear* has been politically mobilized as a pervasive discourse for daily life and has dynamically changed our experience of spaces and places: fear is being instrumentalized as a powerful logic to curtail debate and dissent, and to redefine the role of the state (from "represent and govern" to "serve and protect"). Fear is a dynamic in the process of spatialization. Each of us can identify ways in which cities we are familiar with have changed in the brief years since "security" and the "war on terror" have been picked up locally, nationally, and globally: Vancouver's waterfront docks are no longer openly accessible by road; New York, the world's "global city," famously known for being open 24 hours a day, has its tunnels guarded and its subways and train stations guarded; and airports around the world are slowly shifting from ports of entry to privatized prisons combined with shopping opportunities.

Although the spatialization of fear has been predominantly urban, it also refigures nature as indefensible, as a security risk. The physically unruly Canadian-USA border is being cleared and trimmed of trees and bush to allow more surveillance from the ground and the air; the Mexico-USA border is becoming more militarized, to block the movement of people who are ironically and tragically necessary for the US economy. Alongside this, nature is intensified as a site of capital accumulation—from national parks to the Arctic, places that were once inhospitable to super exploitation have been opened up as capitalism itself is naturalized, and nature capitalized. Nature has become capital's playground, or else an unenclosed space where danger can hide out, hatching plans in caves, training furtive armies.

As the fortress mentality of fear expands, borders, edges, seams, and unenclosed spaces are redefined as vulnerable. *Fugitive (Unbidden)* (2004) leaps, skulks, crawls, and burrows into the production of space through fear by marking geography bodily. Other attributes of the space are blurred as it is produced by fear—for *Fugitive* (*Unbidden*) makes the landscape a generic and transferable landscape of fear. But, as this spatial production is dialectical, the ambiguously gendered and racially marked body in *Fugitive* (*Unbidden*) is also caught in fear, peering askance from behind brush, hiding in a swamp.

As dramatically as I've portrayed this, *Fugitive* (*Unbidden*) adds the jab of the comic into the production of space by fear. This comic intensity is a critique of the goofy depths that the US-defined, yet globally circulated, discourse of fear has sunk to. The color chart of fear, readiness, and alert that the Department of Homeland Security in the US devised, essentially had no function (or infrastructure) other than to map fear and danger as if it were a sort of new-age chart ("Today is orange")—and this comic aspect was intensified by the fact that the former director of Homeland Security looked like he had wandered out a Cold War-era cartoon, speaking a parody of official state language. Like-wise, an image in *Fugitive* (*Unbidden*) in which a black-clad figure creeps, all menacing stealth, along the worn path leading up a bluff to the undefended edge of a suburban expansion is comic, drawing on a cultural stock of images from martial arts movies, spy thrillers, and suburban horror flicks. At this aerosol edge where life-style architecture extends into surplus nature, the docile houses the color of band-aids are fleshy targets.

This staged and performed photograph is a remarkable twist on how geography marks bodies, for— as I've suggested—it is the geography that is marked by the body and its gestures. The space of *Unbidden* is not a text or a message that can be read through national myths of belonging, for to read social space as text, as Henri Lefebvre argues, is to "evade both history and practice."[4] The various images of *Unbidden* produce space by torquing together a general feeling of fear—what Madeline Bunting has called "the dominant currency of our public life"[5]—with poses and staged scenes drawn from a visual culture of suspicion, caution, and vulnerability. Drawn from a grammar of film, the images of the knife-wielding mysterious intruder walking in a shallow waterway (to hide footprints, as we all know), pushing aside the thin branches, or the crouched figure set in the centre of the image, using the foreground of dirt and underbrush as cover, are known to us, and their visual reference constructs the landscape, marking the geography. More actively, the triptych of the fugitive boy/ girl leaping into shallow water with knife raised is an action shot with continuity problems: hanging mid-air above the water, in the cinematic grammar of Bruce Lee, the fugitive enters! Space and an understanding of geography are produced here by an interplay "between the concrete and material and the psychic conditions and metaphorical articulations of the relations between subjects, places and spaces."[6] The material landscape with its recognizable features—industrial infrastructure, recreational sites, housing developments—takes meaning on by a politically mobilized discourse of fear being projected onto the landscape and space. Unlike an inner or psychic landscape, this projection is not from the viewing subject, but is culturally produced frame through which the landscape is viewed. *Fugitive (Unbidden)* taps into how space is currently produced through a discourse of fear, but unravels this as a set of codes, gestures, and poses that are deeply embedded socially and historically, extending a Trumanesque splitting of the world in two in order to freeze geopolitics into a Cold War—George W. Bush's "axis of evil," which equates North Korea, Iran, and Iraq.

One final turn. This spatialization through fear is deeply and troublingly temporal. For fear constructs the present as a time for defense that preempts any discussion of the shape of the future. Unfortunately this is the model of time that the present form of globalization urges. As Jerome Binde argues,

> By giving precedence to the logic of "just in time" at the expense of any forward looking deliberation, within a context of ever faster technological transfer and exchange, our era is opening the way for the tyranny of emergency.[7]

That this echoes Walter Benjamin's thesis that a state of emergency is the rule, not the exception, merely emphasizes how fear—fear of others, fear that the moment for super profits will flash by—is dominant in the present.

[1] Susan Edelstein, "A Transfer of Power," *Unbidden*, Jin Me Yoon, Kamloops Art Gallery, Kamloops, 2004, p. 20.
[2] Irit Rogoff, *Terra Infirma: Geography's Visual Culture*, Routledge, London 2000, p. 23.
[3] Ibid., p. 145.
[4] Henri Lefebvre, *The Production of Space*, trans. Donald Nicholson-Smith, Blackwell, Oxford 1991, p. 7.
[5] Madeline Bunting, "The Age of Anxiety," *The Guardian Weekly* (October 29–November 4, 2004), p. 5.
[6] Rogoff, *Terra Infirma*, p. 16.
[7] Jerome Binde, "Toward an Ethics of the Future," Arjun Appadurai (ed.), *Globalization*, Duke University Press, Durham, North Carolina 2001, p. 90–113.

The Ends of Culture: The Temporality of Cultural Critique

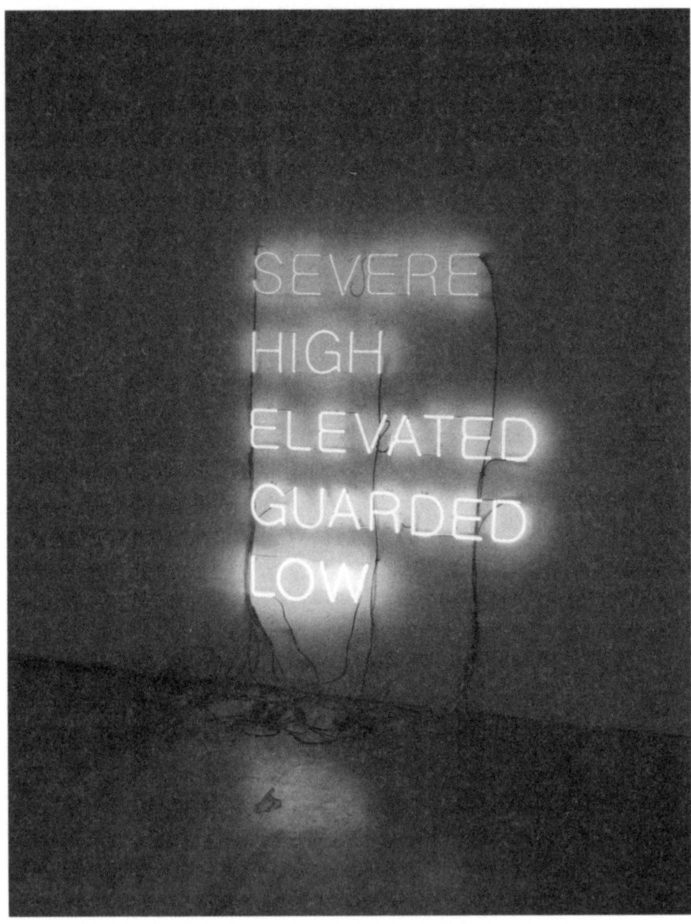

Ron Terada, *Five Coloured Words in Neon*, 2003
Red, orange, yellow, blue, and green neon; each word 17.8 cm high

Raymond Williams forcefully characterized culture as a long revolution of process and change, yet culture is often experienced more abruptly as events cut across our everyday lives, and as moments merge into a collective interruption of the making and remaking of social relations. This cross-cut of moment and event, in contrast to the grain of long duration, characterizes the temporality of September 11, 2001. Yet the temporality that emerged from that day—through the media representation and political fall-out of the attacks on the World Trade Center and the Pentagon—has been deeply contested and has shaped the critical frames and language used to grasp the present. If September 11, or 9/11, marks either a rupture or break in the historical moment that signals a new reality collaged together from the bad history that led to it, or, conversely, if it is an event that requires a longer analysis to properly locate, this tension rattles the temporality of cultural critique and the languages of globalization.

This critical disruption became evident when terms such as *imperialism, hegemony, primitive accumulation*, and *creative destruction* began to reappear at all levels of cultural and political discourse. Beginning with the worldwide anti-Iraq war march and then the peace protests in February and March 2003—massive gatherings that conjured either a public sphere located in globalized cities, a cohesive global public opinion, or the merging of the inchoate multitude— and then accelerating after the invasion of Iraq turned from triumphal event to into a relentless occupation, these terms that had previously been relegated to bygone stages of political and cultural analysis began to circulate as explanations of the moment. Arif Dirlik, in his analysis of global modernity, situated the ground that these terms pushed up from:

> In some contemporary works, the colonial and imperial pasts appear merely as stages of an inexorable globalization that has presently replaced an earlier modernization discourse as the paradigm for understanding the development of the modern world.[1]

Here the logic and language of development provides a paradigm of stages and a temporal unfolding of the modern world that leads to the present configuration. Yet, with Iraq, the historical repetition of invasion, occupation by a (coerced) coalition force, the promise of liberal democracy, and the privatization of common resources (since repeated stealthily in Haiti) has led to the timely re-emergence of these concepts as active processes of the present rather than past stages. As Dirlik asserts, *imperialism* and *colonialism* do not "disappear into a new teleology of globalization," but rather they are forces that have created the unevenness—in the distribution of wealth, in social stability, and in political and cultural power—of the present.[2]

Strikingly these relaunched terms draw on a powerful, if somewhat submerged critique that brings forward the language of resistance to colonialism and imperialism—that is, a language of critique and possibility that Fredric Jameson

periodizes as the 1960s. For instance, Retort, the collective
of writers centered in the Bay Area near San Francisco, argue
the necessity to reclaim *capitalism* and *primitive accumulation*
as terms of analysis in their engaged and enraged analysis,
Afflicted Powers:

> We take it the time is over when the mere mention
> of such categories consigned one—in the hip acad-
> emy, especially—irrevocably to the past. The past
> has become the present again: this is the mark of the
> moment we are trying to understand.[3]

Retort are sharp in their parenthetical assertion that

> It is "the end of Grand Narratives" and the "trap of
> totalization" and "the radical irreducibility of the
> political" which now seem like period pieces.[4]

Yet Retort also cautions that *imperialism* should stay where
Lenin put it in early 1916, as the highest stage of capitalism,
rather than an imperialism that could occur again (as
modernity is continually allowed to do!) in forms not
identical to Lenin's vision. The Retort collective

> find[s] it understandable, if in the end a mistake,
> that imperialism is used in a smug or even relieved
> manner, denying the dialectic of the moment and
> instead driving back to the past once again.[5]

But the question that emerges is not whether the past has
flipped forward again, but whether imperialism (along with
other historical strategies of accumulation) are unfinished
projects that migrate or surge in an uneven moment, in
a temporality that is not so easily relegated to the past,
mirrored in the present, or predicted in the future.

Reflecting on the constellation of culture after the
euphoria of a globality in which cultural criticism had grown
weary of, or even fed up with, concepts such as *capitalism*
(oddly as a determinant, not as a phenomenon), archiving
them as too obvious or too over-determined for investigation while seeing everyday life opened by the possibilities of
resurgent cosmopolitanism, emergent forms of citizenship,

and the connectivity of globalization, it is possible to say today that the rejection of such hardened terms is a hangover from a developmental theory of globalization. Despite a spatial view of globalization as a complex net of connections, nodes, and flows, its temporality has been fairly straightforward—development, flow, localized resistance, and market opportunity brought us to the present global moment. This view of globalization was not cracked by September 11 as an event, but in the ways in which September 11 scuttled the terms such as *progress* and *presentism*. This break happened on both the Left and the Right— the Cold War language of two worlds popped up again (this time coded in terms of good and evil, light and dark, "cave dwellers" and "modernity"). As the route of culture in globalization theory—a narrative of the jumping over of the national scale toward a mash-up of place-specific cultures that have greater connectivity—has shifted the site of critique downward to borders, cities, bodies, things, and events while moving away from larger categories and constellations, this view of globalization as synonymous with linear narratives of connectivity and inevitability begins to crumble. Against the supposed unmapped present, the return of terms that gesture upward sets up a historical reverberation with the era in which *imperialism*, for example, carried a forceful note of critique linked to the past but also articulated in and to the present.

Get Your Imperialism On

Plodding and monologic, *imperialism* is often figured as the unidirectional application of state power now nudged under by fluid globalization and its promise of mobile citizenship, ineffective nations, and hybrid cultural formations fermented in the dynamic mix of the global-local. So, imagine the rusty creaking as *imperialism* and *hegemony* made their way back even into the mainstream media. The American shock political commentator Rush Limbaugh, felt *hegemony* was an accurate marker for the ambitions of the right, and recommended Gramsci as useful reading. Curiously, some liberals, on the other hand, saw new forms of imperialism as an inevitable and ethical way of managing the world (what Michael Ignatieff termed "the burden") and gathered

strength in the moment of the run up to what we were told
was an unwanted yet right war to rebrand imperialism as
a reasonable political strategy to maintain or develop the
happy hegemony of liberal democracy. Ignatieff, who has
since left his position at Harvard University and returned to
Canada to see his political ambitions fail rather spectacularly, identified the present form of imperialism in a manner
that is both careful in its philosophical positioning, yet
startling in its dehistoricization and condescending in its
explanatory tone:

> Imperialism used to be the white man's burden. This
> gave it a bad reputation. But imperialism doesn't stop
> being necessary just because it becomes politically
> incorrect. Nations sometimes fail, and when they do,
> only outside help—imperial power—can get them
> back on their feet. Nation-building is the kind
> of imperialism you get in a human-rights era, a time
> when great powers believe simultaneously in the right
> of small nations to govern themselves and in their
> won right to rule the world.[6]

Ignatieff goes on to outline imperialism as a necessity in
which there are no winners, no losers, just good global
neighbors helping each other out when one falls on bad
times through no fault of capital.

This post-political view of imperialism, an imperialism with no real conflict or economic interest but instead
imbued with a reluctant humanism, is what Fred Moten
identifies as part of "The New International of Decent Feelings," an affective alliance that "will ultimately align itself
against evidence and analysis, as if proper thought will have
taken place only in the obsessive oscillation between false
alternatives."[7] Here, of course, the false alternatives are
liberal democracy forced through imperial rule or the risk of
failure. Ignatieff, as he has already narrowed the possibilities
of the political, does not have to obsess between "temporary
imperial rule" or states slipping further into disrepair, for
his proper thinking does not imagine other forms of political engagement. For Neil Smith, who analyzes liberalism
over the long haul, Ignatieff and other liberal hawks provide
a clear view: "Rarely since 1898 has the vice of liberal

American Imperialism been so honestly on display."[8] Yet, for Smith, this moral order of "liberal realism" is tied to the historical roots of liberalism rather than being a shocking rupture from it. The past is not flipped forward, but the project of capitalism continues astride, upping its "shock doctrine" as Naomi Klein observes, but using a language that buffers, even normalizes, the shock.[9] The "shock therapy" that Jeffrey Sachs recommended for the transformation of first the Bolivian economy and then the Russian economy in 1991 has given way to a language of "liberalization" of trade and "harmonization" of national economies through trade pacts.

Curiously, this resurfacing of *imperialism* occurs precisely at a moment when the cultural discourse of globalization has settled into a set of images that smoothes the surface of the world, eroding uneven development with transnational flows of people, finance, images, and ideas. And for Ignatieff and the other "illiberal liberals," imperialism is posed merely as an idea that migrates easily on these post-political flows. Without touching on capitalism's real effects, and instead seeing uneven development as a complication of center and periphery, such a view presents a world where borders and the nation state become more immaterial, and the barbed edges of interstate rivalries appear as cultural rather than economic. While global flows and "relations of disjuncture," as Arjun Appadurai designates them, navigate the global tension of cultural homogenization and cultural heterogenization, the complex structures of power of this disjunctive global economy nonetheless move through national spaces and take shape in the dynamic production of a geography of globalization that cuts through all spatial scales, altering and being altered as it follows paths of both beckoning and resistance. Imperialism, understood as a crude power with military and economic tentacles, enters into this fluid world conception as an irritant that is insufficiently disjunctive and still troublingly geographical. It takes place.

Retrospectively, the post-geographical view of empire that Hardt and Negri popularized tapping into, as it did, the language of deterritorialization that was once invigorating, has taken a number of hits, and not only from the radical geographers. Eric Lott, writing on the disappearance of the liberal intellectual, observes,

> How musty now seems the globalization theorizing of
> just a few years ago, when Antonio Negri and Michael
> Hardt could argue in *Empire* that global relations are
> today dominated by a set of imperial, but not imperi-
> alist, interests.[10]

In contrast to such a center-less imperial focus, and in
a harsher critique of *Empire*'s "dreamlike desire of fluid
social boundaries [that] effectively blur the crude imperialism of American realpolitik," Timothy Brennan points to a
longer-term "infrastructural necessity of imperialism."[11] And,
previous to *Empire*, Gayatri Spivak described the "continuing
narrative of shifting imperial formations" and the intense
"financialization of the globe" in which capitalism's "seeming
advance is caught back into its transformation into imperialism by way precisely of the money circuit: finance capital."[12]
For Spivak, this seeming advance is a transformation that
confounds a stage theory of imperialism and invigorates new
forms such as "aid-trade imperialism."[13] This is what Ignatieff
happily defines as "empire lite," "a global hegemony whose
grace notes are free markets, human rights, and democracy."[14]
This also seems to mark the end of Ignatieff's humanism
(coinciding ironically with his move toward the highest
public office through the Canadian Liberal party) as well as
the apparent end of irony that 9/11 was to have signaled: now,
when human rights and democracy can be the grace notes of
free markets and imperialism.

Cultural studies, the institutional methodology
for *reading* the world and its cultural effects, also can be
questioned for shading its view from a global hegemony
in which imperialism takes hold in both the stability and
expansion of capital. As Rey Chow argues,

> cultural studies contains within its articulations this
> fundamental *theoretical* understanding of the need
> to challenge the center of hegemonic systems of
> thinking and writing.[15]

Challenged in this way, "standard cultural imperialism"
was decentered and replaced with the constricting

and commoditizing project of tolerant multiculturalism
and a politics of recognition that left little space for forms
of the political while expanding the spaces of the post-
political.

For cultural studies, cultural imperialism was figured
as a staid Galina Khrushchev alongside globalization's
Chanel-clad Jackie O. Interlaced with military and imperialist
adventures globally, and the neoliberal transformation
of state structures along with the push to privatize public
resources and spaces, global flows have hardened against the
tropes of cosmopolitanism, complex connectivity, cultural
dialogue, and emancipation that were once used to describe
the cultural effects of globalization.

Do flows ever rust? Do flows have points of origin
or do they have philosophical wellsprings in neoclassical
economic theory? Imperialism, once the problem of the
periphery, did not end as a tidy stage. Yet a renewed investigation of imperialism, or a new kind of engagement with the
term, can ask how it may have morphed into unrecognizable
forms, how it may dig in at new scales, and how a new or
a different language that bypasses the state to pledge alle-
giance to the mercurial and ephemeral market have become
imperialism's new oaths. The inward turn of colonialization
that gave rise to the slogan of "the colonization of everyday
life" may today help us identify a stealth imperialism
of everyday life. A more brutal imperialism aimed at the
dispossession of territories and resources (what the Mid-
night Notes Collective pointed to in 1990 and what David
Harvey has called "accumulation by dispossession") might
be tied with the denial and dispossession of a non-market
imagination of the social. But an imperialism of everyday
life which forecloses deliberation beyond the false alternatives of liberal democracy or failure might well be cohering
underfoot.

Back to Culture and Other Useful Tools

After the cultural turn in critical theory, *culture* has become
an overworked term, signifying everything, taking place
everywhere. In the theoretical struggle to loosen the bolts
of economic determinism, the relationship of the economic
and the cultural were variously separated and folded into

one other: but culture, as a category, emerged as the reified dominant, the expanded category of life and the everyday across scales. Seeking to embed culture into the processes of everyday life and retrieve it from a superstructural adjunct, Raymond Williams' famous definition of "the theory of culture as the study of relationships between elements in a whole way of life"[16] echoed through cultural studies. But this expansion has only added to the difficulty of defining this "noun of general process."[17] And beyond definition, as Don Mitchell has continued to argue, culture is wielded as explanation to the extent that

> the emptying out of the abstraction of culture—
> the very fact that it means nothing—allows for
> an imperialization of culture: a world in which
> culture is everything (because it is nothing).[18]

For Mitchell, the evacuation of the term has led to an "abandonment of explanation" and a culturalism in which "'culture' is used to explain culture (or cultural forms)."[19] When culture is figured in this way, Mitchell proposes, it becomes a "phantom," a "superorganic mysterious thing," and a default determinant of the social—a "prison-house of social life."[20] Mitchell argues that the political consequences are costly: "It is precisely because the term 'culture' has no clear reference that it becomes a useful tool for arraying power, for organizing distinctions in the world."[21] In place of this Mitchell asks that

> "Culturalism" in geography ... be replaced by a fuller,
> richer dialectical argument about "culture" as a
> social product and a social practice, one that is fully
> implicated in systems of domination, oppression,
> and exploitation.[22]

This compelling argument is a reaction against *cultural studies* as much as it is against the *category of culture*: the theoretical challenge is to effectively open the cultural to the social without falling into the binds of culturalism ("the doctrine," Terry Eagelton argues, "that everything in human affairs is a matter of culture"[23]), of not reducing the cultural to a sphere detached from real materialist and systemic concerns, nor to have culture explain differences that are also rooted in and derived from many other spheres. That is, to look at culture as variously determined and not only determining.

Without explicitly forming a definition, Chow gives a working model of culture that better answers Mitchell's challenge while also generating a cultural politics:

> "culture" is an unfinished process, a constellation—never in pristine form—of social relations that are continually unworked and reworked.[24]

Chow's view does not fetishize culture as a process of open-ended representations, but locates the "unfinished quality" of culture in the social; in

> the lingering effect of massive inequalities inherent in the international divisions of labor; in the access to social representation and political power; and in the possession, exchange, and consolidation of cultural capital.[25]

Yet when culture is not viewed as a process as Chow provides, nor contested as a category as Mitchell does, it can be a tool for dividing up the world and generating area knowledges with little historical depth—this area knowledge constructs regions as static spaces rather than contested territories and socio-historical processes. Culture, as a reified category, can then be used to explain a range of imperial and foreign policy projects—particularly, as we see today, that the "region" of the Middle East has not "known" democracy due to a cultural lack rather than due to the very type of imperial interventions that are now called up as the solution. It is difficult to hear Ignatieff do anything other than invoke an old form of imperialist knowledge when he muses, "The case for empire is that it has become, in a place like Iraq, the last hope for democracy and stability alike."[26] This culturalism also allows for a binaristic rhetoric to emerge: civilization versus the barbarians, skyscrapers versus caves, enlightenment versus primitive darkness, democracy *or* totalitarianism, and the greater mythic simplification of "good" and "evil." As many commentators have asserted,

a lack of geographical and political knowledge allows
or generates such justifications and mystifications. But this
works in tandem with a static view of culture, and the result
is a cultural-spatial politics tied into foreign policy architecture. A reified application of culture as traits and distinctions
results in a static map of the world. What is lost here is
the kind of geopolitical jockeying and hegemonic shoulder
bumping that propel nation-states to take positions in
relation to the world economy, and increasingly, access to
resources.

The Other Ends of Culture

While the theories of the use and consumption of culture by
particular communities and institutions that have convinc-
ingly argued for agency at a number of scales, ties into
notions of global civil society, insurgent citizenships, and
emergent publics—the ends toward which culture is
deployed—have to be examined and negotiated as both
restrictions and possibilities of what artists, writers, and
cultural groups actually do. The uses of culture cannot be
so easily pried from the places, conditions, and discourses
of its production—particularly if we view globalization as
a mechanism of capital and not a network of connections
between things and ideas or people and places. It is through
this nexus that I approach questions of another seemingly
old term of analysis, a term that illuminates the very type
of cultural tensions that a global view of connectedness and
flows drifts away from—this term, a merging of two difficult
words, is *cultural imperialism*. What uses of culture and what
order of culture does a resurgent imperialism aim for? To
counter these ends of culture, I want turn to oppositional
forms of creative practice in literature and visual art today.
In the term *creative practice*, Raymond Williams was sifting
for a term to bring culture into a productive realm as both
cultural production and mental labor. I use it here as part of
what political economist Michael Lebowitz identifies as one
"red thread" amongst many woven through Marx—the push
for living with the potential for creativity in life which is
stymied by capital—and as a counter to the "creative
destruction" that often drives globalization.[27] The estrange-
ments and alienations of work and of life that are structural

under capital are now spread over the globe to a greater extent. As Peter Hitchcock argues, "This is the crisis in activity that globalization seeks to globalize."[28] Here the crisis and potential and limitations of everyday life are thoroughly if unevenly globalized. Yet Hitchcock points to a historical, cultural, and economical nexus that frames globalization as a cultural and philosophical problem:

> The problem with globalization is not only the nefarious economic system it represents, but that it lacks a coherent or logical basis for its apprehension. Within the time/space compression of the moment ... and with all the loud trumpeting that because of technological and economic integration the world is a smaller place, there is relatively little discussion about how globalization can be understood without expounding on some cognitive, imaginative, or sensate means to do so.[29]

The problem of understanding globalization becomes cultural in a different way when artists and writers try to explain or intervene into the apprehension and definition of globalization through the imaginative. The question for artists and activists then is how to join the everyday of globalization—the goods, the information, the cultural drifts—to the systemic. This problem itself is not new, nor unique, but perhaps what is different from previous interventions into everyday life, into public space, and into the larger relations that shape our lives, is that the very structure of globalization is rendered more opaque.

From Old to New Imperialism?

Cultural imperialism has returned as tragedy and farce within cultural theories of the present. Imperialism now has to be designated as *new* or *neoliberal*, or *neoconservative* to be differentiated from imperialism as *the final stage* of capitalism. Mohammed Bamyeh clocks out the "logic of the old imperialism" with the Tuesday, September 11, 1973, coup against Salvador Allende in Chile, while others begin a stage of new imperialism through American hegemony from the 1970s leading to the declaration of infinite war after Tuesday,

September 11, 2001.[30] This runs against the grain of the
temporalities of globalization and its compressed moment
of triumphal capitalism's continuous present. Globalization,
charged with a neoliberal urgency, is imagined as the
immediate now and the replicant future. But the spatiality of
globalization submerges theories of imperialism: globalization imagines no outsides to itself, yet theories of imperialism assumed an outside, a non-capitalist environment as an
outlet for expansion.[31]

Theories of "traditional" imperialism progress from
a strong state pushing its reach beyond its borders, so
establishing an imperial center and a colonial periphery.
Theories that have privileged global processes of fluidity,
deterritorialization, and complex connectivity tend to
propose a porous state adrift without a function: its borders
and boundaries breached on multiple levels ranging from
the economic (via global finance and trade), the cultural
(through the global circulation of images and ideas), to the
citizen (made global through transnational migration or
enabled through technology). But in existing globalization,
capital needs a "global system of multiple states and local
sovereignties, structured in a complex relation of domination and subordination"[32] to maintain itself. Cultural
theories of globalization that scale jump the nation-state
and privilege global-local connections tend to see cultural
imperialism deflected, in the final instance, by the local,
rather than it being administered by a system of states and
localities.

Ellen Meiksins Wood argues in *Empire of Capital* that
no overall theory of imperialism "designed for a world in
which all internal relations are internal to capitalism and
governed by capitalist imperatives" exists.[33] For understanding the forms—and functions—of cultural imperialism, this
means that the ideological function of cultural imperialism
must, in a sense, guard its borders against the cultural
imagining of another world order or social order while
simultaneously trying to contain or deflect critiques internal
to the system. Cultural imperialism is both expansive
and limiting: economically expansive, yet socio-culturally
limiting. Expansively, cultural imperialism pushes the project
of global capital as the only possible form of life, yet as
a limitation, it also ships neoliberalism as its only proper

guiding philosophy. "Neoliberalism" as Brian Massumi picks it up,

> defines freedom as the right of individuals to act according to their personal interest, as rationally indexed to the needs and opportunities of the market economy that sustains them.[34]

Individual consumption, personal (rather than collective) property rights, and privatization of public resources become hallmarks of a neoliberalism that saturates everyday life. With this ramping up of individualism and property, and the state of continual or permanent war that is spread across the globe, *fear* has become, as Massumi argues through Foucault, "the correlate of neoliberal freedom."[35] Picking up on this correlation of fear, affect, and the state, a neon work by Vancouver artist, Ron Terada, *Five Coloured Neon Words* (2003) deploys Pop conceptualism to bring the USA's Department of Homeland Security's color-coded words of warning into another context. Terada's ironic flipping of politics into art through the material of a nostalgic form of commercial signage (and a material with a solid conceptualist heritage, particularly with Bruce Nauman) is a counter to the DHS's rather non-ironic (and unintentionally humorous) approach (duct tape as a deterrent for chemical weapons and flour spills shutting down airports, for example). Terada's shift in context foregrounds the lack of self-reflexivity that seems to typify the DHS. *Five Coloured Neon Words* does not seek an autonomous space for art: its political value is that it brings the social into the aesthetic without the cultural anxiety that the political context will override all crack-downs on the multiple meanings available. In fact, the reverse is set in motion: art is used to open up the suppressed ambiguities of the political and to let out the absurdist nature of the color-coded warning semaphores. In this case, the element of farce that seems to be part of the Department of Homeland Security comes into clarity—despite the tragedy of its origins.

Terada's work also defuses (pun intended!) the wearying repetition and tug of affect that the color-coded fear spectrum seems to have been set up to sustain.

Massumi describes the system in this way:

> The alert system was introduced to calibrate the
> public's anxiety. In the aftermath of 9/11, the public's
> fearfulness had tended to swing out of control in
> response to dramatic, but maddeningly vague, govern-
> mental warnings of an impending follow-up attack.
> The alert system was designed to modulate that fear.[36]

The result, Massumi proposes, was that "[a]cross the
geographical and social differentials dividing them, the population fell into affective attunement."[37] In Massumi's reading,
the system creates an affect that harmonizes the public
to the same register of fear and insecurity, this register then
becomes the new normal (as Massumi points out, there is
no hue for "Safe").[38] Terada's deployment of the spectrum
cracks the unity of affect that is tied together in what
Massumi calls "the affective fact":

> So what is an affective fact? The mechanism is quite
> simple: Threat triggers fear. The fear is disruptive.
> The fear *is* a disruption.[39]

Terada's reworking of this mechanism takes a step back
into the conceptualizing or shaping of the fact about to be
launched:

> Codes for alert create fear. The codes are disruptive.
> Disrupt the code (and derail the affective fact).

The color-codes of alert ignite the affect of fear, and then
fear itself becomes the affective fact—but with Terada,
rather than a hot spectrum of fear, we get the cool conceptual glow of neon as the artist retakes affect into an artistic
context to deploy it as laughter, or even the type of disgust
one can feel when a scenario for duping becomes clear.
Terada does not empty the political signs, he redeploys
them.[40] Here I think we can apply Sven Lütticken's recent
call to "always aestheticize,"

> For it is not that the reign of sign-value must be
> iconoclastically smashed in order to resurrect some

state of normality. Rather, what is needed are interventions in the complexity and contradictions of signs, to question the conditions under which their programmed surfaces came into being.[41]

Further In, Reaching Out

The cultural wing of neoliberalism, a wing also deployed during the Cold War, is aired at everything from World Fairs (think of the Kitchen Debate between Nixon and Khrushchev as a particularly sweaty instance of this) and the Olympics (think of the transformation of Vancouver's inner city and the economic distortion of the city in the lead up to the 2010 winter Olympics) through forms of popular culture and even in the marketization of conceptual artistic production. By limiting the discussion and imagination of other shapes of the world and of other forms of social order, universal cultural imperialism tries vainly to enact Althusser's call of interpellation at a global level; national cultures are expected to turn to the call of "hey you" from neoliberalism, and further embed themselves into its systems and logic. This cultural wing is writ large and *turned inward* toward culture itself. Everyday life, then, begins to reshape itself along the lines of this new commonsense. The triumphant language, or the hectoring talking heads of neoliberalism have shut down the social horizon that cultural production strains at, or what Ernst Bloch calls "real utopian critique" which speaks out for the "particular *tendency to come.*"[42]

Yet cultural imperialism still has an expansiveness based on interstate rivalry, even though culture is dispersed through transnational ownership of the "entertainment industry" and administered by a network of states and local sovereignties. For instance, Sophie Coppola's successful film *Lost in Translation* (2003) does not merely reflect a sympathetic but slightly askew American view of the cultural strangeness of the Japanese—a kind of comedic ethnography —but shows a fascination with Japanese adaptations and rejigging of forms of American culture that result in things both familiar and odd (yet never defamiliarized). From crazy talk-show hosts not presenting the facade of Letterman and Leno to commercials that buff the luster of fading American stars, the Japanese mimic but do not invigorate American cultural forms in this film. The obsequious forms of capitalism the film portrays are also held in a parodic frame as they are represented as lacking the sincerity or robustness of the US version. The film's question seems to be not, "Why do the Japanese appear so sympathetically strange to Americans," but, "Why can they not correctly reproduce American forms of doing cultural and economic business."

Yet this film of cultural disconnection, of the lack of real interface between two cultures despite their connectedness, comes at the moment when Japan has a rapidly increasing "content industry" and the economic aspect of its culture is growing. As an article on the website of Japan's American Embassy points out,

> Japanese cultural exports, i.e. revenue from royalties and sales of Japanese music, video games, anime, art, films, and fashion, soared to $12.5 billion in 2002, up 300 percent from 1992.[43]

And in the seamless inversion of the cultural into the economic that neoliberalism seeks, this cultural expansion is tied to a stronger position within the system of states. In an article that measures Japan's "gross national cool" as a form of soft power, Douglas McGray positions Japan globally:

> Yet Japan is reinventing superpower again. Instead of collapsing beneath its political and economic misfortunes, Japan's global cultural influence has only grown. In fact, from pop music to consumer electronics, architecture to fashion, and food to art, Japan has far greater cultural influence now than it did in the 1980s when it was an economic superpower.[44]

However, Coppola's film portrays a weak Japanese culture that tries to copy American cool rather than a culture revved up with the possibilities of globalization's productive hybridity, a culture that reworks the cool of American culture by lifting it out of its own determinates. In this way, *Lost in Translation* is in a line of American films that represents Japan as out of synch and locked in a losing competition with the US. From Tom Selleck's *Mr. Baseball* (1992) to the Michael Keaton vehicle, *Gung Ho*

(1986), *Lost In Translation* reflects a transnational war of positions in culture.

While this interstate form of cultural imperialism is a rivalry over cultural capital, it can also be a struggle over control of cultural institutions and of national cultures (even though they must be understood as multiple!) that are a part of capital accumulation. In Canada, and particularly during its more cultural nationalist moments, cultural imperialism was understood as structured into the Canadian-USA relationship. The late London Ontario artist Greg Curnoe was driven to produce a work that inverts the stripes of the American flag and replaces the stars with the suggestion "Close the 49th Parallel" (a process that is ironically underway post 9/11, although not for the reasons Curnoe originally had in mind). Post-NAFTA, Curnoe's work takes on a complex temporality, both reflecting its moment, but commenting on the present.

Cultural expansion—via treaties and, in the case of Iraq, by military force—go hand in hand with restrictions and clampdowns on culture internally. The sacking of the National Museum in Baghdad on April 10, 2003, made possible as the "coalition of the willing" guarded the ministry of oil and oil rigs but left key cultural sites unguarded (despite warnings from advisers and archaeologists that museums and libraries would need protecting and despite the museum looting in the 1991 Gulf War), is a cultural example of Harvey's "accumulation by dispossession—an accumulation strategy within the new imperialism" as well as a part of the "inside-outside dialectic" of capitalism.[45] This decidedly old-school imperialist expansion into Iraq has dispossessed the country of its cultural institutions and archives of its cultural history—the National Museum was looted (yet some works have been sleuthed off of the black market and returned), the national library burnt out, and the education system left in ruins. Into this void, American cultural products and models of education continue to be poised to step. Iraq is caught between the "authoritarian statism" (Poulantzas) of Saddam Hussein and the neoliberal weakening of the state as a result of the occupation. Culture, as a sphere where the shape of the state and the role of the public sphere would be debated, has crucially been disassembled.

This disassembling of the institutions and archives of culture, and the intense bombing and segregation that the city of Baghdad has endured, is invoked by Jamelie Hassan's public work *Because … There Was and There Wasn't a City of Baghdad* (1991) at the Morris and Helen Belkin Art Gallery on the campus of the University of British Columbia. The image on the billboard, a cropped cityscape with a copula in the foreground, was first photographed in 1978 when Hassan was in Baghdad studying Arabic. But the billboard itself was generated after the 1991 bombing of Baghdad and the American Desert Storm attack on Iraq. In terms of the temporality of cultural critique that I have been outlining, Hassan's work not only spans (rather than links) the period of air assaults on the city, but it can be read as a chronotope (Mikhail Bakhtin's term for the fusing of time *into* place) of Baghdad. The text of the billboard, *Because … there was and there wasn't a city of Baghdad*, invokes the opening narrative of *One Thousand and One Nights* and asserts Baghdad as a center of Arabic culture: yet it is also a statement that carries a complex temporality that captures the ruin and renewal (or perseverance) of the city. The cruelty of the accuracy of this statement is that the past tense of the phrase not only locates the city in the narrative time of the fable (what Bakhtin called "adventure time") in which the city always exists (albeit in the past), it also points to the present destruction and perseverance of the city.

Shifting this temporality into a relationship with capitalism, and particularly the "shock doctrine" of neoliberalism, the phrase also describes the process of "creative destruction." *Creative destruction* was adopted from a biological term by Joseph Schumpeter in the early 1940s to describe "an essential fact about capitalism." For Schumpeter the continual making and remaking of the economy was not just an *effect* of capitalism but central to capitalism itself: "Capitalism, then, is by nature a form or method of economic change and not only never is but never can be stationary."[46] This change is not simply an evolution, or stage, or progression of the economy, but a process "that incessantly revolutionizes the economic structure *from within*, incessantly destroying the old one, incessantly creating a new one."[47] Isn't this the destructive process that is at work with culture in Iraq? An argument can be put forward that somehow culture *endures*, but it is vital to see culture as also central to the dispossession of national resources, and not merely a form of "collateral damage." *Because … There Was and There Wasn't a City of Baghdad* is a constant reminder of the adventure time of capitalism, a "type of time," that, as Bakhtin notes, "merges only at points of rupture … in normal, real-life, 'law-abiding' temporal sequences."[48] This is the time of "creative destruction," "the shock doctrine," and "the state of exception."

Creative Practice versus Creative Destruction

If cultural imperialism is a central aspect of the new imperialism, and works through various forms of dispossession and creative destruction—both materially and philosophically—new cultural strategies counter this process in ways that can angle toward explanation and toward an understanding of how social relations are determined and how neoliberalism has narrowed the imagination of the social by narrowing the definition and possibility of culture (that is, as Mitchell argues, looking at how culture itself is determined). Bruce Andrews, in writing of the possibilities of poetry and poetics similarly proposes a grasping of the limits of cultural practices and social limits as a determining and, more optimistically, a guiding factor: "The grasp of these social limits can help to define the projected future of the [poetic] work."[49] In this frame, I'd like to identify two types of critical cultural practices that grasp at social limits: one type that counters the claims and ideology of neoliberalism; and one that is more spatial, engaging with particular globalized contexts or localized struggles at the scale of the nation and below. These two types of creative practice are not disarticulated, indeed they can overlap in a joining of a particular scale with ideological issues.

As an example of creative practice that addresses neoliberalism and universal capitalism yet is grounded in a region, Larissa Lai's speculative fiction novel *Salt Fish Girl* describes a futuristic and fully destabilized Pacific Northwest of North America where the region has broken down to a section called "Serendipity" and another, "The Unregulated Zone." In this corporate landscape, Nextcorp has bought out the Diverse Genome Project and used the DNA of "so-called

Third World" laborers mixed in with fish DNA to clone
a variety of workers. One group manufactures shoes in the
sweatshops of Pallas shoes. The Sonias, as this worker clone
is called, begin to organize themselves and start sending out
anti-capitalist messages imprinted on the very soles of the
shoes they make:

> I noticed the footprints when the unpaved shoulder
> gave way to newly poured sidewalk, all kinds of
> footprints, from all kinds of shoes and boots. Because
> I was not on foot myself, I didn't notice that some left
> a textual imprint behind … The wet soles of the shoes
> functioned like rubber stamps, the wet mud like ink
> … One set of footprints was just a price list:
> *materials: 10 units*
> *labour: 3 units*
> *retail price: 169 units*
> *profit: 156 units*
> *Do you care?*[50]

While *Salt Fish Girl* can be read as both a narrative that
explains our present globalization through an allegorical
move to a future anti-globalization dystopia with its focus
on the power of corporations and the absence of nation-
states, it also carries an anti-capitalist perspective that is
braced through explanation. In the scene above, the labor
theory of value is made material and visual: by illustrating by
the price list that outlines the equation of surplus capital,
Lai firmly places this type of exploitation within the machi-
nations of capitalism—as part of "the crisis in activity that
globalization seeks to globalize" (Hitchcock)—rather than
an effect of isolated corporate greed and sweatshop out-
sourcing that leads to an apology, a vow to shift production
sources, and monitoring by an NGO. Here cause and effect
are stamped together.

This strain of anti-capitalism in *Salt Fish Girl* also has
a Utopian impulse, for, as Fredric Jameson concludes in
Archaeologies of the Future, "it is still difficult to see how future
Utopias could ever be imagined in any dissolution from
socialism in its larger sense of anti-capitalism."[51] *Salt Fish
Girl*'s moment of rupture, its revolution, marks the shift
from the dystopic to the utopic by imagining an ideological

and organized resistance that springs from productive forces—the Sonias—to counter the zombie passivity of the consumer citizen in the novel. Here *Salt Fish Girl* fits Jameson's proposition that

> Any formal solution [to producing new versions of utopia's tensions] will, then, need to take into account both the historic-originalities of late capitalism … and the emergence, as well, of new subjectivities [52]

In the emergence of new formations of old subjectivities (for the Sonias are "workers" and new technologically produced subjects), *Salt Fish Girl* unties a bind in one formation of identity politics. The Sonias, clones from the same corporate Petri dish, find unity through their exploitation by Pallas, and establish their collective identities and resistance on that. The unregulated or guerilla society that they set up is based on their common identity—a common identity literally *produced* outside of them—as exact clones. This inside-outside politics troubles the dichotomy of the universal and the particular while fusing the politics of identity with a class-based point of production organizing: that is, as Jameson poetically captures it, "The collectivity is thus inside of us, fully as much as it is outside us, in the multiple social worlds we also inhabit all at once."[53]

A gallery installation project from The Speculative Archive (a collaborative project from Los Angeles between Julia Meltzer and David Thorne) addresses past collectivities attached to specific places, times, and utterances rather than future utopian collectivities. The full title is *Free the, Demand Your, We Want, All Power to the, We Must, Stop the, End All, Don't, Fuck the, The People Will, You Can't, Those Who, Women Are, If You, Resistance Is: some positions and slogans recollected from an archive of political posters* (2002). This installation universalizes forms of social protest—and the conditions that give rise to the protest—through a two-part reading process that engages the social imagination and memory of the viewer. Small monochrome text-paintings provide a neutral description of, but not an image of, protest posters that range from the SILENCE=DEATH Project, the anti-Vietnam Art Worker's Coalition, the Black Panthers, etc.

The text-paintings simply and clearly describe the slogans, but do not quote them. This invokes a strange act of reading through displacement as these descriptions lead one to a recognition of the poster and the possible slogan as well as to one's own position ideologically (or historically) in relation to the poster and that particular struggle. It is a curious experience of social amnesia in reverse in which reading brings back the loaded context: you recall the familiarity of the poster or the slogan, recall your relationship (if any) to the struggle it boosted. A sound element based on the "seemingly endless calls to action" drawn from the posters plays in the gallery space:

> Would you buy a used war from this man? Si, se puede. The Vietnamese never froze my wages. When history cannot be written with a pen, it must be written with a gun. Support the copper strikers. Join the campaign for human rights for all immigrants. Free Los Tres. Attica. Make love not war. Join el movimiento … again. Was your shirt made by Guatemalan women making $3 an hour? The time is now to smash Jim Crow. Let's rap rap. Stop child labor. Don't buy grapes or Gallo wine. Ahora es cuando. For all these rights, we've just begun to fight …

The list of approx. 250 slogans ends with "Never again," and then starts up again. The temporality of this installation is not a bleak looping of oppression, but an insistence on the structural necessity of protest and resistance, a different creative destruction.

Such creative practices also operate out of a social necessity. As consent has taken over the North American mainstream media, and as the mass media is widely understood to have missed the key questions that surround the invasion of Iraq—as comic Stephen Colbert's address to the White House Correspondents dinner in 2006 sharply satirized—there has been a rise of semantically dense, information laden, cultural production. Visual art, poetry, and documentaries in particular, have stepped in to provide a range of information that has been withheld from, or distorted within the public sphere. This has emerged in the last years in the prominence of critical documentary films becoming popular, even approaching box-office hits, and the impulse toward relaying the context and intensity of localized and regional struggles and conditions that was displayed in *documenta 11*, curated by Okwui Enwezor. Another part of this is demonstrated in the type of remining of the archive of social struggle that the Speculative Archive engage in and a rise of works that record or socially map information.

Addressing the bad side of the connectivity of globalization—and doing it in relation to the invisibility of many of these connections—Mark Lombardi's drawings of corporate or governmental "narrative structures" appear more as linked and looped lines forming a global flight path of corruption. Lombardi gathers massive amounts of information from the media on "the interaction of political, social and economic forces in contemporary affairs," as he puts it in an artist statement. The connections he traces out form the titles of the drawings: *banca nazionale del lavaro, reagan, bush, thatcher, and the arming of iraq, c. 1979–90* (1990), *pat robertson, beurt servaas and the UPI takeover battle c. 1985–91* (2000), and *george w. bush, harken energy, and jackson stevens c. 1979–90* (1999). The results are dense map-like loops of connections that are part a world systems narrative (with the title of each work demarcating that world) and part conspiracy theory grids. Here, mapping as a form of knowledge is used to produce dense and opaque narratives to relations that generally remain invisible. In a similar form and impulse, the Bureau d'études from France have initiated a *World Monitoring Atlas* (2003), which provides maps of global issues and resistance groups.

Outside of galleries, political theater also provides a media platform for information that does not circulate in the public. Tricycle Theatre in London, for instance, mounted a play simply titled *Guantanamo* (2004), which uses the letters home from "the detainees," as well and the testimonies recorded after the release of political prisoners from Guantanamo Bay. In an art context, a multi-channel video installation, *9 Scripts From a Nation at War* produced by Andrea Geyer, Sharon Hayes, Ashley Hunt, Katya Sanders, and David Thorne for *documenta 12* (2007) also derives its scripts from the military tribunals at Guantanamo Bay, as well as interviews of American soldiers, blog entries from

soldiers active in Iraq, and other public blogs. These scripts were read by actors in various locations, and each of the scripts (comprising around nine hours of video in total) is an edited mix from the various source materials. Each script circulates around the relationship of speaking and speech, reporting and reportage, and writing and position-taking, while destabilizing or displacing the narration and positioning generated by the speech or text: the video aims to break the expectations, or frames, of the gathered material.
The initial displacement is achieved through the medium of video, but also through various formal devises such as the mannerisms of actors reading written text, the writing of recorded speech on a blackboard, the non-correlation of the identity of the actor reading with the self-description of the author, multiple readings of the same text by different actors, and staged readings of press conferences. Operating through these defamiliarizing devices, *9 Scripts from a Nation at War* breaks the seams between media reception and accepted fact, and between media presentation and affective fact: the dropping out of affect by the form of the readings and the various displacements, blocks the generation of Massumi's "affective fact." And in that gap between affect and fact, critique steps in.

As *9 Scripts from a Nation at War* shows, the nation as a scale of critique has emerged strongly post-9/11, but the nation is still a troubled scale when it comes to the type of "revolution" that is imagined in *Salt Fish Girl*. Gerald Raunig argues that,

> Even though … variations of national revolts still take place, from the separatist regional insurrections and the African civil wars of recent decades, to South American examples in Argentina and Venezuela, to the insurrectionary aspects of the protests against right-wing governments in Europe, the phenomenon of the national revolt today seems to have become too large and too small at the same time.[54]

There is a temporality to Raunig's spatial problem of the nation being both "too large and too small": the nation is too "old" as a site for transformation, having missed its chance before we proceeded to a post-national view of globalization; yet the nation is also too "new," for it is still imagined as a bound container, an absolute space, from which a revolution spurred by new social movements, which do not necessarily aim to seize the state, cannot spread (whose "less spectacular uprisings" are overshadowed by mass media coverage of the spectacular national scale, Raunig agues).

Yet, national uprisings are vexed by neoliberal politics as well as scale. This theoretical scale blockage and temporal problem is reflected in the particular case of Venezuela, the "oil-rich" nation that has been historically deeply divided by poverty and the structural inequalities of colonialism (which are not memories, but extremely present). Since the election and reelections of Hugo Chávez as president (although obviously less so after his recent death), Venezuela has been a bullhorn for the rejection of the globalized neoliberal project at the national scale, which has drawn a responding call of populism to the regime. Countering neoliberalism, the "Bolivarian Revolution" ("el proceso" as it is called locally) has renationalized the oil industry and moved toward securing resources as common good and toward the redistribution of national wealth through literacy and health projects. At a regional scale, Venezuela has done such reverse structural adjustments as loaning other nations in the region money to pay off their World Bank debts and withdraw from this neoliberal sphere of influence. Politically there has been an emphasis on participatory democracy that is constitutionally enacted, rather than a reliance on individual participation in liberal democracy. Yet both Right and Left overlap at points with their view of Chávez as a strongman increasingly detached from grassroots movements. What is overlooked by both sides, is the potential of a nation-scale project that falls outside of conventional histories and turns back to the potentials of anti-colonial nationalisms, but within the long neoliberal moment. As Partha Chatterjee argued more than ten years ago, these nationalisms carry a powerful, creative, and historically significant project and can today be turned against the neoliberalization of the state.[55]

Yet cultural engagement with this anti-neoliberal project (at the national scale and beyond) is so symbolically weighted due to Venezuela's failure to fit into a post-Marxian account of revolution laid out through Hardt and Negri's rejection of closure, that a controversy flared up at the show *Now-Time Venezuela: Media Along the Path of the Bolivarian Process* at the University of California, Berkeley Museum, in 2006. The curator, Chris Gilbert, resigned from his position when the gallery asked that the curatorial statement—the benign welcoming wall text of the exhibition, asserting that the show was "in solidarity" with the Bolivarian process that had "evolved from a modest critique of neoliberalism to a broad and internationalist plan for socialism for the 21st century,"[56] be changed. Despite the softened use of "process" instead of "revolution," the gallery asked for a shift from "in solidarity" to the nonaligned and neutral "concerning." The ensuing tussle, played out over the international critical art scene via the internet, led to Gilbert's departure. What is compelling here is that Gilbert's formation of the "now-time" of Venezuela complicates a temporality of critique that imagines the nation as out of time as a site of social transformation. The temporality of social transformation itself is a future horizon and holds its power exactly in this futurity (and this is perhaps why speculative fiction has so strongly been the negative dialectical space that holds the imagination of "other worlds").

The temporality of the Bolivarian revolution in Venezuela itself has been uneven, but a key speech act by Hugo Chávez in 1992 saw a social and political weight cohere around it. At the beginning of February 1992, Chávez, then a colonel, coordinated a coup with other army officers against President Pérez. Yet, as the government caught wind of the coup beforehand and the military had failed to ultimately bring in sufficient civilian participation, the attempt fell apart as Chávez, with his soldiers, tried to take the Historical Museum in Caracas (which was to be their communications center). After surrendering to the inevitable, Chávez was asked to go on national television to draw the coup down and ask the other colonels to surrender. His very brief speech (just over a minute) addressed the colonels and citizens but, as a speech act, addressed to the future: Chávez said,

> Comrades: unfortunately, for the moment, the
> objectives that we have set ourselves have not been

achieved in the capital. That is to say that those of us here in Caracas have not been able to seize power.[57]

With this temporal turn, "for the moment" or *por ahora* in Spanish, Chávez had set up the futurity of the seizure of power. As Richard Gott describes it, *por ahora* "caught the popular imagination," and "this was read by most people optimistically: as a sign that Chávez would return to the struggle at some later date."[58] While this speech act may have touched off a futurity in a more linear way than Benjamin's less causal "now-time," the temporality of social transformation is multiple (rather than linear or nonlinear), which is precisely why neoliberalism seeks to limit the multiplicities of history in order to lock in the present (even as the neoliberal dream of a market "now-time" falls away under its own edifices!).

At the heart of the cultural Left's hesitation toward Venezuela as a *process* is the relationship between Negri's categories of constituent power and constituted power (see Raunig for an extended discussion in relation to art), which pits an open-ended constituent power-in-process that resists closure, against a constituted power that figures as the opposite in that it has an end game of closure at the levels of the state and below. Jon Beasley-Murray summarizes these positions in a recent commentary in *Radical Philosophy*:

> The alternative is less the tired choice between social democracy and populism, and more the question as to whether we are seeing the emergence of a new form of governmentality sealed by a renovated social pact, or whether by contrast this is but the start of a radically open process in which all pacts and contracts are kept permanently in suspense. Is this a renegotiation of the postcolonial settlement designed above all to relegitimate the state and its institutions? Or is it the rebellion of a multitude, a historical inversion in which what Simon Critchley would call "infinitely demanding" social movements ensure that any attempt at hegemonic closure is now perpetually deferred?[59]

From Raunig's position, the Bolivarian revolution initiated a

> two-fold process in which a grassroots social revolu-
> tion was to be impelled ... [and] the institutions of the
> state were to be made functional again within the
> framework of a process of re-institutionalization.[60]

Yet in Raunig's reckoning, Venezuela falls outside of the
triad of the revolutionary machine because it "stands more
for a consistent radicalization of the ideas of constitutional
law" and has, in a manner, mistaken (or worse, displaced)
the national constitution (as a process) for constituent
power. The poetics of this analysis parallel the dynamic
moments of poetry avant-gardes after the textual turn.
Following a critique of language and power, these movements forced the homology between language and social
order, where a radically open text leaps across a chain of
possibilities toward a rejection of closure at the social and
political level. Raunig's synthesis of Negri's constituent
power could ring as a slogan of a radical poetics:

> Constituent power means here the permanent
> conflictual exchange of differences and, at the same
> time, the potentiality of a radical reformation of
> social organization, which conjoins the rupture in
> the event with an uninterrupted formation process.[61]

Aiming at politicizing the act of reading across the social
field, the Language Poets (a North American avant-garde
formation that began in the late 1970s) worked through
a temporal dialectic of "at the same time": a dialectic of an
open poetic text and a closed social text, a dialectic of
constituent power (of the reader) and constituted power
(of language understood as homology for social order), and a
dialectic of radical openness at the level of form punctuated
with counter-hegemonic moments of "closure" at the level
of the phrase. The result was some of the most politically
and aesthetically engaging poetry of the 1980s. Coming out
of the fertile possibilities of this moment is the long poem
Fantasies in Permeable Structures. In this book, Laura Elrick
steps into the overdetermined time of *representations* of
Venezuela, and Chávez, into the social project under foot.

But this poem also forcefully spatializes a transnational subject that is grounded in the everyday social reproduction of a life in New York, while being acutely tied into a global anti-capitalist ethos that is philosophical, ethical, aesthetic, and affective. The subject in this poem moves through the literal city space (one of the many permeable structures in the poem) as well as discursively carved and linked spaces of this hemispheric anti-neoliberalism. Within this broad and densely structured poem, one section turns to the representations of Venezuela in both the mainstream media and within left cultural discourses. In one view, this is a turn to an avant-garde publicness. Yet, in a more contemporaneous and social manner, Elrick dodges into a pointed engagement with the "news."

Through a diachronic analysis of the dominant frames of meaning utilized by media representations of Venezuela, Jules Boykoff shows that a set of shuffling frames produce an image of "Chávez" as a "jack-booted" populist thwarting democracy and running though Venezuelan wealth with ill-conceived policies. Boykoff identifies four dominant media frames from the last nine years: the Dictator Frame, the Castro Disciple Frame, the Declining Economy Frame, and the Meddler-in-the-Region Frame. Elrick's critique of media frames and of relationship of the state to social transformation troubles the binary of constituent *or* constituted power:

> … When radical claims
> are dupes for big media as in the *Tropical*
> *Fascism* [sic] of Chávez because some
> struggles never wither out of the state. It's
> *Strange, this military's for popular reform …*
> *The soldiers found they workers were …*
> *If oligarchs are people too (it's oh so true)*
> *The "thug" can also* back *be thrown …*
> To redistribute centuries of siphoned wealth
> what're the odds? And *that* in the same
> //
> hemisphere as Texas!⁶²

The result is a long poem whose extended publicness takes on other public discourses such as *The Washington Post* (a paper particularly rattled by Venezuela) as well as the more secret publicities (see Lütticken) of the cultural sphere that had such difficulty in breaking the frames of the dominant media. Yet Elrick also foregrounds the power of the dominant media to frame social movements in a manner that entraps the left cultural critique, or with which they unintentionally overlap. By spatializing the politics ("And *that* in the same // hemisphere as Texas!"), Elrick gives a greater *actual* geopolitical frame rather than a frame determined by a particular philosophical debate regarding the nation—this is not a crude materialist versus discursive analysis, but rather a realpolitik that acknowledges the mess and excess of any social process.

These examples of creative practice against the logic of neoliberalism and against the turns and returns of imperialism foreground cultural production and cultural knowledge within a social project. These works, and the impulse of using cultural representation as a method of altering the temporality of critique, can be situated as both timely and untimely gestures. Wendy Brown eloquently defines a trajectory of a "time for critical theory" through Walter Benjamin's revision of historical materialism:

> Untimely critique that seeks to speak to our time
> is launched not from outside time, or indifferently
> to the times, but rather from historical materialism
> in control of its powers and wielded as a power.[63]

While not outside time in a materialist sense, several of the works I have pulled in try to step outside a dominant conception of time in order to find an opening to address the present. In the four problematics of critical theory that Brown develops, this corresponds to her third, a "thinking against the age, or being untimely."[64] This untimeliness is doubled however; one move is to think against the structures of feeling that both shape and are shaped by the present (and its longer cohesion), and the second is to *rethink* or refigure the very temporality of the times. That is, to counter the inevitability of the present. A focus on a social horizon not solely determined by a temporality that puts liberal democracy and the market as the only possible future ignites this doubleness.

[1] Arif Dirlik, *Global Modernity: Modernity in the Age of Global Capital*, Paradigm Press, Boulder, Colorado 2007, p. 102.

[2] Ibid., p 103–104.

[3] Retort, *Afflicted Powers: Capital and Spectacle in a New Age of War*, Verso, London/New York 2006, p. 9.

[4] Ibid., p. 9.

[5] Ibid., p.18.

[6] Michael Ignatieff, *Empire Lite: Nation-Building in Bosnia, Kosovo, and Afghanistan*, Penguin, Toronto 2003, p106. Originally published as "The Burden," *New York Times Magazine*, (January 5, 2003).

[7] Fred Moten, "The New International of Decent Feelings," *Social Text*, 20.3 (2002), p. 189–199.

[8] Neil Smith, *The Endgame of Globalization*, Routledge, New York 2005, p. 44–45.

[9] Naomi Klein, The Shock Doctrine: The Rise of Disaster Capitalism, Alfred A. Knopf, Toronto 2007.

[10] Eric Lott, *The Disappearing Liberal Intellectual*, Basic Books, New York 2007, p. 184.

[11] Timothy Brennan, "The Empire's New Clothes," *Critical Inquiry* 29:2 (Winter 2003), p. 337–368.

[12] Gayatri Chakravorty Spivak, *A Critique of Postcolonial Reason: Toward a History of the Vanishing Present*, Harvard University Press, Cambridge, Massachusetts 1999, p. 101.

[13] Ibid., p. 102.

[14] Michael Ignatieff, "The American Empire: The Burden," *New York Times Magazine* (5 January 2003). http://www.nytimes.com/2003/01/05/magazine/the-american-empire-the-burden.html?pagewanted=all&src=pm (last accessed July 2013).

[15] Rey Chow, *Ethics After Idealism: Theory—Culture—Ethnicity—Reading*, University of Indiana Press, Bloomington, Indiana 1998, p. 4.

[16] Raymond Williams, *The Long Revolution*, Harper Torchbooks, New York 1961, p. 46.

[17] Raymond Williams, *Marxism and Literature*, Oxford University Press, Oxford 1977, p. 17.

[18] Don Mitchell, "The End of Culture? Culturalism and Cultural Geography in the Anglo-American 'University of Excellence,'" *Geographische Revue* (Germany), 2 (2) (2000), p. 3–17

[19] Ibid., p. 9.

[20] Ibid., p. 10.

[21] Don Mitchell, "There's No Such Thing as Culture: Towards a Reconceptualisation of the Idea of Culture in Geography," *Transactions of the Institute of British Geographers*, 19 (1995), p. 102–116.

[22] Mitchell, "The End of Culture?" p. 3–17.

[23] Ibid., p. 11 (quotation of Terry Eagleton).

[24] Ray Chow, *Ethics After Idealism*, p. xiv.

[25] Ibid.

[26] Ignatieff, "America's Empire is an Empire Lite," *New York Times*, January 10, 2003, http://www.globalpolicy.org/component/content/article/154/25603.html (last accessed July 2013).

[27] Michael Lebowitz, *Beyond Capital: Marx's Political Economy of the Working Class*, Palgrave MacMillan, Houndsmill 2003.

[28] Peter Hitchcock, *Imaginary States: Studies in Cultural Transnationalism*, University of Illinois Press, Urbana 2003, p. 194.

[29] Ibid., p. 185–186.

[30] Mohammed A. Bamyeh, *The Ends of Globalization*, University of Minnesota Press, Minneapolis 2000.

[31] Ellen Meiksins Wood, *Empire of Capital*, Verso, London 2004, p. 126.

[32] Ibid., p. 141.

[33] Ibid., p 127.

[34] Brian Massumi, "The Future Birth of the Affective Fact," http://browse.reticular.info/text/collected/massumi.pdf, p. 1 (last accessed July 2013).

[35] Ibid., p. 1.

[36] Brian Massumi, "Fear (The Spectrum Said)," *Positions* 13:1 (2008), p. 31–48.

[37] Ibid., p. 32.

[38] Ibid., p. 31.

[39] Massumi, "The Future Birth of the Affective Fact," p. 8.

[40] For a very different reading of Terada's *Five Coloured Words in Neon*, see William Wood, "Offensive," *Public* 28 (2003), p. 84–97. Locating it in a trajectory of conceptual art, Wood reads the context of this work through Nauman, Kosuth, and a critique from Jeff Wall. Ultimately Wood writes, "*Five Coloured Words in Neon* takes the embodiment of bureaucracy in the Homeland Security Advisory System, the nostalgic publicness of neon signage, and the tainted 'academicism' of the reference to Kosuth in order to compose an image of the likenesses, continuities, and also the incommensurate influence of each of these components to give the impression that conceptual art's 'bad faith' compact was with the masterminds of the Vietnam War; yet Terada follows this misprision" (96). This leaves Terada's work as a representation of the "withering-away of the energies and the analysis which saw through the cant and linked together the components of the 'war machine,' making the linkages public" (96), yet toward an ineffective gesture.

[41] Sven Lütticken, "Attending to Abstract Things," *New Left Review*, 54 (November/December 2008), p. 101–122.

[42] Ernst Bloch, "The Meaning of Utopia," Maynard Solomon (ed.), *Marxism and Art: Essays Classic and Contemporary*, Alfred A. Knopf, New York 1973, p. 581.

[43] Junya Ishii, "'Cool' Japan: Spreading Japanese Pop Culture in the United States," http://www.us.emb-japan.go.jp/english/html/embassy/otherstaff_ishii1115.htm (last accessed July 2013).

[44] Douglas McGray, "Japan's Gross National Cool," *Foreign Policy* (May/June 2002), p. 44–54.

[45] David Harvey, *The New Imperialism*, Oxford UP, Oxford, 2003, p. 140–141.

[46] Joseph Schumpeter, *Capitalism, Socialism and Democracy* (1942), Harper, New York 1975, p. 82.

[47] Ibid.

[48] M.M. Bakhtin, *The Dialogic Imagination: Four Essays*, trans. Caryl Emerson, Michael Holquist, University of Texas Press, Austin 1981, p. 152.

[49] Bruce Andrews, *Paradise & Method: Poetics & Praxis*, Northwestern University Press, Evanston, Illinois 1996, p. 41.

[50] Larrisa Lai, *Salt Fish Girl*, Thomas Allen Publishers, Toronto 2002, p. 238.

[51] Fredric Jameson, *Archaeologies of the Future: The Desire Called Utopia and Other Science Fictions*, Verso, London 2005, p. 196–197.

[52] Ibid., p. 214.

[53] Ibid.

[54] Gerald Raunig, *Art and Revolution: Transversal Activism in the Long Twentieth Century*, trans. Ailen Derieg, Semiotext(e), Los Angeles 2007, p. 57.

[55] Partha Chatterjee, "Whose Imagined Community?" Gopal Balakrishnan and Benedict Anderson (eds.), *Remapping the Nation*, Routledge, New York 1996, p. 214–225.

[56] Dario Azzellini and Oliver Ressler, *Now-Time Venezuela: Media Along the Path of the Bolivarian Process*, BAM/PFA, Berkeley, California 2006. Not paginated.

[57] Richard Gott, *Hugo Chávez and the Bolivarian Revolution*, Verso, New York 2005, p.70–71.

[58] Ibid., p. 70.
[59] Jon Beasley-Murray, "Fear of Heights: Bolivia's constitu-
       ent process," *Radical Philosophy* 148 (March/April 2008),
       p. 2–6.
[60] Raunig, *Art and Revolution*, p. 64.
[61] Ibid., p. 254.
[62] Laura Elrick, *Fantasies in Permeable Structures*, Factory
       School 2005, p. 57–58.
[63] Wendy Brown, *Edgework: Critical essays on Knowledge and
       Politics*, Princeton University Press, Princeton, New Jersey
       2005, p. 14.
[64] Ibid.

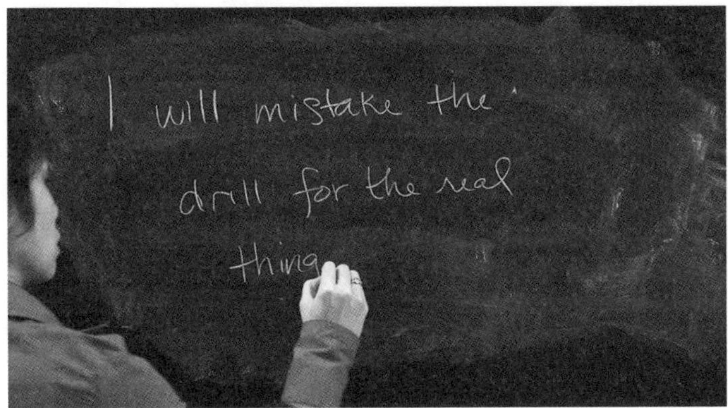

Andrea Geyer (with David Thorne, Katya Sander, Ashley Hunt, and Sharon Hayes),
Script: Citizen: 248 predictions of what I will do when democracy comes. 9 Scripts from a Nation at War, 2007
Installation with 10 videos (HDV), color, sound, 75 minutes

For Now: On Holly Ward's
Persistence of Vision

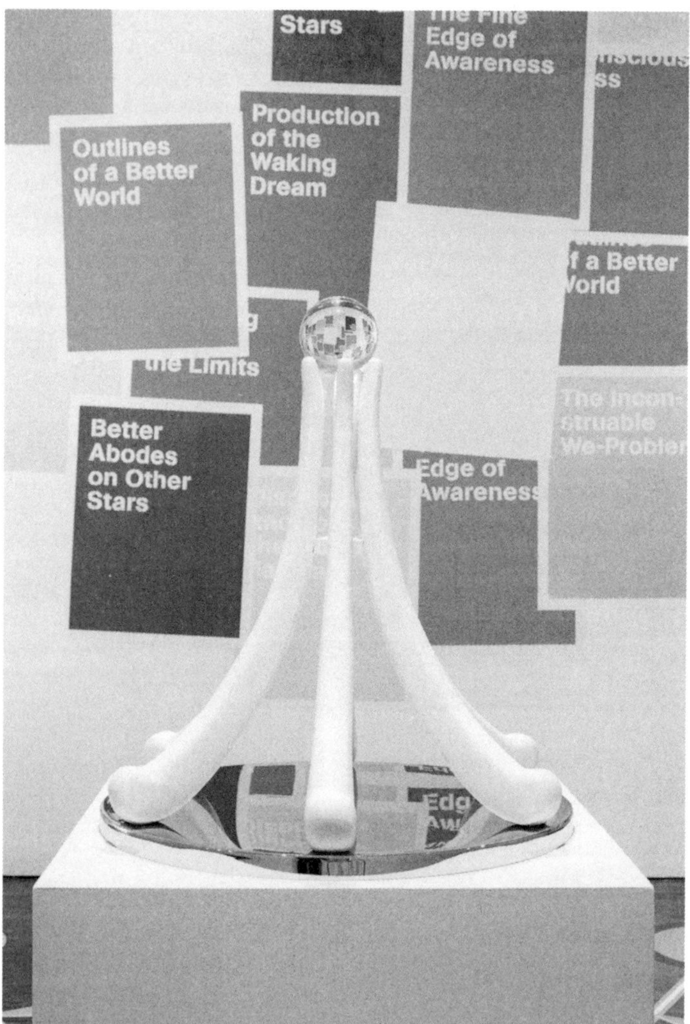

Holly Ward, *Persistence of Vision*, 2011
Installation detail

Yellow, blue, green, gold, silver,
and pink silk-screened signs
carrying appropriated slogans
from the utopian thinker Ernst
Bloch spill out of Artspeak's space,
accentuating the division of
inside and outside, of common
and enclosed spaces. These signs
disperse onto Carrall Street,
a newly demarcated border
in Vancouver's urban geography.
For several years, Artspeak's
programming has gone onto the
streets as well, initiating acts
of artistic publicness against the
embourgeoisment of this block
by the *big window gentrification* of
restaurants that extend their
inside onto the street. In this city,
where acts of publicness make
the heads of the town, and the top
of the cops, nervous to the point
of seeing ghostly images, past and
present, of "anarchists" at every
moment, it is culture, activism,
and affect that generate rare
chances to assert non-administered
publicness.[1]

Holly Ward's *Persistence of Vision* (2011) takes a semiotic spatial act of publicness to draw contour lines between the gallery space, utopian urban visions, and the recent explosion toward social transformation, sparked in Tahrir Square in Cairo, Egypt, that has spread across the Arab world.

> From Tunisia to Egypt to Libya, to Yemen … to Morocco and to Bahrain, and, yes, even now to Syria, the young and brave have told the world they want freedom. And freedom, over the coming weeks and months, they will undoubtedly obtain,

the reporter Robert Fisk wrote in March.[2] Yet history has not been as hopeful as Fisk and the spontaneous uprisings. This great hope appears stalled and unfolding in a more predictable manner than it began. These calls for transformation, which are national in scale, began at the urban level and have hit difficulties as they jumped from city to city— particularly in Libya, where cities have become fronts in a civil war, or in Syria where the cities are sites of intensified repression.

Bahrain, from which Ward draws the central imagery for this show, is another story: calls for freedom and democracy have been oppressed by that nation's security forces as well as troops from the Gulf Cooperation Council— "military riff-raff," as Fisk calls them, crossing the bridge from Saudi Arabia.[3] In Bahrain, Pearl Square became the focal point of the protests, the space that countered the dictatorial governmental space. Its name is derived from a 100-meter monument that commemorated the main industry of the Gulf region before oil brought wealth into petro-plutocracies: the six curved spires that held the "pearl" at the apex represented the six nations whose troops were now brought in as a show of force.[4] The monument reflected this particular history of the region, yet its aesthetics balanced the grand symbolism of public monuments with a universal monumentalizing of prosperity, pride, and futurity.[5] The protestors appropriated the monument's symbolism, shifting it from economic development to political futurity, as a result of which the state pulled it down. Ward has rescaled and reproduced this monument with a futuristic twist: the pearl is now a transparent globe,

a light-reflecting orb held high. Altered in this way,
the monument could be placed into fictional utopian urban
spaces such as the city in Ursula K. Le Guin's utopian-
dystopian classic, *The Dispossessed* (1974), or Kim Stanley
Robinson's anti-capitalist epic *Red Mars* (1992). Appropriately,
the plinth that holds the sculpture is set on a diagrammatic
floor design referring to utopian city designs. This crucial
detail illustrates the centrality of cities to the utopian
tendencies that Ward, via Ernst Bloch, brings to the project.

Bloch argues against a denigration of utopias by
proposing that utopias intensify tendencies to come
that already exist in our present, but which are unformed.
Therefore utopias project tendencies into the future
via a "concrete utopia" (Bloch's term) that both anticipates
and affects the future. As Ruth Levitas writes,

> Concrete utopia, on the other hand, is anticipatory
> rather than compensatory. It reaches forward to
> a real possible future, and it involves not merely
> wishful thinking.[6]

This contrasts an "abstract utopia" that is compensatory
wishful thinking not backed by willful action.

Looked at from Bloch's perspective and from the
historical view of utopia, two utopian tendencies emerge
from this exhibition—the spatial and the temporal.
The spatial tendency of utopia has historically begun with
a negation; that utopia, as the Greek root of the word points
to, is "no place." But *Persistence of Vision*, in its linking of the
urban sites of the Arab Spring and the streets of Vancouver,
where Bloch's words resonate on the posters, poses
a question regarding the *where* of utopia. Do we in the global
north continually look elsewhere, and compulsively to the
global south, for the possibility of utopia? From the shifts in
forms of democracy in Latin America and now to the Arab
Spring, it seems *elsewhere* holds the hope of what has become
culturally and socially unimaginable in North America.
This touches off a larger cultural and artistic question for us:
How did we arrive at a moment when utopia can only be
compensatory (or "abstract" in Bloch's terms) and hope
reduced to electioneering?

Yet, in its articulations, *Persistence of Vision* points
to a tendency within our present that gestures to the *where*
of a concrete utopia. Margit Mayer has recently written that,

> we can say that, while the neoliberalisation of the city
> has in many ways created a more hostile environment
> for progressive urban movements, it has also allowed
> for a more global articulation of urban protest: and
> it has brought about a renewed convergence of some
> of these strands under the umbrella of the 'Right
> to the City' slogan.[7]

But the Arab Spring has shown that this "Right to the City"
is not just a slogan that Henri Lefebvre concocted, but
that its scale and outcomes are much more dynamic and
unpredictable. From city squares such as Pearl Square,
to entire urban territories and up to a national imagination
of social transformation across "the Arab world," cities
have become the scale where the utopian tendencies that
Bloch helped illuminate have accelerated. Ward's contour
lines, an aesthetic articulation of signs and sites within
an imagination toward a future that does not willfully ignore
the present, move from city squares to these questions:
Are utopian tendencies now also urban tendencies? And
what, actually, can utopia mean in the present, other than
the possibility of change?

[1]   Some urban critics point to Vancouver's lack of a public square as a reason why the city does not have a "natural" gathering point, but this design question seeks to spatialize rather than politicize publicness.

[2]   Robert Fisk, "Right across the Arab world, freedom is now a prospect," *The Independent*, http://www.independent.co.uk/opinion/commentators/fisk/robert-fisk-right-across-the-arab-world-freedom-is-now-a-prospect-2248975.html (last accessed July 2013).

[3]   Ibid.

[4]   Ethan Bonner, "Bahrain Tears Down Monument as Protesters Seethe," *New York Times*, www.nytimes.com/2011/03/19/world/middleeast/19bahrain.html (last accessed July 2013).

[5]   In this way, the monument has a resemblance to Soviet-era symbols of futurity and prosperity *in the present*: I'm thinking particularly of the 1980 Olympics emblem for the boycotted Moscow Games: sweeping spires holding aloft a star.

[6]   Ruth Levitas, "Educated Hope: Ernst Bloch on Abstract and Concrete Utopia," Jamie Owen Daniel, Tom Moylan (eds.), *Not Yet: Reconsidering Ernst Bloch*, Verso, London 1997, p. 67.

[7]   Margit Mayer, *Social Movements in the (Post-)Neoliberal City*, Civic City Cahier 1, Bedford Press, London 2010, p. 29.

Slogans for Slade and Vancouver

All that is air
Solidifies into "air credits."

Beneath the paving stones
Indian land!

The developers develop
The envelope of their Dream City.

Nature: what have you done
For me?

We will, we will
Evict you!

Keep your hands off my
Conceptual art collection!

Acknowledgments

As a collection of essays gathered over a period of time—
in this case from 2003 to 2012—this book is a collaboration
of people and places. Firstly it is a collaboration with Kathy
Slade, editor of Emily Carr University Press and the editor
of this collection, who first asked me to devise a book from
existing essays and then encouraged directions and engagements for other texts. Kathy's own collaborations with
Christoph Keller and Lionel Bovier lead to the book being
graciously included in the Documents Series at JRP|Ringier.
This book is also the conversations with many artists,
writers, and editors in Vancouver, Vienna, and New York,
where I have been fortunate enough to live and work,
including Lyndl Hall and Michael Barnholden who tied the
text together when the text got tough. Secondly, this book
reflects collaboration with the artists whose work I write
about, and marks both the occasions for these texts and
the outcomes of longer conversations and friendships. And,
thirdly, this book gathers collaborative texts that I have
written with Christian Parenti and the late Neil Smith—two
people whose work and spirit I admire greatly. Neil's death
was, and continues to be, a great loss to critical thought and
revolutionary spirit—this book is dedicated to him and to
the community of writers, activists, and artists who work in
the spaces that he imagined, produced, bent, and defended.
And, lastly this book holds the textures of conversations
with many people— Jules Boykoff, Reinhard Braun, Clint
Burnham, Cindi Katz, Bart Lootsma, Kristina Lee Podesva,
the late Nancy Shaw, and Helmut Weber, among others—
and most significantly Sabine Bitter, whose support,
suggestions, impatience, and sincerity fueled the writing of
these texts.

I would also like to formally acknowledge The
Canada Council for the Arts for financial support during
the writing and editing of this book. Likewise, research
was funded by Simon Fraser University, and the Spanish
Ministry of Economy and Competitiveness, through
the Project Globalized Cultural Markets: the Production,
Circulation and Reception of Difference (Reference
FFI2010-17282), headed by Dr. Belén Martín-Lucas.

Text Credits and Acknowledgments

"How High Is the City, How Deep Is Our Love?"
This text was commissioned by *Fillip* magazine and was
published in *Fillip* 12, 2010. It was also published and as Fillip
Edition pamphlet. Thanks to Jeff Khonsary and Kristina
Lee Podesva.

"Art and Cities During Mega-Events: The Olympics in
Vancouver and Beyond"
Originally published as four columns to cover the cultural
scene in Vancouver during the 2010 Winter Olympics for
Camera Austria in issues 108/109/110/111 in 2009 and 2010).
Thanks to Christine Frisinghelli and Daniela Billner.
The first column was also printed in the catalogue for
Upon Arrival. Spatial Explorations, curated by Margit Neuhold
at Malta Contemporary Art, 2010.

"Citizens of the [World] [Nation] [City] Unite and Take
Over!"
Catalogue essay for Andrea Geyer, *Parallax*, at the Secession,
Vienna. Published in *Andrea Geyer*, ed. Rike Frank, Vienna:
Secession/Revolver, 2003.

"Fixed City & Mobile Globe: Urban Facts & Global Forces
in Ken Lum's Art"
A catalogue essay for Lum's retrospective show, *Ken Lum
Works in Photography*, at The Canadian Museum of
Contemporary Photography. Published in *Ken Lum Works
in Photography*, Ottawa: National Gallery of Canada, 2002.

"Making and Breaking Neoliberal Spaces"
Catalogue essay with Neil Smith for Sabine Bitter and
Helmut Weber exhibition at Camera Austria. Published
in *Live Like This!: Bitter & Weber*, ed. Reinhard Braun, Graz:
Camera Austria, 2005.

"The Flâneur Could Not Take the Monorail: Representing
Vancouver in Three Temporalities"
A text regarding Dennis McNulty's work *skytrain/monospan
twin ride*, which was part of the exhibition *The sound I'm
looking for (part 1)* at the Charles H. Scott Gallery, Vancouver,
October 2008, curated by Cate Rimmer.

This essay was subsequently published in *Dennis McNulty 2004–2011: Obscure Flows Boil Underneath*, Dublin: IMMA Associated Press, 2011.

"The Poetics of Bad History"
An altered version of a catalogue essay for Sam Durant's show at Catriona Jeffries Gallery, Vancouver, Canada. Published in *CJ Press: Anthology of Exhibition Essays 2006/2007 Vancouver*, Vancouver: CJ Press, 2008.

"After Big Failures"
A text commissioned by Truck Gallery, Calgary, Canada, for publication in their *Resonant Histories: 25 Years of the Second Story Art Society in Calgary*, Calgary: Truck Contemporary Art, 2009.

"A Geography of the Difficult"
Catalogue essay with Neil Smith for Alfredo Jaar, *Let One Hundred Flowers Bloom?* at Macro, Rome. Published in *Alfredo Jaar*, ed. Dobila Denegri, Rome: Macro Gallery, 2005.

"A Private Riot Going On?"
A catalogue essay with Christian Parenti for the project *European Corrections Corporation*, a container installation by Martin Krenn and Oliver Ressler in Graz and Wels, Austria, in 2003/2004. Published in *European Corrections Corporation*, Graz, Austria/Munich, Germany: 2003.

"National, Global, or Neoliberal Suburb?"
Published in *Uropean Urbanity: Europan 7 and 8*, eds. Bernd Vlay, Paul Rajakovics, Marko Studen, Vienna/New York: Springer, 2006.

"Frontiers of Use"
Published in *Artificial Arcadia*, ed. Ed van Hinte, Rotterdam: 010 Publishers, 2004. Thanks to Michael Lamb of the Center for Place, Culture, and Politics at the City University of New York Graduate Center for research assistance.

"Fugitive Spaces"
An exhibition folder essay for Jin Me Yoon, *Unbidden*, at Catriona Jeffries Gallery, Vancouver, Canada, 2006.

"The Ends of Culture"
A different version of this text is published in the anthology
Transnationalism, Activism, Art, ed. Kit Dobson and Áine
McGlynn: University of Toronto Press, 2012.

"For Now: On Holly Ward's *Persistence of Vision*"
A catalogue essay for Holly Ward's exhibition at Artspeak
Gallery, Vancouver, summer 2011. Published in *Every Force
Evolves a Form*, Vancouver: Artspeak, 2012.

"Slogans for Slade and Vancouver"
This series of up-dated Situationist slogans are for the artist
Kathy Slade, the glam rock band Slade, and the city of
Vancouver. They were published in *Pyramid Power 5* (2008).

Imprint

Edited by Kathy Slade

EDITORIAL COORDINATION AND COPY-EDITING
Michael Barnholden, Lyndl Hall, and Clare Manchester

DESIGN CONCEPT
Gavillet & Rust, Geneva

DESIGN
Rémi Brandon

TYPEFACE
Genath (www.optimo.ch)

PRINT AND BINDING
Présence Graphique, Monts (Indre-et-Loire)

© 2013, the author, the artists, and JRP|Ringier Kunstverlag AG

IMAGES CREDITS
Page 26: courtesy of the artist; p. 44: courtesy of the artist (top) and courtesy of the artist and the Audain Gallery (bottom); p. 60: courtesy of the artist; p. 72: collection of the Winnipeg Art Gallery—Gift of Denise Oleksijczuk; p. 84: courtesy of Grita Insam, Vienna; p. 98: reproduced by permission of Laura Cohn; p. 112: courtesy Catriona Jeffries, Vancouver; p. 122: courtesy of the artist and the Charles H. Scott Gallery, Vancouver; p. 134: courtesy of the artist; p. 146: courtesy of the artists; p. 164: courtesy of the artist; p. 172: courtesy of the artist; p. 180: courtesy of the artist; p. 212: courtesy of the artists; p. 214: courtesy of the artist and Artspeak Gallery, Vancouver

Every effort has been made to contact copyright holders
and to obtain their permission for the use of copyright
material. The publisher apologizes for any inaccurate
acknowledgement or omissions and would be grateful if
notified of any corrections that should be incorporated
in future reprints or editions of this book.

PUBLISHED BY
JRP | Ringier
Limmatstrasse 270
CH–8005 Zurich
T +41 43 311 27 50
E info@jrp-ringier.com
www.jrp-ringier.com

IN CO-EDITION WITH
Les presses du réel
35, rue Colson
F–21000 Dijon
T +33 3 80 30 75 23
E info@lespressesdureel.com
www.lespressesdureel.com

ISBN 978-3-03764-197-2 (JRP | Ringier)
ISBN 978-2-84066-668-4 (Les presses du réel)

This volume is co-published with ECU Press, Vancouver

Emily Carr University Press
1399 Johnston Street
Vancouver, BC
Canada V6H 3R9
Tel: +1 604 630 7411
chscott.ecuad.ca/ecupress

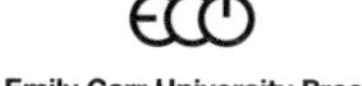

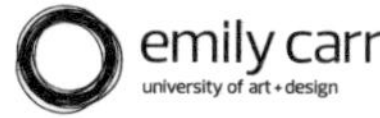

The ECU Press would like to acknowledge the generous
financial support of Dr. Yoseph Wosk, OBC

Distribution

JRP|Ringier publications are available internationally
at selected bookstores and from the following distribution
partners:

GERMANY AND AUSTRIA
Vice Versa Distribution GmbH, Immanuelkirchstrasse 12,
D-10405 Berlin, info@vice-versa-distribution.com,
www.vice-versa-distribution.com

FRANCE
Les presses du réel, 35 rue Colson, F-21000 Dijon,
info@lespressesdureel.com, www.lespressesdureel.com

SWITZERLAND
AVA Verlagsauslieferung AG, Centralweg 16,
CH-8910 Affoltern a.A., verlagsservice@ava.ch, www.ava.ch

UK AND OTHER EUROPEAN COUNTRIES
Cornerhouse Publications, 70 Oxford Street,
UK-Manchester M1 5NH, publications@cornerhouse.org,
www.cornerhouse.org/books

USA, CANADA, ASIA, AND AUSTRALIA
ARTBOOK|D.A.P., 155 Sixth Avenue,
2nd Floor, USA-New York, NY 10013, dap@dapinc.com,
www.artbook.com

For a list of our partner bookshops or for any general
questions, please contact JRP|Ringier directly at
info@jrp-ringier.com, or visit our homepage
www.jrp-ringier.com for further information about
our program.

Documents Series 14:
Jeff Derksen
After Euphoria

This book is the fourteenth volume
in the "Documents" series,
dedicated to critics' writings.

The series is directed by
Lionel Bovier and Xavier Douroux.

Also available